HISTORICAL AND SOCIO-CULTURAL ASPECTS OF NORTH-EAST INDIA

About the Editor

Dr. Sikhamoni Konwar (Gohain Boruah) is presently Principal of Karmashree Hiteswar Saikia College, Guwahati (India). She did her schooling in North Lakhimpur, graduated from Cotton College in History (Major) and obtained her Master degree with specialization in ancient Indian history from Gauhati University. She was awarded JRF by Indian Council of Historical Research and received her PhD from Gauhati University on the subject "Charaideo: The Religious and Cultural Centre of the Ahom Royalty" in 2006.

She has the credit of contributing 22 research papers in the International seminars and 22 in National seminars. Her research papers and articles have been published in the proceedings of the seminars, in the reputed journals, magazines, souvenirs and local newspapers. She has authored a book "Charaideo: A Cultural Heritage Site of Assam". She has also edited the book "Diversity and Integrity of North-East India".

She is a life member and is associated with North-East India History Association and served two consecutive terms in its executive body. Besides, she is also the life member of South and South-East Asian Association for Study and Culture and Religion (SSEASR), All India Oriental Conference, Indian History Congress, Kamarupa Anusandhan Samity, Indian Association for Asian and Pacific Studies also associated with International Associations of Historians of Asia (IAHA). Her major areas of interests are the history and culture of Assam.

HISTORICAL AND SOCIO-CULTURAL ASPECTS OF NORTH-EAST INDIA

Volume One

Editor

Dr. Sikhamoni Konwar

Principal

Karmashree Hiteswar Saikia College, Guwahati

CONCEPT PUBLISHING COMPANY PVT. LTD.

NEW DELHI-110059

ISBN-13: 978-93-5125-196-5 (Set)
ISBN-13: 978-93-5125-197-2 (Vol. I)
ISBN-13: 978-93-5125-198-9 (Vol. II)

First Published 2016

Published and Printed by

Concept Since 1974

Concept Publishing Company Pvt. Ltd.
A/15-16, Commercial Block, Mohan Garden
New Delhi-110059 (India)
T: 25351460, 25351794, *F*: 091-11-25357109
E: publishing@conceptpub.com, W: www.conceptpub.com
Editorial Office: H-13, Bali Nagar, New Delhi-110 015, India.

Cataloging in Publication Data--*Courtesy:* D.K. Agencies (P) Ltd. <docinfo@dkagencies.com>

Historical and socio-cultural aspects of North-East India /
editor, Dr. Sikhamoni Konwar.
volumes cm
Contributed articles.
Includes index.
ISBN 9789351251965 (set)
ISBN 9789351251972 (vol. I)
ISBN 9789351251989 (vol. II)

1. Folklore--India, Northeastern. 2. Values--India, Northeastern. 3. Moral education--India, Northeastern. 4. India, Northeastern--Social conditions. 5. India, Northeastern--Economic conditions. I. Konwar, Sikhamoni, editor.

GR305.5.N67H57 2016 DDC 398.209541 23

PREFACE

India is a multi-cultural country bound by the spirit of unity in diversity. And this socio-cultural phenomenon is much reflected in North-East India. The North-East India region consists of seven States of India known as seven sisters. It is the hub of cultural diversity in terms of ethnicity, language, literature, diasporas, migration etc. North-East is known as the anthropological museum of the country. Historically, North-East India is a strategic location for its proximity to India's international borders with four countries — China, Myanmar, Bhutan and Bangladesh. India's North-East region has distinct geographical unit connected with the rest of the country by only 24 km slender thread of the Siliguri corridor that connects with the country. North-Eastern state share 98 per cent land with International border, only 2 per cent with the mainland of the country. So the North-East region is like a land bridge and Gateway to South-East Asia. Keeping this in view, it is pertinent to mention here that we thought of highlighting the rich historical and socio-cultural aspects of North-East India by publishing a collection of research articles in a form of book. It is our earnest attempt to bring forth the historical and socio-cultural aspect of North-East India from an academic point of view. In recent years, we have noticed that ignorance about North-East India has degenerated into deep-rooted societal misconceptions about the region which needs to be transformed highlighting the basic facets of its history, culture, life-style, geography etc. The present volumes discusses various issues relating to North-East India and tries to project it in proper light. It is hoped that the present book will be beneficial to all concerned of the society, students, academicians and, above all, will pave the way for the assimilation of the North-East culture with the mainstream in this era of globalization.

Most of the chapters are well researched. Scholars of high repute have contributed to this book of two volumes. We have also encouraged the younger and new scholars to contribute for these volumes.

It is my bounden duty to express my gratitude to the academic advisers and editorial board for entrusting me with the responsibility of editing the book and here I must admit my limitations.

I want to place on record my deep appreciation to the Academic Advisers, Members of the Editorial Board, all the fraternity of our College Prof. Paromita Das and Mr. Ranjit Konwar who helped us in varied ways in preparation of these volumes.

My sincere thanks are also extended to the esteemed contributors, who readily responded to our request, and other well-wishers, who have been source of support and encouragement. We apologize to our readers for our unintentional shortcomings, errors or omissions and commissions. Despite our best effort, we may not be able to cover the whole aspect of the historical and socio-cultural aspects of North-East India, as such many relevant aspects may have been left out. Finally, we would like to thank Concept Publishing Company Pvt. Ltd., New Delhi for their interest in the work.

Dr. Sikhamoni Konwar

CONTENTS

VOLUME TWO

SECTION III — Socio-Economic Scenario

SECTION IV — Traditional Practices and Culture

CONTRIBUTORS

Dr. Akunthita Borthakur, Asst. Prof., Department of History, Cotton College, Guwahati

Dr. Anup Kr. Deka, Asst. Prof., Department of English, K.H.S. College, Guwahati

Dr. B.K. Gohain, I.A.S. (Retd.)

Biju Rajkhowa, Asst. Prof., Department of Assamese, K.H.S. College, Guwahati

Dr. Biman Hazarika, Associate Prof., Department of History, Dhing College, Nagaon

Dr. Daisy Nath Choudhury, Asst. Prof., Department of Education, K.H.S. College, Guwahati

Dr. Deepi Rekha Kouli, Director, Directorate of Archeology, Govt. of Assam

Dr. Gargee Sharmah, Asst. Prof., Department of Hisotry, Pragjyotish College, Guwahati

Gitika Das, Librarian, K.H.S. College, Guwahati

Dr. Jagadish Patgiri, Associate Prof., Department of Philosophy, Cotton College, Guwahati

Dr. Kanan Medhi, Asst. Prof., Department of Assamese, K.H.S. College, Guwahati

Dr. Manjula Phukan, Associate Prof. & Head, Department of History, B. Baruah College, Guwahati

Manoj Barpujari, Senior Journalist

Dr. Manoj Kumar Choudhury, Principal, MAC Memorial Academy, Sonai Road, Silchar

Dr. Marami Choudhury, Asst. Prof., Department of Philosophy, K.H.S. College, Guwahati

Nivedita Brahma, Academic Councilor, K.K.H.S.O.U.

Dr. Paromita Das, Prof., Department of History, Gauhati University

Dr. Rajib Handique, Professor, Department of History, Gauhati University, Guwahati

Dr. Ritu Thaosen, Associate Prof., Department of History, Cotton College, Guwahati.

Dr. Saswati Baruah Bhuyan, Asst. Prof., Department of Education, K.H.S. College, Guwahati

Dr. Sweta Pegu, Associate Prof., Department of English, Guwahati Commerce College, Guwahati

Tulika Choudhury, Asst. Prof., Department of Economics, Dispur College, Guwahati

SECTION I

Folk Culture and Tradition

1

NOTIONS OF TRADITIONAL HEALING AND FAITH AMONG THE DIMASA

Ritu Thaosen

Traditional healing among the different ethnic groups of Northeast India is a product of their own specific social and cultural milieu. As tradition is a continuity, it involves both the process and the product. The large number of ethnic groups including the Dimasa have their own socio-cultural traditions which are distinguishable from one another. Like in many other tribal communities, shamanic practices of divination, incarnations, etc. of traditional healing are prevalent in the Dimasa community. Knowledge of traditional healing among the Dimasa has been handed down from generation to generation, through oral traditions, practices and beliefs. Healing is tied with the belief system, faith, and the support of the community. The chapter, therefore, seeks to understand the ancestral way of healing or the traditional healing practices and the continued faith among the Dimasa.

Sickness and diseases are believed by the Dimasa to be caused by malevolent spirits and deities and so they ascribe every petty ailment of a person to the influence of some evil spirits and deities which has to be propitiated for the recovery of a sick person.[1] Hence, in the event of a person falling ill, a healer or a medicine-man is consulted to identify the plausible cause of ailment and figure out the responsible deity to be worshipped[2] after which the people make arrangements for the rites and rituals. The healers are all self-employed and supposed to have special magical powers. By means of divination they make a prognosis of the ailment and figure out the probable remedy for recovery. As the art of divination cannot be learnt, different healers employ different methods to find out the symptoms which in Dimasa is known as *Sma Naiba.*[3] Some of the chief means of divination employed by the medicine-man to find out the causes of diseases are by measuring a rope or stick, observing the intestine of a sacrificial chicken, the falling position of the cowrie, the broken egg shell, etc. The healer explains the cause of the disease and the nature of the sacrifices to be made in order to assuage the responsible spirits and also the deities. However, the most common means of divination is examining the chicken intestine. The healer takes out the intestine of a sacrificed chicken and examines it closely and if any wound or hole is noticed in it, then it is believed to be a bad sign. But if the intestine is intact, thick and coated with fat then it is the symptom of a healthy and prosperous life.[4]

After due suggestion is offered by the healer, the people prepare for the corresponding nature of sacrifice, the rites and rituals to be performed to appease the evildoers and withdraw the wrath of the spirits from the affected person. This process of worship is known as *Mdai Huba* or *Mdai Khilimba*[5] which means offerings and prayer to the deity. Hence, the first reaction of a Dimasa to fight a disease is to take recourse to supernatural means.[6] Any ritual has to be conducted only by their own priest called *Hojai* or *Jonthai* who is aided by an assistant as the devotee cannot offer a worship directly to the deities.[7] It is only the priest who has the knowledge of all the rites and rituals. A particular day is fixed taking into consideration the deity or the spirit to be appeased. For example, to worship the deity *Heremdi* it can be done only on Monday and Friday.[8] On these days she may be appeased just for the general welfare of the people of the community but in the event of an extreme emergency arising like ill-health or disease, she may be worshipped on Thursday.[9]

Elaborate arrangements are made for the rites and rituals and the offerings of the rituals are common in all the worship. Animal sacrifice like chickens, goat are a must, and even eggs are required for the worship.[10] Both the birds and animal should neither be complete black nor white. Sometimes, the requirement of eggs could increase according to the numbers of the family members. During the rituals, the intestines of the sacrificial chickens, the falling position of the broken egg shells and also the sacrifice of the goat are observed.[11] A large number of banana leaves are required which are stitched to hold together layers of fifteen, thirteen, eleven leaves and so on in the name of the deities.[12] However, the deities and spirits of the Dimasa do not have any anthropomorphic shape and belong to either sexes and some have their spouses too.[13] The most malevolent spirits are collectively called *Sagainjik*, which are seven in number and they are propitiated with great fear and respect. *Sagainjik* is generally associated with witchcraft and hence, Dimasa women with wicked nature are often referred to as *Sagainjik.*[14]

As there are no structured shrines, small earthen mounds are made during the rituals and covered with the banana leaves.[15] The rituals of this worship is generally carried out on the outskirts of the village or in the forest. Any food is first offered to the deity.[16] People who attend the rituals are also offered the consecrated food. The leftovers are thrown away and cannot be brought back home. During the rituals the priest chants the incarnations which says:[17]

> Wherever we go
> Whether we climb the hills
> Or cross the streams,
> We face obstacles
> But now,
> After worshipping you,
> We can climb the hills
> Without stumbling on the way
> We can cross the streams easily
> We can walk through the forests
> Without the creepers blocking the way.

These incarnations speak of the faith the people have in their healing tradition. Through the observance of different rituals, the Dimasas believe in the recovery of a person from ill-health and disease. Some healers also infuse charm into water by incarnation and gives it to the person suffering from sickness to drink it.

Another female deity, known as *Khandisa* is usually propitiated whenever a baby suffers from any sickness. She is regarded as the deity for the welfare of the baby. *Khandisa* is propitiated to restore the lost health and energy of the baby. The rituals for propitiating this deity is generally done in the morning in the forest.[18]

However, the most visible shamanic characteristics are seen in a *Phatri* who exhibits varied forms of divination. He is consulted during any natural calamity in the village, outbreak of an epidemic or failure of crops and the villagers ask him questions on remedial measures.[19] At the same time individuals go to him seeking advice for the symptoms of their personal ill health while eggs and rice-beer are offered to him.[20] It is considered that a man must be wise and well versed in the religious rites to be regarded as a *Phatri.*[21] The *Phatri* exerts influence on the people through some miraculous activities and revelations. He is called to the village at the place of annual worship after some calamities occur.[22] He observes customary restriction and wearing new clothes he takes his seat and he falls into a trance in accompaniment to musical instruments — the *Khram* (drum) and the *Moori* (blowing instrument).[23] The beating of the drum perhaps allows the *Phatri* or the *shaman* to achieve an altered state of consciousness. While in a trance the *Phatri* or the *shaman*, trembling and with eyes closed answers the questions of the people and suggests remedial measures.[24] The replies given at this moment are considered to be a direct communication from God. In clear terms he mentions the ceremonies and rituals to be performed and the sacrifices to be made to get rid of the present state of troubles and to have a better prospect in future.[25] The Dimasas believe in the *Pathri's* prediction and hold it as true.

From the above study, it can be said that the Dimasas are still found to be dependent to a great extent on the traditional means of healing. Rituals of traditional healing are still practiced in the villages as an alternative to modern medicine due to the inaccessibility of modern medical facilities. Often the healer's remedial measures and the rites and rituals performed might not produce any effective results. Even when the means of treatment might have met with repeated failures, the belief of the people in the power of the supernatural agencies remain firm and unchanged. In most cases when modern medical aids are sought at the eleventh hour, the treatment proves unsuccessful. This lends support to their belief in the indigenous healing and way of treatment. People continue to consult the medicineman or the healer and perform different set of rituals with the help of the priest. As the indigenous healing tradition takes a much larger view of the individual and the disease, the people's faith on the healer, therefore, continue to hold good. The main strength of the traditional healing system, therefore, lies in the faith of the entire community. Faith is an important element in the healing process. And so long as the people have faith in the system they own, it helps them to tide over periods of crisis and reduces the mental conflicts that they evoke. These religious ideas, beliefs and practices of the Dimasa like many other indigenous tribes have been evolved over a long period of time in response to adoptive needs and strategies for survival in different ecological systems and so rooted in nature. Healing practices reinforces faith in the people and the act of faith itself is the recognition that we can do nothing on our own.

NOTES AND REFERENCES

1. Ramdina Lalsim, *Tribes of N.C. Hills, Assam*, North Cachar Hills Autonomous Council Publication Series, Haflong, 2005, p. 17.
2. Dipali G. Danda, *Among the Dimasa of Assam*, New Delhi, 1978, p. 129.
3. Bhadreshwar Bodo, "Traditional Healing Among the Dimasa" in *Traditional Systems of the Dimasa*, VKIC, Guwahati, 2006, p. 17.
4. *Ibid.*, pp. 17-18.
5. Junu Devi, "Divination" in *Traditional Systems of the Dimasa*, VKIC, Guwahati, 2006, p. 2.
6. Dipali G. Danda, *op. cit.*, p. 142.
7. *Ibid.*, p. 135.
8. Personal Interview with Manomohan Nunisa of village Dehangi, Dima Hasao (Assam) on 15.1.2013.
9. *Ibid.*
10. *Ibid.*
11. Personal Interview with Dhanjanon Nunisa, Priest of Dehangi Village, Dima Hasao on 23.1.2013.
12. *Ibid.*
13. Dipali G. Danda, *op. cit.*, p. 130.
14. *Ibid.*; B.N. Bordoloi, *The Dimasa Kacharis of Assam*, Assam Institute of Research for Tribals and Scheduled Castes, Guwahati, 1984, p. 70; Partha Sarathi Misra, "Myths and Rituals of the Dimasa Kacharis of Assam", in *Folklore in North-East India*, edited by Soumen Sen, Guwahati, 1985, p. 110.
15. *Ibid.*; Manomohan Nunisa had more details on this.
16. Information collected from Dhanjanon Nunisa on 24.1.2013.
17. Recited by Dhanjanon Nunisa and further explained by his younger brother Hamdao Nunisa.
18. Dipali Danda, *op. cit.*, p. 129.
19. B.N. Bordoloi, *op. cit.*, p. 70.
20. Personal Interview with Ramesh Thaosen, an Assam Civil Service Officer on 4.2.2013.
21. Dipali Danda, *op. cit.*, p. 136.
22. Junu Devi, *op. cit.*, p. 3.
23. Personal Interview with Ramesh Thaosen on 4.2.2013; Information collected from Manomohan Nunisa on 15.1.2013.
24. Dipali G. Danda, *op. cit.*, p. 136.
25. Junu Devi, *op. cit.*, p. 3.

2

RIFT IN MAHAPURUSHIYA ORDER
A Critical Review

Biman Hazarika

The history of neo-Vaisnavism in Assam cannot be treated without reference to the rift that developed in the later phase[1] of the movement just after the death of Sankaradeva (1449-1568 A.D.). Katha Guru Carita first uses the term '*samhati*' to denote such rift within the Mahapursushiya order. This term was usually employed in the sense divisions of the original order emerged out of a fissure. The term schism[2] has been in vogue in the History of religion at least from the eighteenth century, if not earlier. In some of the early biographies of Vaisnavite saints the division was never termed as Sampradaya or simply Samprada instead of often cited term samhati.[3]

The phase of sub-sect began to claim its independence soon after the formation of the Damodari sub-sect. The earliest mention of this four-fold division seems to occur in Aniruddha's *Guru Varnana* where Damodara, Caturbhuja's successor is made to explain to King Jayadhvaja Simha (1648-1663 A.D.) that all these four samhaties follow Sankaradeva's faith by worshipping Krishna, abstaining from the cult of older deities and celebrating *nama-kirtana.*[4] There is, however, no unity of opinion on the manner and nature of such divisions among Mahapurushiyas. About the origin of this religious fissure; we find some fantastic and mythological accounts in different Caritas. Katha Guru Carita, the most trustworthy amongst them gives an elaborate account and throws much lights on the organizational aspects of the Vaisnavite movement, the nature the structure of later group of Sattra institution, method and hardships undergone in its propagation, history of schisms and accounts of different sects. This work gives an account of an event, which indicates the future division of the religion after Sankaradeva. It records 'one day when Purusottam, the grand child of Sankaradeva tore up leaves of Dasama into three pieces, the savant asked Madhava why the baby (*parama brahma*) did so ? Madhava could not reply properly; Sankaradeva himself explained the matter thus — 'after our departure'; the religion would be divided into three pantheons — *niguna* (*brahmaghati*), *kewala* (*nikaghati*) and *bhagawati* (*kalaghati*).[5] It was Damodara, whom Sankaradeva entrusted to initiate Brahman disciples administered the first such rift proclaiming itself as separate sect within the Mahapurushiya order. Some other accounts refers how Sankaradeva before starting on his second pilgrimage asked his one of the most trusteed disciples Damodara to manage the Sattra ceremonials and to initiate persons specially Brahmanas to the faith. One day Sankaradeva said to him, "you please start initiating Brahmans, nobles and kings without any difference", to this Damodara replied: "you are burdening me with a noble responsibility when your ownself is present".[6] It is a possibility after Sankaradeva's return that Damodara established the first Sattra at Patbausi on his own. Immediately after the death of Sankaradeva, Damodaradeva (1489-1598 A.D.) and Harideva (1489-1598 A.D.) who had so long been cooperating with Sankaradeva seceded from the orthodox Church led by Madhavadeva. They are said to have declared independence and separate identities of their own which is not borne out by the Carit puthies of Sankaradeva as well as those of Damodaradeva and Harideva.[7] The first schism was thus more important as it ultimately divided the order into two distinct groups. It was the rejection of communion with the authorities of the main order, and this term has historically been applied to the break when there was no dispute about doctrine of neo-Vaisnavism. It seems the main cause of discontent that led to the schism was Damodara being one of the principal followers naturally expected to succeed Sankaradeva to the pontifical position. But when this expectation was belied by the nomination of Madhavadeva he found it difficult to regard him, whom he treated as an erstwhile colleague not as his superior. Some scholars argue that it was not a solitary event that marked the breakdown. Some other factors relating to this development is found in the pages of biographies of both the *gurus. Guru Carita* narrates how Damodara administered some modifications to accommodate *smartta* rituals in the neo-Vaisnavism and even accepted his fold a few persons who were expelled earlier from the order by Madhavadeva. When Madhavadeva called for an explanation, Damodaradeva replied 'though I deviate from the original preaching of Bhagavata, I consider Bhagavata to be more authoritative than Sankaradeva. Further I do not owe any explanation to you (Madhavadeva) as I am not a member of your order.[8] Damodara's refusal to attend the sraddha ceremony disowning Madhava's leadership strained the relations further between him and the followers of the orthodox order. Daityari Thakur's Carita narrates another episode, which said to be helped in creating a gulf between the early apostles. It says, after the passing away of Sankaradeva, Haricarana refused to accept the financial aid offered by Damodara when he came to know that *Sarana* (initiation) system of Damodara had some way different from that of Sankaradeva. As the path of devotion shown by Sankaradeva leaves no room for esoteric ritualism; so Madhavadeva being an ardent follower of pure Vaisnavism simply sacked him from the order. However, it can be gauged that owing to the critical socio-political situation of that period Damodara might have slightly altered his path of devotion. It is said Damodara could clearly see that the wholesale abolition of Brahmanical rites and rituals would not only estrange the sympathy of the Brahmans but the opponents of the Bhakti movement would make a capital of it by interpreting the movement as a revolt against the Vedas.[9] This modification helped in accelerating the proselytizing activities of the new order with growing number of Brahmin disciples and setting up good number of Sattras. The total number of Sattras affiliated to the sub-sects of Damodara exceeds one hundred in the entire Brahmaputra valley and the number of disciples is larger than that of any other sub-sects. According to some scholars, earliest apostles of *Brahma Samhati*, one of the largest denominations in neo-Vaisnavism, found it difficult to believe that Sankaradeva divinely ordained Madhavadeva as his successor. The debate and controversy as to what if any arrangements Sankaradeva made for a successor have continued to this day. Nilakantha, the biographer of Damodara says that Madhavadeva performed the *sraddha* ceremony of Sankaradeva at Rangiyal-ghar of Barpeta with Ramananda. Damodaradeva separately performed the same with Haricharana at Patbausi, where Sankaradeva's family lived. (*Nilapada*, 457-464) So, the controversy relating to the *sraddha* ceremony should not be taken into account as a matter of disregard of Damodara. It is evidently related with the customs of *sraddha* ceremony only.[10] Nilakantha further says that Damodaradeva also duly celebrated the death anniversary of Sankaradeva. If he was free from any spiritual tie with Sankaradeva, why did he perform the ceremony?[11] However, it can be safely concluded why Sankaradeva nominated Madhavadeva as his successor, instead of his sons or a Brahmin disciple. The spiritual accomplishment, personality, organizing zeal and skill that the Master observed on him prompted to take the decision. Besides, Madhavadeva was acknowledged as the second in rank in the order while Sankaradeva was alive.

With this the ideal, which Sankaradeva and his immediate successors carried further the movement that soon started melting in a more pronounced way after the death of his immediate successor Madhavadeva. Subsequently, three more sub-sects originated within the main body of the order. An early biographer presents an account of the prevailing situation on the eve of the death of the master like this "when the end of Madhavadeva was approaching, *bhakatas* asked him as to who would lead the order after him. After observing three days of silence he told them that he saw nobody fit for guruship and that those desired to might find, in his work Namaghosa. Daityari, therefore, says that guruship is applicable to none, but Sankara and Madhava alone".[12] Following his death in 1568 A.D. Madhava's creed developed certain sectarian divisions within itself and within a short period ranging up to a few decades of the next century four separate branches cropped up under different heads belonging to his Brahmanical followers. Damodara seceded during the lifetime of Madhavadeva. Narayanathakur, the friend and colleague of Madhavadeva was then too old to shoulder the responsibility of wielding together the different sections of the devotees. Naturally, therefore, a good number of disciples found themselves in three sections under the leadership of Gopala Ata, Purusottama Thakur and Mathuradas respectively.[13]

Sivanath Barman observes "it was the towering personality of Sankaradeva that binds the devotees of different caste and creeds during his life time, but germs of divisive forces sprang up after his death".[14] Likewise, in the third stage of the tradition of Gurubad; we find four further divisions which follows fourth, fifth and the sixth in due course. It is found the *acaryas* of post-Sankarite period were of firm conviction in maintaining two principles — *Guru agya* (guru's enjoin) and *Bangsanukrama* (inheritance) on which the tradition built-up and extended later on.

Followers of orthodox type explain the terms, *viz. Purusa*, *Nika*, *Kala* and *Brahma* in a fantastic or mythological way without any rational basis. According to them the *Brahma Samhati* is so called because it originated from Brahma, the creator. The *Purusa Samhati* derived its names from *Purusa Narayana* who is supposed to be its first initiator. In this way, they try to explain the designations attributed to different sub-sects without any logical basis.[15] Dvarika Nath Dwija in his work *Santavaoli* first tried to explain the history of evolution of *Samhati* in a mythological way.[16]

However, S.N. Sarma gives a rational explanation of the origin of divisions. He explains, "It is because of the predominance of Brahmanical elements, the sub-sects of Damodaradeva and Harideva have been known as *Brahma Samhaṭi.* The origin of the term has nothing to do with Brahma *sampradaya* of Madhava acarya as explained and believed. As regards *Purusa samhati*, he holds, the sub-sect is so called because Purusottam Thakur, the eldest grandson of Sankaradeva founded it. He refused to accept the generalized explanation in which the term is said to have derived its name from the term *Mahapurusa*, the honorific titles applied to Sankaradeva. He asserts this sub-sect had not existed at all during the time of Sankaradeva.

It is said that Sankaradeva's tolerance had enabled Damodaradeva and Harideva to work unitedly for the spread of the new cult, but after him they found Madhavadeva too rigid and therefore, declared independence and his section is commonly known as *Brahma samhati.*

S.N. Sarma further observe this development and situation like this —

". . . by the end of the first quarter of the seventeenth century three sub-sect and two seceding sects having minor difference in exoteric and esoteric observances sprang up. By the end of the Century the most faithful period of the Vaisnavism in Assam also came to an end and the galaxy of Vaisnava stalwarts disappeared from the religious firmament. The later history of the faith and the sub-sects is marked by the expansion of the Sattra institution throughout the entire Brahmaputra valley and the stereo typed proselytizing process and religious activities continued unabated. Difficulties, hardships and opposition from the state that confronted the religious reformer of the first two centuries of the history of the movement practically ceased with the beginning of the eighthteenth century".[17] Sarma argues that perhaps a Brahmanical swing back to orthodoxy impelled Damodaradeva and the followers of Harideva too to disown their connection with the original sect. On the other hand Caturbhuja Thakur who headed the *Purusa samhati* order held Sankaradeva as the only *guru*, resulted in a difference of opinion with the *Bhakatas* of the Barpeta Sattra. Caturbhuja admitted that he only followed Madhavadeva and Purusottam's edict in maintaining the tradition of *Gurubada* or *Guru parampara. Santavali* narrates —

> *Suniyaka bhai kaho sare sar/Sankarata pare guru nahi kaiya ara//*
> *upadesa data Sankarat pare nai/*(648)
> *aponi Madhabe mota kahise dahai//*

Sankarar pare guru nai nai nai/
laiuka pramana tan ghosa puthi cai//(649)[18]

This view was supported by a considerable number of associates and disciples of the two Thakurs and that led to the growth of different groups in succeeding period. It is generally believed and accepted that what we know today as the Gopala Ata and Mathuradasa Burha Ata were appointed by Madhavadeva, the forerunners of the Mahapurusiya order. They took up the cause of their new sect with zeal and enthusiasm and in a few years grew remarkably in power and own Guru and tarnishing others.[19] Members of a particular *Samhati* might have felt their own salvation, or achievement, or success of their particular objectives, requires of increasing number of converts from other groups; adherents of a given fraction might have believed that for the achievement of their own religious goods their internal opponents own religious project their internal opponents must be purged. It was not the religion that caused it to fall but rather the moral and ideological degradation that caused it to fall apart. The idealistic differences that cropped up among the acaryas and followers of various groups for petty reasons had damaged the very fabric of the noblest religion. Personal jealousy and weakness, conventional social rituals and customs, lack of far-sightedness, complex sociological situation and above all the influence inserted by the royal houses from time to time compelled the Vaisnavite apostles to think differently. This led to the separation of most of them from the universally acclaimed tradition and ideals of guruship propounded by Sankaradeva.[20] Proselytizing methodology of the apostles of post Sankarite period seemed to differ as they tried to spread *nama-dharma* amidst various ethnic groups of Assam by applying different methodology for their convenience. This resulted in differences of opinions that led to the formation of four *samhati*.[21]

Pioneer of neo-Vaisnavite studies like Maniram Dewan, Lakshminath Bezbarua, Banikanta Kakati, Maheswar Neog, Satyendra Nath Sarma, Bapchandra Mahanta and some others offer a penetrating and incisive evaluation of secessionist ideology, with a clear eye to the priority of apostolic history of succession and its development. The principal source on which the analysis is made certainly on close scanning of Caritputhies and genealogical accounts, the sources are worthy of exploitation. Most of the critics in a mood of embarrassment call the entire situation as '*Guru biparjaya*' (Guru-crisis) and to which some spurious literature of that period added fuel to fire. They observe that deliberate attempts were made in this period to interpolate even the existing early works and to write some new ones both in prose and verse. Most of the works are anonymous, where Caturbhuja, Madhavadeva and even Sankaradeva are said to have foretold about the real successorship of the order.[22] Some *Vamsavalis* even tries to twist the genealogy of some families and some of them have made serious departure from the early accounts. Observing this; M. Neog referred a list of apocryphal works with dubious authorship in '*Sankaradeva and His Times*'.

It has been observed the sub-sects grew after the death of the Masters created a network of Sattras throughout the entire Brahmaputra valley. This division weakened the old unity and strength of neo-Vaisnavite movement but created a force within each of the sects to compete each other for expansion of its own organization in different parts of the state. The rapid growth and development of various sub-sects and their overzealous proselytizing activity under various *samhaties* practically converted more than half of its population to Vaisnavism. However, the history of sub-sects has not mentioned any friction between the different sub-sects of Vaisnavism, rather a spirit of co-operation and harmony marked the relation between the different sub-sects throughout the history of Vaisnavism.

D. Nath, stated that the growth of schism leading to the multiplication of the Sattras and the expansion of the Ahom political power over the valley and formation of kind of national monarchy with a comparatively peaceful and secured situation that paved the way for the growth of the Sattras in established institutional form under the protection and patronage of the Ahom rulers. With this socio-political background, it soon became apparent that most of the Sattras would grow in different places of Assam, particularly in upper Assam significantly under the Ahom patronage, which remained outside the spell of neo-Vaisnavism till the at least close of the sixteenth century.[23] The district gazetteer of Assam, 1905 have recorded two hundred eighty eight (288) Sattras including many branches spreading over the entire Brahmaputra valley all of them are not uniform in size and affluence, but are marked by the some fundamental characteristics.[24] Under the feudal administration of the Ahom and Koch rulers and subsequently under the imperial British, Sattras gained fertile ground to grow in their own way. These sects and sub-sects tried to establish their own identity, but in cardinal principle there is practically little or no difference amongst them.

Conclusion

The above discussion reveals that the divergence of the Mahapurushiya order was a process of many years, influenced by a host of socio-economic and primarily theological factors. With the passage of time and changed conditions, attitudes and approaches among different samhati began to more soften, doctrines becomes flexible and the sectarian outlook to liquidate. No doubt, the rift weakened the old unity and strength of neo-Vaisnavite religion but it seemed to develop a force within each of the sects to compete with each other for expansion of its own organization, in different parts of the state. It is worth noting that in the beginning when the schism materialized, the differences between the sects were acute but did not take the form of a dogmatic and doctrinaire rigidity as is clear from the fact that the Vaisnavism by and large agreed that preaching of *Bhakti dharma* in the simplest form was the highest ideal as it is the characteristic of a neo-Vaisnavism.

NOTES AND REFERENCES

1. For the origin and development of rift or schism in neo-Vaishnavite movement one may consult Upendra Nath Lekharu (ed.), *Katha Guru Carita* (ed.), Guwahati, 1987; M. Neog, *Sankaradeva and his Times*, Guwahati, 2008; S.N. Sarma, *The Neo-Vaisnavite Movement and the Sattra Institution of Assam*, Guwahati, 1999; Bapchandra Mahanta, *Aitihashik Patabhumit Mahapurusa Sankaradeva*, Dibrugarh, 1999.
2. *Oxford Advanced Learners Dictionary* (2005) defines schism as a strong disagreement within an organization, especially a religious one, that makes its members divide into separate groups.
3. Kesavananda Devgoswami, *Post Sankaradeva Vaisnava Faith and Culture of Assam*, New Delhi, p. 35.
4. M. Neog, *op. cit.*, p. 153.
5. *Kathaguru Carita*, 1987, p. 618.
6. *Damodara Carita*, p. 71, quoted in S.N. Sarma, *op. cit.*, p. 102.
7. H.K. Barpujari (ed.), *The Comprehensive History of Assam*, Vol. III, 2004, p. 239.
8. Ramacarana, *Sankara Carita*, p. 305: Daityari, *Sankaradeva Madhavadeva Carita*, p. 299; *Katha Guru Carita*, p. 229.
9. S.N. Sarma, *op. cit.*, pp. 103-104.
10. Bapchandra Mahanta, *Aitihashik Patabhumit Mahapurus Sankaradeva*, Jorhat, 1987, p. 141.
11. S.N. Sarma, *op. cit.*, p. 103.
12. M. Neog., *op. cit.*, p. 133.
13. S.N. Sarma, *op. cit.*, p. 93.
14. Sivnath Barman, *Srimanta Sankaradeva and Terar Uttar Suri Sakal*, Guwahati, 2004, p. 101.
15. S.N. Sarma, *op. cit.*, p. 95; *Santavali*, V.V., 1734-1786.
16. *Santavali* (ed.), S. Hazarika, Guwahati, 2007. This is a descriptive biography and historical analysis of Assamese Vaisnavite santas and various Sattra institutions by Sri Dwarikanath Dwija of nineteenth century.
17. S.N. Sarma, *op. cit.*, p. 262.

18. . . . listen brothers, after Sankaradeva we don't have any *guru*, there is no body to guide us. Madhavadeva himself tells this. Take the proof of this notion from Ghosa puthi. Supporting the view the Bardowa group of *Sattras* and other institutions affiliated to it claim that Madhava nominated Purusottam Thakur as his rightful successor.
19. Bapchanda Mahanta, *op. cit.*, p. 140.
20. *Ibid.*, p. 139.
21. Anil Roy Choudhary, *Asamiya Samaj Aru Navavaishnavabada*, Guwahati, 2007, p. 12.
22. Maniram Dewan, *Buranji Vivek Ratna*, (ed.) Dibrugarh, 2002, p. 124.
23. D. Nath, *Sattras in Colonial Assam: Their Response to the Emerging Socio-Political Issues* (1st edn.), 2007, New Delhi, p. 4.
24. *Assam District Gazetteers:* 1905, p. 53; p. 93; p. 95; p. 96; p. 123.

3

A RELOOK INTO THE STATUS OF TANTRIC GODDESS IN EARLY ASSAM

Gargee Sharmah

The wave of *Tantra* that swept over Assam during early medieval period was very strong. Tantric elements associated with the goddess, which were given mature shape in medieval Assam can be traced even in the epics and the *Puranas*. The process of the growth of the cult of Mother Goddess as depicted in the Tantras has associated with her personalities of a large number of goddesses who may be classified as *Mahavidyas*, *Matrikas*, *Yoginis*, etc. This chapter focuses on the status of Tantric goddess in early Assam in the light of literature and archaeology.

Tantricism generally refers to the religious beliefs and practices which are intricately connected with Saktism. Tantricism greatly developed in early medieval period in Assam and impacted practically every major religion. The scriptures that present these practices are generally known as *Tantras*. The word *Tantra* is derived from the Sanskrit word '*tan*' meaning 'to draw out', or 'to spread'.[1] According to Carl Clemen, *Tantra* means literary production dealing with religion, philosophy and natural sciences and is of a later date than the Vedic literature.[2] Though the germ of Saktism can be traced to the *Vedas*, in reality Saktism has developed only in the *Tantras* and the *Puranas*.[3] The "union of male and female energy is the evidence of *Tantra*".[4] Some scholars opine that *Tantra* ought to be restricted to the text connected with Sakti worship which emphasizes *prakriti* or the female principle, the main aspect of Tantricism. The worship of the phallus, *Linga* and *Yoni*, personified later on as Siva and Devi respectively formed the basis of Saktism and Tantricism[5] and according to a group of scholars it is found in the pre-historic finds including those from the Indus.

However, regarding the origin of the Tantricism it is said that Assam and Bengal were the birth places of Tantricism in India from where it spread to the rest of India. Smith points out that Kamarupa (ancient Assam):

> . . . Is a gate through which successive hoards of immigrants from the great hive of the Mongolian race in Western China have poured into the plains of India and many of the resident tribes are still almost pure Mongolians. The religion of such tribes is of more than of local concern, because it supplies the clue to the strange Tantric development of both Buddhism and Hinduism which are so characteristic of medieval and modern Bengal.[6]

This view is corroborated by the evidence of *Tantra* which point to the importation of Tara worship from China to India. Tantricism has been intimately connected with Kamarupa-Kamakhya, the *Mahapithas* of *Tantras* and *Puranas*.[7] *Hevajra Tantra*, which is a Buddhist Tantra (composed around 690 C.E.) mentions four noted centres of Tantricism: Kamarupa, Purnagiri, Uddiyana and Jalandhara. Pratap Chandra Choudhury observes that another centre was definitely Bengal with which region Kamarupa and Magadha (Bihar)-Utkala (Orissa) had close contacts.[8] It is believed that Tantricism travelled from Assam and Bengal to Dravidian India. Wilson holds that Assam or at least the north-east of Bengal seems to have been in a great degree the source from which the Tantric and Sakta corruption of the religions of the *Vedas* and *Puranas* proceeded.[9] Assam was one of the great centres of Tantricism which is proved by *Tantras* themselves. Probably ancient Assam with her non-Aryan elements contributed greatly to the origin and growth of the system. Choudhury states that:

> The Austrics and the Tibeto-Burmans, as shown by the phallic megalithic remains, really laid the foundation of the system, the final form of which was given by the assimilation of both Hindu and Buddhistic ideas. In short the origin and later growth of some of the important elements of Tantricism are to be attributed to the non-Aryans in ancient Assam, one of the fertile fields in eastern India for the development of those ideas.[10]

There are two schools of thought regarding the origin of Tantricism. One group including scholars like Prabodh Chandra Bagchi argues in favour of the Vedic origin of the Tantricism as some features of the Tantricism are clearly found in the *Vedas*. However, it is to be noted that in Buddhist and Jaina canonical works there are several references to mystic rites, which are akin to Tantric rites.[11] There is, also a contradictory theory that was suggested by scholars like Nagendra Nath Vasu that the Tantric cult had a foreign origin as is evident from the verses in the *Kubjika Tantra* (5th century A.D.) and *Mahachinachara Tantra*. Probably, Tantric goddess Tara was imported from China as we have a reference to the peculiar practice of using the twig of a tree in her worship, a custom unknown to the Indians.[12] From *Tara Tantra* it is clear that the cult of Cina Tara came from the Mahachina. Levy finds in Cina Tara an echo of secret societies in China. Mahacinatara is identified with Ekajata whose cult is said to have been taken by Nagarjuna from Tibet. Kanak Lal Baruah has tried to establish that Nagarjuna had close association with Kamarupa and may have actually hailed from there.[13] In *Rudrayamala* and other Hindu *Tantras* including *Yogini Tantra* the worship of Tara is said to have been brought by Vasistha from China and meditated on Goddess Tara on Nilachala hill of Kamarupa. Thus, Kamarupa was associated with early part of Buddhist Tantricism.

Devi Purana states that Devi was worshipped in Kamarupa, Kamakhya, Bhottadesa and other places. According to some writers the deity was formerly a goddess of spirits worshipped in a cremation ground. The *Yogini Tantra* confirms this in stating that Kamakhya is the Kali-*smasana*. Kamarupa is the noted centre of Tantricism and the temple of Kamakhya has the reputation of the worship of Devi with Tantric rites and sacrifices details of which are given in the *Kalika Purana* and the *Yogini Tantra*.

Both epigraphy and literature testify to the widespread prevalence of Tantricism in Assam. The reference of magic practices in inscriptions of ancient Assam shows that the Tantric rites had already appeared in the field of Brahmanical religion and reached predominance during seventh century C.E. The text of the Tezpur Copper Plate Inscription begins with the sign *Anji* which is a Tantric symbol representing *Kundalini*. Tantricism laid principal emphasis on joint worship of Siva and Sakti. This inscription also refers to the temple of Kameswara (Siva) and Mahagauri (Sakti).[14] The Guwahati Grant of Indrapala (960-90 C.E.) of Pala dynasty of Assam refers to *Tantra* as a subject and King Indrapala was well versed in the subject.[15]

Another text *Kalika Purana* written in ancient Assam in ninth or tenth century C.E. prescribes the Tantric mode of worship to appease Kamakhya or Kameswari of Kamarupa. It is said that Vasistha who was practicing penances to Siva was forced to go out by the goddess Ugratara.

Vasistha cursed Ugratara with these words — "You being a women (*vama*) are expelling me, you will henceforth be worshipped only according to *Vama* rites, your hosts (*Ganas*) roving about like '*mlechchhas*' will henceforth be degraded to the rank of '*mlechchhas*".[16] According to Bani Kanta Kakati the figure of Vasistha is made to stand at the cross-roads of political and social changes in Assamese legends. Vasistha's curses led to changes in religious and social customs and the result was the initiation of *Vamacara* (left hand) rites in ancient Kamarupa.[17]

The erotic sensual elements that are an integral part of Tantric religion are recognized in the above mentioned *Puranas*. In the *Devi Purana* there is a *stotra* where Devi is said to be the better half of Siva. She is worshipped along with Siva. An emphasis is laid on the union of Siva and Sakti as the basis of creation and preservation of the universe. The *Kalika Purana* also gives an account of Siva's marriage with Devi and mentions that Kali is very dear to Siva and she is half of Siva's body.[18] The union of Siva and Sakti has its philosophical foundation in the *Samkhya* system and is also reflected in the esoteric Tantric Yoga practices connected with awakening of *Kundalini*, the Primeval Energy dormant in the microcosm (human body). Representation of the union of Siva and Sakti in the art of Assam is very common. A large number of images of Uma-Maheswara, Ardhanarisvara, etc. can be noticed in the art of the region which prove the popularity of the Tantricism.

In Assam and Bengal the *Tantras* were composed not earlier than twelfth/thirteenth century C.E. However, the study of both *Devi Purana* and *Kalika Purana* indicate that much prior to the composition of the *Tantras* in these regions, Tantric practices were in vogue in connection with the worship of the goddess.

The Saktis bearing different names and forms seem to have been worshipped by different sects. But the variety of names and forms of Sakti has been brought under the most famous division of ten *Mahavidyas* (*Dasamahavidyas*), each having a distinct literature of its own. The concept of *Dasamahavidyas* is of Tantric origin. According to the *Yogini Tantra* those are *mantras*, which are applied to the worship of gods, and those applied to the goddesses are known as *vidyas*. *Mahavidya* means great goddess. The popular myth behind the origin of the *Dasamahavidyas* is that when *Sati* came to know that her father Daksa was going to perform a sacrifice where he had invited all but Siva and *Sati*, she wanted to go there without an invitation. Siva forbade her and at this *Sati* became ferocious and angry. At the sight of her anger, Siva became perplexed and wanted to flee hither and thither. Then *Sati* expressed herself in ten images in ten directions. Siva was perplexed and accorded her permission to go to Daksa's place.[19]

The ten *Mahavidyas* are Kali, Tara, Sodasi, Bhubaneswari, Bhairavi, Cinnamasta, Dhumawati, Bagala, Matangi and Kamala. According to David Kinsley the *Mahavidyas* emerged about a millennium ago. However, some individual goddesses like Kali have significant early and independent footing.[20] The ten forms, while lacking any obvious internal coherence, are overlapping embodiments of the great goddess (*Mahadevi*)[21] representing many of her paradoxical aspects — benign and horrific, creative and destructive. The terrible aspect predominates. The *Dasamahavidyas* defied conventional Hindu norms regarding the ideal woman as a controlled and obedient wife.

The Siva-Sakti union is best explained by *Dasamahavidya* concept. Except Dhumavati who is represented as a widow the other nine *Mahavidyas* are to be worshipped along with their Bhairavas. Most popular among these ten incarnations of the Goddess was no doubt, Kali. The *Mahanirvana Tantra* ascribes her as the progenitor including of animate and inanimate object.

According to David Kinsley the *Dasamahavidyas* lack strong association with the theme of fertility and nurturance.[22] None of the ten is portrayed as a mother. *Dasamahavidyas* can be treated as symbol of liberation from the confines of a world strictly governed by rules of caste, of purity and pollution.[23] *Dasamahavidyas* are worshipped in ancient Assam. There are temples of *Dasamahavidyas* on the Nilachala hillock in Guwahati where regular worship has been performed since the remote past. It is said that the worship of *Dasamahavidya* is equally ancient as that of Kamakhya.[24] The existence of the *Dasamahavidya* temples in Nilachala hillock proves that it was a great centre of Tantric worship for a long time and inscriptions prove that they were rebuilt in the late medieval period over earlier remains dating back to the 10th/11th C.E.

In the *Puranas* we may trace the beginning of the Tantric elements. The *Matrikas* who are associated with the Devi in the *Puranas* are given more importance in the *Tantras*. In the *Markandeya Purana* it has been said that the *Matrikas* aided Goddess Ambika along with Camunda in causing death to the most powerful ally of the demon king Sumba, named Raktabija. Similar was the case with Andhakasura who fought against Siva. Generally, the *Matrikas* are seven in numbers. However, there are occasional variations in the list of *Matrikas* with regard to their number. *Sapta-Matrikas* (seven mothers) represented the *Saktis* (female energy or counter part) of important familiar gods. They are Brahmani, Maheswari, Kaumari, Vaisnavi, Varahi, Indrani and Camunda. However, Aindri, Yami and the others also added in different texts. From the *Sadhanas* in the Buddhist literature, it appears that the Tantric Buddhist literature has also incorporated the *Sapta Matrikas* in their religious fold.[25] The characteristics of the *Matrikas* are that they are fierce in nature in the most part, and they are formidable in battle, terrifying their enemies. This concept of the cult as war-goddess is borne out of the political turmoil of the time. This is an identifiable political construct of the Mother Goddess. In the worship of the divine mothers, it was intimately associated with the Tantric form of Shakti worship, as primarily fear played the prominent part.

Matrika worship is prevalent from a very early period in Assam. Four of the *Matrikas* are known to have been represented in the art of Assam. An image in the Assam State Museum is seen to represent Varahi that has the face of a boar. **Camunda** is a common image usually with four hands and sometimes with six or eight hands too. The following are the general characteristic features of the Camunda image: She is depicted with skeletal appearance with — flesh dried up, bones showing through the skin, eyes sunken and abdomen contracted; she wears a necklace of skulls and bones; she is often dressed in a tiger skin and has a corpse and an owl as her vehicle; her complexion is generally of dark or blue colour. Camunda images are common in Assam. Images of Camunda found in Na-bhanga, Kamakhya, Barpathar, etc. depict these features. She is often accompanied by a jackal and vultute, associated with death.

Vaisnavi is one of the *Saptamatrikas*. Vaisnavi, the power or Sakti of Visnu is described as seated on Garuda (vehicle of Visnu) with four or six hands. She holds *sankha* (conch), *chakra* (discus), *gada* (mace) and *padma* (lotus). Sometimes her hands are depicted in *varada mudrā* (blessing hand gesture) and *abhaya mudra* (boon of fearlessness hand gesture). Like Visnu she is adorned with ornaments like necklace, anklets, bangles, etc. A terracotta plaque depicting goddess Vaisnavi, was recovered from the excavation at Bhaitbari now in Meghalaya.

In Tantricism the Great Goddess appears with *Yoginis* as her followers. From the *Kularnava Tantra* it is learnt that the followers of the goddess were emanations from the goddess herself and assumed different forms. In the Sanskrit literature, the *Yoginis* have been represented as the attendants of various manifestations of Durga engaged in fighting with demon Sumbha and Nisumbha and the principal *Yoginis* are identified with the *Matrikas*. The number of *Yoginis* varies from eight to sixty-four. *Kalika Purana* (Chapters 60, 61, 63, 65) gives a description of *Yoginis*. Goddess Durga has eight associates known as Saktis, called Ugracanda, Pracanda, Candogra, Candanayika, Canda, Candavati, Camuna and Candika. Goddess Kausiki, Uma, Bhadrakali have eight, eight and twelve *Yoginis* respectively. In Kamrupa also *Yogini* cult was popular. *Kalika Purana* mentions Bhuvaneswari and Dirgheswaris as *Yoginis*. Dirgheswari has her shrine in Rangmahal in northern Guwahati. An idol of sixteen armed Chandanayika was recovered from the Ambari excavation in the heart of Guwahati city, identified with ancient Pragjyotisapura.

Tantricism has been intimately connected with Kamrupa Kamakhya where the chief Goddess Kamakhya is a *yoni* goddess. Kamakhya temple is unique because it enshrines no image. Only the symbol of *yoni* or genital organ is worshipped. This *yoni* worship is certainly a strong reference to old fertility cult associated with agricultural economy. Here, we may refer to fertility ritual called *ambuvaci* which is observed by the women of Assam on and from the seventh day of the third month of the Hindu calendar. It is believed that during the four days of the said ritual mother earth menstruates in order to prepare herself for procreation. In many parts of India, great importance is given to the menstruation of goddess Parvati. Reference should also be made in this connection to the menstruation of the goddess Kamakhya of Assam. The basic ritual of Tantricism is *pancamakara* which consist of *madya* (wine), *mamsa* (meat), *madira* (intoxicating drink), *mudra* (hand gesture) and *maithuna* (sexual intercourse). According to James Frazer sexual rites related to fertility magic are common to all forms of primitive religion. Erotic practices, associated with the Mother Goddess cult, are very old concepts.[26]

Goddess Kechaikhiati of Sadiya region of eastern Assam is regarded as a form of Kamakhya and also of Tripureswari of Tripura. She was the same Goddess of Dikkaravasini of *Tantras* and *Puranas*. She is known as Tamreswari who has two forms *tikshna* (fearful) and *lalita* (lovable). The former was black, pot-bellied and with one lock of matted hair (*Ekajata*). She was also called Ugratara (According to legend the present Ugratara temple of Guwahati marks the spot where Sati's navel fell when Visnu's discus dismembered her corpse carried by Siva). Her attendants are Bhaga, Subhaga, Camunda, Karala, Bhisana and Vikala — all are dreadful name which suggest her Tantric character. In general she was worshipped like Kamakhya. Her offerings consisted of strong liquor, human sacrifice, *modaka*, etc.

With the popularity of the cult of Mother Goddess, custom like human sacrifice became common in ancient and mediaeval Assam which effected the society. Barua clearly stated that Ranchandi and the Mahamaya of the Kachari Tribe, Tamresari of the Chutias, Jayanteswari of Jayantiyas and the fourteen *devatas* of Tipperas were worshipped by resorting to human sacrifices.[27] Generally, human sacrifice was mainly to please the goddess. The head of the victim was very precious in Tantricism. In the *Kalika Purana* Kali is imagined as wearing a garland of human skulls. Some tribes of this region offered human sacrifice when they faced common danger like natural calamities, drought, etc. They believed that the Mother Goddess would save them being appeased human sacrifice. By the tenth century human sacrifices were given canonical sanction by the Hindu tantrist. A chapter titled 'Blood Chapter' (*rudhiradhyaya*) in *Kalika Purana* is devoted to injunctions in regard to the sacrifice of animal and human beings to the Mother Goddess.

There are several *thans* which are open places regarded as sacred to the Mother Goddess in early and mediaeval Assam which prove the influence of the Sakta Tantric cult all over the region and, therefore, shaped the religious history of the land. Among them Malini *than* is noteworthy. There are several local legend regarding Malini *than* in the lower part of the West Siang district of Arunachal Pradesh. However, Malini is the name of one of the sixty-four *yoginis*. The temple was probably erected during the period of the Pala rulers of ancient Assam. Malini *than* originally fell within the zone of the early Mother Goddess Cult which later received Sakta Tantric oriention.[28] Malini *than* is described as belonging to the spiritual kingdom of Dikkaravasini. In Tezpur cults of Candi, Mahabhairabi, etc. and in North Lakhimpur the cults of Kali, Keohaikhaiti, Nila Gosani, etc. were prevalent since the pre-Ahom days which influenced the socio-cultural fabric of ancient Assam.[29]

N.N. Bhattacharyya in his work Indian Mother Goddess states that:

> "The glorification of Kamakhya as found in the *Kalika, Brihaddharma* and *Devibhagavata Purana* as well as in the *Kubjika, Yogini* and *Cudamani Tantras*, etc. is suggestive of the fact that the region bounded by the Himalayan extention on the north, the river Dikrang on the east, the confluence of Lakhya and Brahmaputra on the south and Karatoya on the west was from the earliest period a zone of the Tantric cult of Female Principle".[30]

Thus, Tantricism not only made its way to mainstream Saktism, but became inextricably linked to it so much so that it became very difficult to differentiate them. The local goddesses became assimilated in Tantricism. The *Puranas* give a realistic picture of the local goddesses. Later, they were identified with the supreme deity of both Saktism and Tantricism. Both *Puranas* and Tantric texts furnish detailed information regarding the *Pithas*, and their respective deities. There are several *Pithas* in Assam and Bengal. Among them some are purely recognized as Tantric in character. Kamarupa of Kamakhya is the most important eastern Indian site of the Mother Goddess cult.

NOTES AND REFERENCES

1. Woodroffe John, *Sakti and Sakta*, Ganesh & Company, Madras, 1975, p. 50.
2. Clemen, C., *Religion of the World*, London, 1931, p. 125.
3. Shastri, B., "Some Aspects of Saktism in Assam" in the *Journal of The Assam Research Society*, Vol. XXXII, Guwahati, 1992, p. 1.
4. H.P. Sastri as cited in Maity, P.K., *Historical Studies in the Cult of the Goddess Manasa*, Punthi Pustak, Kolkata, 2001, pp. 63-64.
5. Choudhury, P.C., *Assam-Bengal Relations*, Spectrum Publications, Guwahati: Delhi, 1988, p. 300.
6. Quoted by P.K. Maity, *Historical Studies of the Cult of Goddess Manasa*, Punthi Pustak, Kolkata, 2001, p. 66.
7. *Kalika Purana*, 51/64.
8. Choudhury, P.C., *op. cit.*, p. 300.
9. *Visnu Purana*, LXII.
10. Choudhury, P.C., *The History of Civilization of the People of Assam to the Twelfth Century A.D.*, Spectrum Publications, Delhi, 1987, p. 416.
11. Maity, *op. cit.*, p. 65.
12. Maity, *op. cit.*, p. 67.
13. Barua, K.L., "Kamarupa and Vajrayana" in the *Journal of Assam Research Society*, Vol. II, No. 2, 1943, pp. 44-49.
14. Sarma, D., (ed.), *Kamarupasasanavali*, Second edition, Publication Board Assam, Guwahati, 2003, p. 173.
15. *Ibid.*, pp. 199-202.
16. *Kalika Purana*, Chapter 85.
17. Kakati, B., *The Mother Goddess Kamakhya*, Publication Board Assam, Guwahati, 1989, p. 30.
18. *Kalika Purana*, Chapter 47.
19. *Brihaddharma Purana, Madhyama Khanda*, VI Chapter, pp. 13-14.
20. Brown, Mackenzie, C., A Review, "Tantric Visions of the Divine Famine: The Ten *Mahavidyas*" by David Kinsley in *International Journal of Hindu Studies*, Vol. 2, No. 1, Springer, 1998, p. 144. http:/www.jstor.org/stable/20106560, Retrieved on 24/06/2011.
21. *Ibid.*
22. *Ibid.*, p. 145.
23. *Ibid.*

24. Goswami, K.P., *Kamakhya Temple: Past and Present*, A.P.H. Publishing Corporation, Delhi, 1998, p. 81.
25. *Sadhanamala*, II, p. 130.
26. Frazer, *The Golden Bough: The Study in Magic and Religion*, MacMillan and Co. Ltd., London, 1957, p. 11.
27. Barua, K.L., "Human Sacrifice in Assam" in The *Journal of Assam Research Society*, Vol. VI, No. 1, Guwahati, 1938, p. 10.
28. Bhattacharyya, *op. cit.*, p. 304.
29. *Ibid.*
30. *Ibid.*, p. 306.

4

IDENTITY AND LIMINALITY IN NORTH-EAST INDIA

A Study of the Ahoms in Colonial and Post-Colonial Assam

Rajib Handique

Questions of identity have become an important aspect of academic discourse. History in the twenty-first century is going through an exceptionally vigorous, lively and innovative period. Many historians claim that history is moving from explanation to meaning and from causes to understanding.[1] Identity whether of individuals or communities is not a rigid or static phenomenon. Rather identity is dynamic and under constant definition and redefinition.

It is under certain circumstances that identity assumes a liminal character. *Liminality* comes from the Latin word *līmen*, meaning "a threshold". It is a psychological, neurological, or metaphysical subjective state, conscious or unconscious, of being on the "threshold" of or between two different existential planes. Liminality has been popularised by the anthropological theories of ritual by such writers as Arnold van Gennep and Victor Turner.[2] As stated by Victor Turner.[3]

> The attributes of liminality or liminal personae ("threshold people") are necessarily ambiguous, since this condition and these persons elude or slip through the network of classifications that normally locate states and positions in cultural space. Liminal entities are neither here nor there; they are betwixt and between the positions assigned and arrayed by law, custom, convention, and ceremonial. As such, their ambiguous and indeterminate attributes are expressed by a rich variety of symbols in the many societies that ritualize social and cultural transitions.

Issues of identity are fundamental in protecting a sense of self and group survival, and they become particularly important during conflicts. At the deepest level, identity is lodged in the narratives of how people see themselves, who they are, where they have come from and what they fear they will become or lose. The movement for identity of the Ahom community in Assam has undergone changes in terms of its demands and methods of articulation. This chapter will try to make an analysis of the changing mores in identity assertion of the Ahom community in the colonial and post-colonial Assam and in the process try to reflect on the phenomena of liminality.

The Ahoms, one of the foremost ethnic communities in the North-East India are a branch of the Tai or Shan people that migrated from South East China to Maulung in Upper Myanmar (Burma) from where they passed through the Patkai range and the Naga Hills and entered Assam in 1228 A.D. They succeeded in setting up a kingdom in the Brahmaputra valley, which lasted till 1826, when it was overtaken by the British Empire. The Ahom kingdom laid the foundations of an Assamese nation by unifying the diverse groups of people that inhabited the Brahmaputra Valley in pre-colonial Assam.

The Ahom kingdom lasted six centuries and could successfully withstand the onslaught of different forces including those of Mughal imperialism. It was the identity of interest regarding driving out the Mughal invaders that largely contributed to the formation of a civil society, a state with a common overlord. It was under these circumstances that a state called Asam or Assam, with a common overlord in the person of the Ahom king and a civil society to be identified as 'Assamese' grew up.[4]

By their own admission, dwelling on the ruling principles of the Ahoms, in a memorandum submitted to the Home Minister of India on behalf of the All Assam Ahom Association (AAAA), on 7 August, 1967, it was stated.[5]

> There were many principalities nominally tributary but self-governing within this vast extent of territory predominantly inhabited by mongoloid tribes and races. Under the hegemony of Ahom rulers, Assam was a sort of fraternal confederacy of friendly states both of the Hills and the Plains. The Ahom rulers scrupulously abstained from intervention in the internal political and social affairs of these states. Every time the Mughal invaded Assam, all the princes and rulers of these States united to fight and drive the enemies out. This experiment of fraternal confederacy of friendly states based on

common allegiance to the strongest of them, namely, the Ahom State proved of unique success in defending this part of South East Asia for nearly the whole reigning period of the Ahom monarchs.

The battle of Saraighat might be considered as a culminating point of this social development that was bringing people of different ethnic groups under a common figurative 'imagined community'.[6]

From the very beginning of their reign, the Ahoms followed a policy of assimilation and peaceful co-existence with the Morans, Barahis, Kachari, Chutiya, Bhuyan and other indigenous communities of Assam. The people of the different communities were made part of a greater societal framework. It was the liberal outlook of the Ahoms and their policy of assimilation that formed the bedrock of their political hegemony. It was in this way that the Ahom Kings from the time of Sukapha wanted to unify the various tribes and communities of Assam to form an Assamese nation.[7]

The Ahoms had their own language, religious beliefs and culture when they came to Assam.[8] They followed exclusively their own religious practices during the early part of their reign. It is worth mentioning that Sukapha had brought with him texts on Tai religion, language, astrology, etc. along with him.[9]

However, with the passage of time, the Ahoms came under the influence of various religions and ways of life. Matrimonial linkages between the Ahoms (exogamous as they were) and the indigenous communities were one significant way of building cultural bridges. The Ahom royalty came under direct influence of Hindu religion during the reign of Sudangpha also known as *Bamuni Konwar* (1397-1407). It was during his reign that the *Lakshmi Narayan Salagram* was installed in the royal household along with that of their titular diety *Somdeo*. This paved the way for entry of Brahmanic religion in the royalty.[10] It was during the reign of Bamuni Konwar that several religious ceremonies were conducted in the royal household.

During the reign of Suhungmung or *Dihingia Raja* (1497-1539) the great saints Sankardeva (1449-1568) and Madhavdeva (1489-1596) started the neo-Vaishnavite movement which spread all over the Brahmaputra valley and even beyond.

Later on, during the reign of Sutamla or Jayadhvaj Singha (1648-1663) Vaishnavism got formal patronage from the royalty. It was during his reign that the Satras were established in Majuli for the spread of Vaishnavism. These Satras became the vital institutions not only for spreading Vaishnavism but also for developing new forms of dance, drama and art forms that became popular as parts of the *Satriya* culture.

The Ahom royalty became interested in Saktism from the reign of Supatpha or Gadadhar Singha (1681-1696). It is said that his son Rudra Singha (1696-1714) was planning to take the *Sarana* of Krishnaram Bhattacharjee, the famous Sakta saint of Nadia in Bengal.

Thus, we find that the Ahom royalty patronized different religious faiths. The syncretism made them followers of different religious practices at the same time. Similar was the case with the Ahom gentry and the commoners. This created a liminal situation that was getting more and more fixed with the passage of time. In other words, the identity of the Ahoms was undergoing a process of transformation and in a way was becoming layered with other larger identity constructs that was necessary to sustain the kingdom.

As already mentioned, the Ahoms had their own religious beliefs and customs and the same continued to be followed by them in spite of their acceptance of other religious beliefs and customs from time to time. However, the common Ahom populace accepted the Assamese language and stopped speaking in their traditional Tai language.[11] Some of the Ahom families also stopped the practice of *dam-phi* or the traditional ancestor worship. There were Ahom families that became fully Vaishnavites, while there were also families that followed different religious practices at the same time though some of them were contradictory to each other. There are many Ahom families that perform among others both the *dam-phi* (where chicken, fish or other non-vegetarian cooked items are used along with the traditional drink *Haz*) and *Nam-Kirtan* (where gram, fruits, and other strictly vegetarian and uncooked items are offered) annually.[12]

British imperialism somewhat stunted the process of cultural syncretism that had developed in Assam. Imperial policies brought about monumental changes in the over-all economy. The revenue maximizing colonial land-use pattern, the advent of the plantation economy and coal and oil industries along with the significant demographic changes in a way traumatized the indigenous populace as age old ties were broken and new challenges emerged.

Quest for identity of self and one's own ethnic group is a natural human behaviour. Identity of an ethnic group may be on the basis of religion, occupation, language, territory, etc. Though the origin of the term 'Ethnic' was associated with the biological formation of populations, in social plane many other criteria including cultural parameters came to be associated with this term.[13] The ethnic groups are not necessarily homogenous. Boundary of an ethnic group is not a static phenomenon. Depending upon the circumstance and specific goal at a certain point or period of time, division and amalgamation of ethnic groups or segment of an ethnic group may even take place.[14]

Unlike the hundreds of princes in other parts of India who could keep their identity intact and could maintain some semblance of autonomous power, both the Ahom monarchy and the aristocracy saw their authority vanish rapidly in the imperial world. Various socio-economic policies introduced by the colonial rulers contributed to the backwardness of the Ahoms. W.W. Hunter, a British officer remarked that the once dominant race of Ahoms had sunk to the level of common cultivators. The regret of the nobility is evident when Kandarpeswar Singha in a letter to the authority politely remarked, "I am only a common ryot, like most of the government ryots, insignificant and destitute'.[15]

The assertion of the Ahom for a distinct identity within India and Assam is more than a century old today. The first major articulation of this identity was visible in the constitution of the *Ahom Sabha* on 13 May, 1893 under the leadership of the noted Assamese litterateur Padmanath Gohain Baruah (who also happened to be first President of the Assam Sahitya Sabha). This Ahom Sabha was subsequently renamed as All Assam Ahom Association (AAAA) in 1910. These organizations tried to overcome some amount of the social lag by pleading for conceding the demands of free studentship, appointment in government services, reservation of seats in local bodies and provincial legislature.[16]

Most of the sectional elite of the region seemed to believe that 'adequate share' of political power is necessary for the all round development of their respective communities. At the same time, it appears to them that that the maintenance of distinct identity is essential to bargain with the ruling elite for 'adequate share' of the decision making process and to realize other benefits for their respective groups. Thus, maintenance of distinct identity and development of the communities appear to be identical and complementary to each other.[17]

The Ahom leadership in the thirties and the forties of the twentieth century was vigorously pursuing the cause of minority status and separate electorate for the Ahom. In 1912, under the 1909 Act, what is also known as the Morley-Minto reforms, a Legislative Council was set up in Assam, after the Province was separated from the Eastern Bengal. One Ahom member was nominated to the Assam Legislative Council. Under the 1919 Act, again one Ahom was nominated to the first Legislative Council, the nominee being a member of the Ahom Royal family. In the subsequent Councils, the Ahom community had their members as nominees from minority community.[18]

However, after the passage of the Government of India Act, 1935, the situation changed and the subsequent beginning of the democratization process, the Ahom elite realized that the socio-economic development of the Ahom was largely dependent on the share in the administration they would enjoy. There was their apprehension of their interest remaining unaddressed or unprotected in an upper-caste dominated Assamese society. Surendra Nath Buragohain, a representative of the AAAA unsuccessfully moved a private Member's resolution in the Assam Legislative Assembly on November 20, 1943 thus:[19]

> This Assembly is of the opinion that the Ahom community of this Province be included among the recognized minorities for future Indian Constitution and that the Government of Assam do move the Government of India and His Majesty's Government for consideration and acceptance of the community as a minority.

In the event of Independence, when the Constitution was being framed, the Ahom leaders collaborating with other ethnic elite pleaded for adequate constitutional safeguards to preserve and protect their distinct ethnic identities. This collaboration might be viewed as a challenge to the hegemonic position of the 'caste Hindu dominated' Congress party of the province. The Ahom leaders particularly felt victimized within the Congress organisation itself. In the AAAA Memorandum on the Ahoms as a minority signed on 2nd July, 1941, it was stated,[20]

> The way in which this minority movement of the Ahoms has gone inside the Congress organisation itself will, however, be shown by the fact of increasing number of Ahom Congressmen having been subjected to disciplinary action during the past five years. The attempt to silence and to frighten the mass of the Ahoms into submission of the so-called discipline of the Congress by taking such actions against their leaders, must, however, necessarily fail.

The Ahom leaders collaborating with the other ethnic elite pleaded for adequate constitutional safeguards to preserve and protect their distinct identities. In the *Demands of the Tribal Communities of Assam : A Memorandum issued by the Conference of Leaders of the Ahoms and Tribal Communities of Assam*, Shillong (July, 1946, p. 2), it was stated,[21]

> These communities must be assured separate political existence in the new constitution by providing for them in the case of Hill tribes, local autonomy, and in the case of others, separate electorate. They must be allowed to live their own life and their own customs and culture without any encroachment either by the Hindus or the Muslims.

There was also serious concern voiced by several Ahom leaders regarding the problems Assam might face as part of an independent India. At the inaugural session of the Assam Tribes and Races Federation on 21st March, 1945, Prof. P. Gogoi had stated, "... Economically she is rich enough in resources, both essentially and strategic to be not only self sufficient but also to be flourishing if the need for capital is met for working plans of development during a period of economic transition. But if Assam remains a part of India she will go dangerously into the economic grip of Hindustan big business under the smoke screen of a national government. Historically and politically, she has a tradition behind which is unique and glorious in the History of the Far East and bears eloquent testimony to the fact that Assam can never be a digestible part of India, now or in the future".[22] Thus in the backdrop of imminent transfer of power there were a section of Ahom leaders that vouched for a separate state.

While demanding special privileges for them in the new constitution, they asserted that the setting up of autonomous unit among the ethnic tribes was 'vital to the peace and tranquility' of the region. The efforts made by the leaders of the Mongoloid communities to send their representatives to the Constituent Assembly became futile and their hopes and aspiration appeared to be shattered. Thus, after Independence, in the changed political circumstances, the AAAA felt the need of a broad based and coherent political organisation to fight against the Congress in Assam.

In 1948, Surendra Nath Buragohain, an Ahom leader collaborated with Muhammad Saadullah, the Muslim League leader, P.M. Sarwan, the leader of the Assam Tea Labourers Association, Capt. Williamson Sangma, and Prof. G.S. Swell, leaders of the Hill tribes and a few others to form a new political party named All Peoples' Party (*Sarba-Dal*) in 1948 in order to challenge the Congress in the First General Election of 1952. However, the Congress was able to make Saadullah and Buragohain defect and join the Congress in 1949, and thereafter the party lost its effectiveness. Buragohain later on emphasised that the interests of the community could be best fulfilled by being with the ruling party. The AAAA came to have an electoral understanding with the Congress.[23]

Thereafter, the political articulation of the Ahoms took the form of a demand for a separate federal unit in Assam comprising the then Sibsagar and Lakhimpur districts. The *Ahom Tai Mongoliya Rajya Parishad* (ATMRP) which was established in 1967 through merger of several Ahom organisations, spearheaded this demand. The ATMRP was rechristened as *Ujani Asom Rajya Parishad* (UARP) in 1970 in order to give it a inclusive image. It contested the mid-term Parliamentary election to the Lok Sabha in 1970 to back up the demand for a separate state. This organisation virtually became extinct after its election alliance with the Janata Party in 1977. The demand for a separate state has also lost its strength in due course of time. However, the demand for recognition of the Tai Ahoms as Scheduled Tribe continues to be raised. Demanding tribal identity, the Tai Ahom Council of Assam in one of its memoranda submitted to the President of India stated:[24]

> We fully claim to our tribal identity and have the reasons to believe that a constitutional safeguard shall alone be the only means and the most imperative need of the hour for a total upliftment of the Tai-Ahom Tribe in social, educational and political spheres by including the Ahoms in the schedule of Scheduled Tribes of Assam and elsewhere.

Political articulation was buttressed by lingo-cultural revivalism. However, this lingo-cultural assertion was mostly a post-Independence phenomenon. It was since the early 1960s that the Ahoms became much concerned with their lingo-cultural identity. The *All Assam Mohan Deodhai Bailung Sanmilan* (AAMDBS) established in 1962 strongly pleaded for the development of Tai language and culture. The All Assam Tai Students' Association formed in 1964, in one of its memoranda addressed to the then Chief Minister of Assam emphasized on the importance of learning Tai language and asserted that:[25]

> It is of utmost importance to promote the study of Tai Language and literature in this part of the country by reason of the fact that Tai is not only a mother tongue of a large section of the Tai population . . . but that there are lots of important and valuable manuscripts in Tai language in possession of the Tai Pundits of Assam, of many Assamese families and also in the Buddhist monasteries in Upper Assam and NEFA dealing with history, religion jurisprudence natural science, astrology and many other subjects.

It has been already stated that the Ahom royalty patronized different religious faiths while the general Ahom populace also developed the syncretism and made them followers of different religious practices at the same time.

Sukapha had brought with him the Ahom priests known as *Mohan, Deodhai* and *Bailung* besides *Chiring* the official chronicler.[26] These Ahom priests continued to practice the different traditional Tai-Ahom religious ceremonies till the contemporary times, though some of them accepted neo-vaishnavism. Some of the important religious ceremonies performed by them are *Ompha, Me-dam-me-fi, Dam-Fi, Jasingpha, Furalung and Rikkhan Myunkhan.*[27] They in a way preserved the Tai-Ahom religion, language and culture. The Ahoms also had their own ceremonies relating to birth, death and marriage. The marriage ceremony *Chaklang* is still popular among many Ahom families.

Revivalism can be considered as natural fallout of identity movements. However, the post-Independence revivalism in Assam was not for the pre-colonial culture of inter-cultural communication and social cohesion. The politicization process and the resurgence of ethnic identity in post-Independent India has resulted more in cultural separatism.[28] This separateness came to be articulated in various ways like:

(i) Using new forms and ways of writing names, e.g. using *Chaw* in place of Shri, or using Garg or Parashar in place of Borthakur or Rajkhowa, etc.
(ii) Using dresses fashioned as being particular to a community, which were not in popular use, e.g. *Chapkon* of the Ahoms, etc.
(iii) Celebrating different religious and other social festivals peculiar to each community. E.g. *me dam me fi* of the Ahoms, etc.
(iv) Laying claims of origin on aspects of common cultural practices and forms.
(v) Forming different literary and cultural organizations to promote and preserve their separateness.

Since, the early 1980s we witness ethnic assertion of various communities including that of the Ahoms in Assam. The revival movement of the Ahom developed sometimes with the patronage of the state. Ceremonies like *me dam me fi, rik khan myun kham* and *ompha* came to be celebrated by the Ahoms. As already stated, the Ahom priestly class consisting of the Mohans, Deodhais and Bailungs had preserved the Ahom religion and language and had continued performing the various religious ceremonies. When the revival movement gained momentum, these preserved religious customs gained acceptance among the larger Ahom community. It is however interesting to note that the revived traditions have not replaced the existing customs and traditions; more so the phenomenon manifests more the acceptance of the old as new.

Religious revivalism amongst the Ahoms is taking interesting turns. The Ahom Royal Society, an organization led by members of the descendents of the Ahom Royal family has claimed to have recovered the statue of *Somdeo*, which is being interpreted as an image of Buddha. This claim is yet to be substantiated, but there is also a likelihood that belief may suppress reason in this case. This development may become a watershed in the religious revivalism that is taking place in the Ahom community. Already, there are sporadic appeals made by the Tai Ahom organisations to mention Buddhist or Phralung as their religion and Tai as their mother tongue in the Census.

The Ahoms are today followers of different religious ways of life. This heterogeneity is likely to survive in the days to come. To understand the religious diversity amongst the Ahoms we need to adopt a flexible approach. As Talai observed, we need "a more flexible approach to ethnicity which does not make an *a priori* assumption that the presence of boundaries between ethnic groups implies heterogeneity between such groups but homogeneity within them". He had also opined that ethnic groups are interest groups which go underground when there is no competition.[29]

Thus, we find that throughout the colonial and the post-colonial periods, the Ahoms have been asserting their identity for various reasons. The articulation of their demands has undergone changes in the different historical contexts. The Ahoms asserted for a Minority status under the British *Raj*, while in the post-Independent context, demands were raised for a separate state and later on for a Scheduled Tribe status. In the context of lingo-cultural identity, there has been revivalism to a large extent, and like many other ethic groups of the region, the Tai Ahoms are involved in rebuilding if not re-inventing their own identities in the contemporary situation. The constitution of the *Tai Ahom Development Council* by the Assam Government marks yet another milestone in the identity movement.

However, in all of these, the liminal identity formations within the Ahoms are a historical reality. Many communities in North-East India have undergone similar experiences. Perhaps the cultural diversity of the region and the historical processes of integration or convergence have led to such liminal situations as identities appear temporally fixated in the throes of being and becoming.

NOTES AND REFERENCES

1. Cannadine, David, (ed.), *What is History Now?* Palgrave Macmillan, Hampshire, 2002, pp. x-xi.
2. Turner, Victor, *The Ritual Process: Structure and Anti-Structure*, Cornell University Press, New York, (Seventh Print) 1991, p. 85.
3. *Ibid.*
4. Barua, S.L., *A Comprehensive History of Assam*, New Delhi, 1989, p. 251.
5. Phukon Girin (ed.), *Documents on Ahom Movement in Assam*, Institute of Tai Studies and Research, Moranhat, 2010, pp. 16-17.
6. Anderson Benedict, *Imagined Communities: Reflections on the Origins and Spread of Nationalism*, Verso, London, New York, 2006.
7. Gait, Edward A., *A History of Assam*, Guwahati, 1926, p. 74.
8. Gogoi, Padmeswar, *The Tai-Ahom Religion and Customs*, Guwahati, 1976, p. 35.
9. *Ibid.*
10. Baruah, S.L., *op.cit.*, p. 227.
11. Gogoi, Lila, *Tai Sanskritir Ruprekha*, Dibrugarh, 1994, p. 142.
12. This is being observed by the author being a member of the Ahom community and may therefore be considered as lived experience.
13. Pranab Kumar Dasgupta, "Quest for Ethnic Identity by the Tribes of India", in Mrinal K. Miri (ed.), *Continuity and Change in Tribal Society*, IIAS, Shimla, 1993, p.158.
14. *Ibid.*
15. Letter issued to government in 1838, as cited in Buragohain, Nirala, "Socio-economic bases of Identity Assertion of the Ahoms: An Historical Perspective", in Phukan, Girin and Dutta, N.L. (ed.), *Politics of Identity and Nation Building in North-East India*, New Delhi, 1997, p. 156.
16. Phukon, 2010
17. Phukan, Girin and Dutta, N.L. (ed.), "Preface" in *Politics of Identity and Nation Building in North-East India*, New Delhi, 1997, p. vii.
18. Phukon Girin (ed.), *Documents on Ahom Movement in Assam*, Institute of Tai Studies and Research, Moranhat, 2010, pp. 16-17.
19. *Ibid.*
20. *Ibid.*
21. *Ibid.*
22. *Ibid.*, pp. 45-46.
23. *Ibid.*
24. *Ibid.*, p. xvii.
25. *Memorandum to the Chief Minister of Assam on behalf of the Tai Student Association*, Shillong, July 25, 1964 also cited in Phukon, 2010.
26. Choudhury, P.C. (ed.), *Kashinath Tamuli Phukanar Assam Buranji Sar*, DHAS, Guwahati, 1964, p. 14.
27. Barua, Sukha, *Ahom Sakalar Utsav Anushthan*, Guwahati, 2007.
28. Miri, Sujata, "Whither Tribal Culture", in Mrinal K. Miri (ed.), *Continuity and Change in Tribal Society*, IIAS, Shimla, 1993, p. 36.
29. Talai, V., "Social Boundaries within and between Ethnic Groups: *Americans in London*", in *Man*, Vol. 21, No. 2, pp. 251-70, as cited in Pranab Kumar Dasgupta, "Quest for Ethnic Identity by the Tribes of India", in Mrinal K. Miri (ed.), *Continuity and Change in Tribal Society*, IIAS, Shimla, 1993, p. 158.

5

HARI-HARA IN THE ART OF ASSAM

Deepi Rekha Kouli

As in other parts of India, religion was the basic force in the evolution of art forms in Assam which was known as *Pragjyotisha* in ancient times and *Kamarupa* in medieval times. It appears from the traditional accounts that the ancient kingdom of *Pragjyotisha* and later known as *Pragjyotisha-Kamarupa* was much more wider in extent than the geographical boundary of modern Assam. But the geographical boundary of kingdom of *Pragjyotisha-Kamarupa* was not static and constant throughout the ages. Both the great epics *Ramayana* and *Mahabharata* mentioned *Pragjyotisha*. The first epigraphic reference of *Kamarupa* has been found in the Allahabad Pillar Prasathi of Samudra Gupta.[1] As a part of Indian art tradition, in ancient *Kamarupa* we find influence of different forms of religious sects and beliefs, basically based on Hinduism and Buddhism, which brought about radical changes to non-anthropomorphic and ancestral worship of Indigenous people as well as Vedic rituals of earlier period.

As mentioned by Gopinath Rao, the worship of Harihara is the result of conflicts between Saivism and Vaisnavism and reconciliation that Siva is Vishnu and Vishnu is Siva and that they are essential for the creation, protection and destruction of the Universe.[2]

According to literary and epigraphic sources Saivism was the most dominant faith in this region from the earliest times. *Siva Purana* refers to the meditation of *Sivalinga* by the *Kamarupa* king.[3] Vidyavinoda mentions that the *Kings* of *Kamarupa* are Saivas. The *Kalika Purana* also refers fifteen numbers of sacred places which was associated with worship of Siva.[4] It also referred Siva as guardian deity before the coming of Naraka, who became worshipper of Mother Goddess, *Kamakhya*.[5] *Mahabharata* refers Naraka as Bhauma which indicates his connections with Vishnu. In *Dronaparva, Vishnu* describes that as requested by mother earth, he gave *Vaisnavastra* to Naraka. The epigraphic reference of the universality of religion is indicated by the Second Copper Plates grant of Dharmapala, wherein Lord Vishnu is highly praised in the initial verse. Further the Copper Plates grants of Indrapala also praised Vishnu as well as Siva. It indicates liberalization of religious cult. In *Kalika Purana* (xxxix.45), *sakti* is described as weapon of Vishnu. Thus, found reconciliation of Vaisnavism and Saivism. In this region, Siva was worshipped both in phallic and iconic forms. The iconic form of Siva has two aspects — *ghora* or *ugra*, i.e. fierce and the other *Sauma*, i.e. benign. Of the *sauma* form of Siva is represented by Sadasiva, Yoga-dakshinamurti, Nataraja as well as composite figure of Hari-Hara and Uma-Mahesvara are found in this region. There are very few composite figures of Hari-Hara, which needs detail study. The figure of Hari-Hara represents syncretise form — combination of Siva and Vishnu thereby manifesting syncretism of both Saivism and Vaisnavism in art form. It represents cordial relation between Siva and Vishnu cult. The figure of Hari-Hara may be in seated or in standing form and represents right half Siva and left half is Vishnu. The iconic reference is found in *Matsya Purana, Vamana Purana, Vishnudharmottara, Devatamurti-prakarana, Rupmandana*, etc.[6] However, as mentioned by Gopinath Rao, the worship of Harihara is the result of conflicts between Saivism and Vaisnavism and reconciliation that Siva is Vishnu and Vishnu is Siva and that they are essential for the creation, protection and destruction of the Universe.[7]

There is a rock-cut image of Hari-Hara at Urvasi island of river Brahmaputra. The figure is in *padmāsana* and it measures 56 × 32 cms. The deity carries *triśūla* in right upper hand and rosary in right lower hand while left upper hand carries *chakra* but other left hand is found broken. The God wears *kirātamukuṭa* and *yajñopavīta*. Below the figure, *vāhana Nandi* of Siva is carved in right and winged *Garuda, Vāhana* of Vishnu is carved in left, on the pedestal. Thus, represents both Siva and Vishnu (Plate 5.1). There is another figure of Hari-Hara found at North Guwahati which is now in A.S.M. The figure is flanked by Gauri and Lakshmi, consort of Siva and Vishnu respectively. The deity is in *tribhanga* posture, while both the consorts are standing cross-leged on either side. The God wears *yajñopavīta, vanamālā* and *kirātamukuṭa*. The God holds *triśūla* and *damaru* in right hand while his left hands carry *gada* and *chakra*. The Goddess Gauri wears *jaṭāmukuṭa* and Lakshmi wears *karandamukuṭa* and adorned with heavy ornamentation.

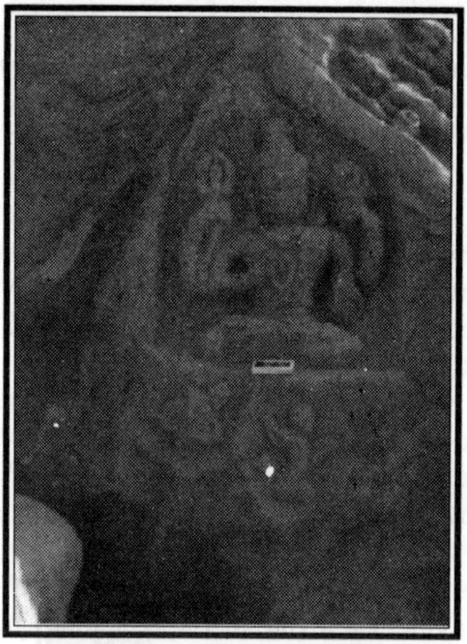

Plate 5.1: Harihara at Urvashi Island.

Uniqueness of the sculpture was that all the figures were of equal height. The stone relic appears to datable to nineth century A.D. It measures 61 × 73 cms. (Plate 5.2). There is found another *caturbhuja* stone figure

Plate 5.2: Harihara in Assam State Museum

of male deity found at Uzan Bazar which is now preserved at A.S.M. The deity was in *padmāsana* on a *visva-padmāsana* pedestal. The figure measures 83 × 55 cms. The God has been identified as Vishnu by earlier scholars but in closer examination it has been found that iconographic features represents that the deity appears to be a figure of Hari-Hara (Plate 5.3). There is a *Prabhāvali* behind the head of the deity on the

Plate 5.3: Harihara in Assam State Museum.

stella. The God wears *kirātamukuṭa, kundala, hara* and *Yajñopavīta.* The upper part of the stella is broken. In one of the left hands, the figure carries *gada* while other three hands were found to be broken. But on the right side of the figure there appears to be impression of a *śūla* on the stella though mutilated. There are four figures — two on the middle of the stella and two on the pedestal on either side of the central figure. Of the two figures on the middle of the stella, one on the right represents Mahishamardini Durga and the other one stands with a *khadga* may be Kalki, while of the two figures below on pedestal, one in right represents Gaṇeśa and the other on left represents Buddha in *dharmachakrapravartana mudrā.* Below on the pedestal there found a figure of Garuda in the centre and a figure of devotee with *Siva-Linga* on the right. Thus, the above observation indicates that the existence of Gaṇeśa and Mahishamardini on the right represents Siva, while presence of Kalki and Buddha on the left represents Vishnu. Thus, the figure may be identified as Harihara. There found two inscribed images of Harihara from Deopani, Golaghat District, now at Assam State Museum (Plate 5.4 and Plate 5.5). Of them, one is inscribed as *Śaṅkaranārāyaṇa* and the deity is four handed and in *samapada-sthānaka* posture on lotus pedestal.

Plates 5.4 and 5.5: Two images of Harihara from Deopani. (A.S.M.)

The right forearm holds rosary and right back arm holds trident, while left forearm holds *sankha* and left back arm holds *chakra*, which is partly broken. The figure has *nandi,* Bull (*vāhana* of Siva) on his right side[8] and *Garuda* (*vāhana* of Vishnu) on his left side below on pedestal. The figure wears *vanamala*, one of the icononic features of Vishnu and on the other hand the figure has *urdhvalinga*, which signifies that the figure is a saivite image. Thus, the figure may be identified as Harihara. While the other image represents similar iconographic features like *samapada-sthānaka* posture, having rosary with *varada mudrā* in lower right hand and *sankha* in lower left hand and *chakra* in upper left hand. Further, bull and *garuda* is depicted below on right and left respectively. The image has *urdhvalinga, jatamukuta* and *trinetra* distinctive features of Siva and wears *vanamala*, the icononic feature of Vishnu. The inscription inscribed on the body of the image described the image as Harihara and carved in low-cut relief. As per epigraphic reference both the images are datable to 8th c.A.D.[9]

Thus, as per archaeological evidence and literary references, it may be concluded that though Saivism was popular cult in prior to 7th c.A.D. Vaishnavism also exists side-by-side. It appears that Vaishnavism was popular cult in the early medieval period. As a result we found reconciliation between two major cults of Vaishnavism and Saivism in the composite form of Harihara image side-by-side saktism in early medieval period.

NOTES AND REFERENCES

1. Barpujari, H.K., *Comprehensive History of Assam*, Vol. 1, p. 73.
2. *Kāmarupaśāsanāvali*, p. 60D. Sarma, (ed.), Publication Board.
3. Sri Sri Jeev Nyayteertha (ed.), *Sivapurana*, Ch. 48.50, p. 184, 1392 Bangabda.
4. B.K. Barua, "A Cultural History of Assam", *Early Period*, Vol. I, pp. 161-62.
5. *Kalika Purana*, ch. XXXVIII, V. 96, p. 421. Translated by Debendra Nath Bhattacharya.
6. *Kāmarupaśāsanāvali*, Dr. D. Sarma (ed.), publication Board, Assam, pp. 150-51.
7. D. Sarma (ed.), *Kāmarupaśāsanāvali*, p. 60.
8. K. Barpujari (ed.), *The Comprehensive History of Assam*, Vol. I, p. 358.
9. D. Sarma (ed.), *Kāmarupaśāsanāvali*, p. 64.

SECTION II

Value Education and Culture

6

AHOM CULTURE

B.K. Gohain

The Ahoms are one of the Tai groups and are distinguished by their distinctive culture and traditions. The group of Tais who entered into the easternmost part of Assam (then called Kamrup) in 1228 A.D. from Mungmao and Mungkhu-Mung-Ja under the leadership of the great prince Chaolung Siu-Ka-Pha was given the name 'Ahom' by the local populace like the Mataks, Barahis, Chutias and Kacharis, while in all the historical manuscripts written in Tai Ahom language and script, they used to call themselves as Tais. The name was accepted and it denotes the name of the tribe.

Siu-Ka-Pha with his retinue of nobles and soldiers numbering nine thousand befriended the Matak and the Barahi tribes. Siu-Ka-Pha encouraged intermarriage with the local populace and even Siu-Ka-Pha married two princes of the Matak and the Borahi kings. His descendants also followed suit and the formation of the Ahom tribe was characterized by inter-marriage with the local tribes and castes. Only distinguishing feature in this process was that the families of the persons with whom the Ahom entered into matrimonial alliances were encouraged to be included into the Ahom fold and to become Ahom. The Ahoms never discriminated any person on the ground of caste, creed and religion and was equally respectful to other religions.

The Ahoms have their traditional religion which is practised by many even to this day. It is a fact of history that the Ahom kings patronized Hinduism and encouraged setting up of the monasteries (*sattra*) in their kingdom. Some of the nobles also embraced Hinduism and Vaishnavism but they never foresook their traditional religion.

Religion

The traditional religion of the Ahoms is called Banphi which is practiced by the members of the priestly classes namely Deodhai, Mohan and Bailung. The priestly classes are the repository of the religious texts written in Thai Ahom language and script which are found in the manuscript form written on Saci bark and on Muga (Silk) clothes.

The Ahoms are animists but they have the basic concept of God Almighty whom they call Pha-Tyu-Shing-Phrong-Hum. Their most sacred text is called "Lit Lai Pak Peyn Ka Ka" which may be termed as the Ahom Bible. This manuscript recounts the story of creation of the universe and of the gods and goddesses of the Ahom pantheon clearly specifying that at the beginning, there was only void and no sky, no stars, no sun, no moon, no earth, etc. It was God Almighty who created everything. There are the gods, and the goddess of the heaven like (1) Pha-Nu-Ru Lengdon, the presiding deity of the Ahoms, and the lord of thunders, storms, lightning, etc.; (2) Khaokham, the lord of waters; (3) Ai Lengdin, the lord of the earth; (4) Jan-Shai-Hung, the preceptor (Guru) of the gods; (5) Ja-Shing-pha, the goddess of learning; (6) Mut-kum Tai Kum, the Sun and moon god; and (7) Chit lamsam, the seven gods associated with thunder, storm, lightning, dew, etc., who are also called the sons of Lengdon. All these goddess and the gods are worshipped on different occasions by the Ahoms with the priests belonging to the priestly classes performing the rituals. They offer blood-sacrifices and each and every ritual is attended by the offering of home made rice beer which is an indispensable item of offering for the gods. They may also be worshipped with the offering of eggs.

The other set of gods worshipped by the Ahoms with blood sacrifices is called the frontier gods or the gods of the wildness. The most important of them are (1) Po-Phi-Su (the lord of the jungles), Langkuri, the most ancient god and Nang-Chi-Chao. Their attendants like Khetor, Bhut, Jokh, Bagh-Baghini, etc. are also worshipped.

In Umpha worship, besides there deities as mentioned hereinbefore, the Hindu gods and goddesses like (1) Mahadeo (one of Hindu trinity), (2) Gossani (Phi-Methao), (3) Saraswati (goddess of learning), (4) Ai Nabhani (nine sisters of Mother goddess), and (5) Jol-Kunwari, Apeswari, etc. are worshipped in a separate pavilion.

While the offering for Lengdon is a white calf which should be killed with a stout stick of guava tree, other white animals and birds are also offered in Umpha worship.

The most important ritual of the Ahoms which is most practiced annually on 31st January is the public Ancestor Worship called Me-Dam-Me-Phi. This public ritual has assumed the proportions of a festival and all people can take part in the public prayers and feast organized. The striking point is that an Ahom of any clan (not necessarily of the priestly class) can perform this ritual as a priest.

Dam-Phi ritual is performed by the members of the priestly classes on all auspicious occasions like the new harvest and feasting festival in every household, on the occasion of the spring festival (Rongali Bihu) and on the Makar Sangkranti (Magh Bihu). Here, the family worships the dead spirits, their grand parents, great grand parents and of the spirits of the persons who died as children or without marriage. They make the offerings of food and rice beer on the raised platforms. The dead spirits are supposed to reside in the mainpost (Pho-Kam) in the kitchen and are worshipped by the family. They believe that the ancestors come down to accept their offerings and to bless them. This is exemplied by one of the hymns chanted on the occasion (The meaning of which is given below).

> "Neither the walls nor the roof
> Nor the gods in the heaven
> Can protect you
> If the household ancient spirits
> Donot Protect".

The Ahoms have the concept of the duality of the soul called Pu and Phu. This concept might have been inspired by the concept of Ying and Yang of Taoism.

The only ritual which is performed without blood sacrifice or without the offering of eggs is Phuralung, which is the worship of God Almighty. Here, the priests worship Pha-Tyu-Shing-Phrong-Hum or God Almighty by lighting earthen lamps and offering only fruits and soaked gram, etc. The holy book "Peyn Ka Ka" is read. This ritual has the overtones of the Buddhist influence on the Tais in the thirteenth century early part when Siu-Ka-Pha and his compatriots left Mung Maolung and Mung Khu Mung Jao, the Tai countries presently located in Dehong Dai prefecture of Yunnan of China.

Literature

The Assamese language and literature developed tremendously with the patronage of the Ahom royalty and the nobles. The Vaishnavite literature got written during the Ahom period. The growth of a peculiar genre of play and the emergence of a prose medium of expression and the composition of religious songs are noteworthy.

It was Swargadeo Jaydwaj Singha who first composed "Padmapuranar Janakar Akhyana" in poetry. Kaviraj Chakraborty was patronized by the Ahom king. Atan Buragohain, one of the most important and influencial Prime Ministers encouraged Ramananda Dwija, a pontiff of a Vaishnavite monastery (Sattra) to compose "Shankardevar Charita" and Ramananda also composed religious songs of very high standard. Other works of literature were "Bhismaparva" and Putala Charitra, one Ramachandra Borpatragohain composed "Hayagriva Madhava". Swargadeo Rudra Singha patronized the Assamese literature in a big way. He composed some songs and encouraged Kaviraj Chakraborty, the Poet Laurate to translate "Geet Govinda" of Joydev into Assamese who also wrote a book of astrology called "Bhaswati". During the reign of Swaergadeo Shiva Singha and Queen Phuleswari, "Shakuntala Kavya" and "Shankhachud Badh" were composed and "Krishna-Janma-Khanda" of "Brahmavaivartta Purana" was composed.

In a book of poetry written by him (Kaviraj Chakraborty) under the royal patronage, some romantic songs of love were also composed by him.

Swargadeo Shiva Singha composed "Shiva Purana" in Assamese and he along with his principal queens Phuleswari and Ambika encouraged writing of books by Ananta Acharjyya who composed "Ananda Lohori". Kavichandra Dwija composed "Dharma Purana", Romananda Dwija composed "Brihat Ushaharana" and Sukumar Barkath composed "Hasti Vidyarnava" and all these books contain some paintings.

During the reign of Swargadeo Shiva Singha and his brother kings, some works of literature are seen. "Shailya Parva" of Bholanath Dwija, "Udyoga Parva" of Dwija Ramananda, "Brahmavaivartta Puranar Prakriti Khanda" of Durgeswar Dwija, "Chandi Pada" and "Kalki Purana" of Kuchinath Kandali, "Shanti Parva" of Lakshminath Dwija and "Hari-Vansha" of Vidyachandra Kavisekhar were some of the important works of the period. Swargadeo Rajeswar Singha also patronized the Assamese literature. He is reputed to have composed a drama "Kichaka Badha" as well as some Shakta songs. Some of the important works of the later period were "Niti-Latankur" of Bagiswar, "Rama Charita Manasa" of Shrikanta Suryavipra, "Mushala Parva", "Mohaprasthanika Parva" and "Svargarohana Parva" of Prithuraja Dwija. Other works are "Sambarasur Badha" of Bhavakanta Bipra, "Kumara Harana" of Lakhsmikanta Das, "Dharmodaya" of Dharmadev Bhatta, "Shri Krishna Proyana" of Vidya Panchanana, "Kama-Kumara Harana" of Kavichandra Dwija "Bighnesh-

Janmodaya" of Gourinath Dwija and "Shankhasura Badha" of Dinanath Dwija.

During the Ahom rule, the Vaishnavite literature grew rapidly. After Shrimanta Shankardeva and Mahadeva left the Ahom kingdom, some of the Vaishnavite preachers like Bangshigopaldeva, Aniruddhadeva, Jadumoni, etc. thrived during the Ahom rule. They contributed heavily towards the Assamese literature Shri Shri Aniruddhadeva distinguished himself by writing a sacred book on Bhakti called "Niz-Sashtra" in coloqual Assamese prose. All these pontiffs were required to write plays to spread Vaishnavism. The patronage of the Parbatia Gossain of Bengal by Swargadeo Rudra Singha and Swargadeo Shiva Singha and his principal queens Phuleswari and Ambika led to the writing of books on Saivism and Shaktism.

Historical Literature

Sir George Abraham Grierson in his '*Linguistic Survey of India*' wrote about the historical literature during the Ahom rule in the following words:

> "The Assamese are justly proud of their national literature. In no department have they been more successful than in a branch of study in which India, as a rule, is curiously deficient.
>
> The historical works, or Buranjis as they are styled by the Assamese, are numerous and voluminous.
>
> According to the custom of the country, a knowledge of the Buranjis was an indispensable qualification to an Assamese gentlemen".

The Buranjis or the historical works written in Assamese were brought to light by the relentless efforts of Dr. Suryya Kumar Bhuyan, Pandit Hemchandra Goswami, etc. During a period of nine years from 1930 to 1938, Dr. Bhuyan compiled and edited eleven Buranjis and published them. They are (1) Assam Buranji by Harakanta Barua (1930), (2) Kamrupar Buranji (1930), (3) Tungkhungia Buranji (1932), (4) Deodhai Asam Buranji (1932), (5) Asamar Padya-Buranji (1932), (6) Padshah Buranji (1935), (7) Kachari Buranji (1936), (8) Jayantia Buranji (1937), (9) Tripura Buranji (1938), (10) Assam Buranji (1945), and (11) Satsari Assam Buranji (1960).

The important feature of these historical texts is that the events were written down from generation to generation by the Ahom priests under the supervision of Chiring Phukan and Barchiring Barua.

Pandit Hemchandra Goswami edited '*Purani Asam-Buranji*' for '*Kamrup Anusandhan Samity*' which published it in 1922. Here, the texts from the first to the fourth chapters were recorded during the reign of Swargadeo Siu-Hung-mung. Pandit Hemchandra Goswami made a very significant observation in the preface of this historical work that the Ahoms had the system of recording the events since 568 A.D. and at first all these works were in Tai Ahom language and script and only afterwards, the historical accounts were written in Assamese which the Deodhai-Bailungs (Ahom priestly classes) continued to record the events in Ahom language and script upto the last Ahom king. He also observed that after the Ahom kings accepted Assamese, they contributed immensely to the development of the Assamese literature and the historical literatures are one of the most important parts of the Assamese literature. These historical works in Assamese dated from the early sixteenth century upto the end of the Ahom rule.

These chronicles constitute an invaluable repository of the old Assamese ways of expression and they reveal many forms and vocables which are gradually becoming obsolete.

Besides these historical works in Assamese, the following works were printed and published thereby enriching not only the historical value but also the literature. They are:

1. Assam Buranji by Kasinath Tamuli Phukan edited by Radhanath Barbarua and published in 1906 from Calcutta and was written in the year 1833 during the reign of Swargadeo Purandar Singha. This was originally a Buranji written in Ahom language and script during the reign of Swargadeo Gourinath Singha.
2. Asom Buranji (1648-1681 AD) edited by S.K. Dutta and published in 1938.

Besides these published works there are many chronicles in manuscript form in Assamese which are yet to see the light of the day.

The wealth of historical texts, chronicles, works on astrology and astronomy, religious works, stories, creation myths, Jataka stories, etc. which are written in Tai Ahom language and script has remained unappreciated by the Assamese as well as the Indian scholars for their lack of knowledge of Tai-Ahom language. *The Tai Ahom script is one of the early forms of script of the eleventh century and unlike other Tai scripts, it has not changed a little bit. The scholars from Thailand, China, Myanmara, etc. are interested in studying this ancient script of the Tais.*

The Government of Assam under the British rule first ventured upon the collection of such manuscripts as a result of which many manuscripts in Tai-Ahom are now available in the library of the Directorate of Historical and Antiquarian Studies, Assam, Guwahati. The first work of translation of a chronicle written in the Tai was accomplished in the year 1930 when Rai Sahab Golap Chandra Barua translated an original Ahom Buranji into English with the assistance of certain Ahom Pandits. The beauty of the work is that it carries the Ahom text with English translation.

Such manuscripts, hitherto unpublished and untranslated from the wealth of the historical texts in Tai Ahom. The works in Tai Ahom language and script are characterized by the following divisions: (a) History (Din Buranji and Deo Buranji), (b) Manuscripts on religion (regarding the details of the various rituals as well as the creation myth), (c) Manuscripts on astrology and astrology like Bansheng, Phelung Phe-Ban and on Tai system of calculations), (d) The manuscripts on the Ahom system of marriage (Chaklong), (e) Amra manuscripts (dictionaries), (f) *Jataka* stories, (g) Other stories.

The most important of the religions texts is Lit Lai Peyn Pak Ka Ka which gives the myth of creation. The astrology and astronomy are different from the Hindu concepts and are unique. The *Jataka* stories are also interesting from the point of view that it indicates the influence of Mahayani Buddhism on the Tai Ahom religion.

Marriage Ceremony

The Ahom marriage ritual which called Chaklong is unique in the sense that no other Assamese holds this marriage ritual. When during the Ahom rule, any non-Tai Ahom princes was married to an Ahom king by observing this ritual, it became a way of accepting the bride as Ahom. The ritual consists of (1) *Juran* or the gift-giving ceremony from the groom's side by his mother and close relations. (2) *Nuoni* or the ceremonial baths to the bride and the groom for three to five times in their respective homes. (3) *Rik-Khwan* or the ritual of longevity performed by the Ahom priests and making offering to Khaokham, the lord of waters. Two to three priests fish in a river or a pond with a bamboo scoop and whatever edible water-creatures like fish, etc. are caught are cooked and offered to the bride and the groom in their respective houses on the first day. (4) *Deoban* or the worship of the Ahom gods Langkuri, Janshaihung, Lareng, Lengdon and Jashingpha by the priests in the houses of the groom and the bride by the Ahom priests on the second day. Offerings are also made to the Dam (dead spirits) of the respective family.

Aptang is the ritual of giving a bath with purified and incarnated water mixed with medicinal herbs to the groom and bride in their respective houses.

Gathean grinding ceremony is performed on the second day by grinding a specific herbs by the mothers of the bride and the groom and giving a holy dot on the foreheads of both.

After the *Juran* ceremony, the family holds the Ancestor Worship or Naparushar Bhojj or the community feasting worshipping the nine generations of the ancestors.

Dayan Diya ritual is the ritual of applying two betel leaves soaked with curd on the faces of the bride and the bridegroom in their respective houses. The mother and the close relations (ladies) apply the betel leaves on the arms, knees and feet.

The marriage party with the groom proceeds to the house of the bride. The mother as well as the ladies on the bride's side welcomes the bridegroom and the party. The mother plants kisses on the cheeks of the groom after a small girl washes the feet of the groom who gives her some money as gift. The groom and the party are led to the *pandal* (stage) where the arrangement for holding the Chaklong ceremony.

The Chaklong pavilion is very colourful where 101 earthen lamps are placed and lit. There is a coloured design generally a lotus on the raised platform made of earth and the lamps are placed on at each and every cross-point with a bigger lamp and four other lamps in the center on a post.

The most important feature is the chanting of *mantras* in Tai language by the priests and conducting the ritual in Tai explaining the meaning in Assamese. After the groom takes his seat beside the bride's father, the bride is invited to the pavilion from the groom's party. The bride is led to the Chaklong pavilion and seated near the groom to his left. The father of the bride honours the priest with the offering of some betelnuts and leaves and dresses, etc. both the bride and groom salute the priest. The priest conducts the ceremony. The genealogies of both the families are told. The priest chants the mantras and the bride and the groom offer flowers and rice in the name of Lord Lengdon and say in Tai the prayer following the priest. Then the bride's father offers the hand of the bride taking the right hand of the groom in his right hand and the right hand of the bride in his hand and placing the hand of the bride on the right hand of the bride and says that he has given his daughter to the groom in marriage in the name of God. The groom says that he accepts the bride as his wife. Then there are exchanges of garlands first by the bride. Then they salute the bride's father at his feet. The priest chants hymns in praise of the presiding deity Lengdon. Then the bride hands over a sword (Hengdan) to the groom asking him to protect the country, the family, etc. which he promises to do. The priest gives them advice for a blissful married life.

After this there are fun and frlicks. After taking of meals by the groom and the bride, the groom's party which was given a sumptuous meal return back to the groom's place to a hearty traditional welcome.

Coinage

The Ahom kings used to mint coins which have become a subject of interesting numistic study as it is reflected of the culture of that time. Generally, the shapes of the coins were octagonal as for the Ahoms, the octagonal shape is sacred and holy. There are square coins also.

Although both Gait and Botham credited Siu-Kleng-Mung as the first Ahom King to strike coins, however, on reading the Ahom texts in Tai script, it becomes abundantly clear that the first Ahom King who minted coins was not Siu-Kleng-Mung but Siu-tam-la or Swargadeo Joydwaj Singha. He also minted coins in Sanskrit in Assamese character. The Tai Ahom coins on the observe gives the *lakni* (year) and *plekni* (cycle) of the King while on the reverse, the salutations to God Almighty are mentioned.

Jaydwaj Singha's Assamese coin bears the Saka era of 1570 and on the reverse it is the salutation to Shri Sri Hari Hara at their feet. In 1681 A.D., Siu-Pat-Pha *alias* Gadadhar Singha became the king after a long spell of Chaos and he minted coins in Ahom language and script. On the obverse of the coins is the year (*lakni*) and the cycle with the name of the king and on the reverse it is the offering of the prayer of the king to Lengdon, the Lord of Heaven. This shows the return to the Ahom faith of the king and the use of Ahom in the Court.

The coins of Siu-Khrung-Pha *alias* Rudra Singha were in Assamese character and in Sanskrit. The coins had the Hindu name of the King on the obverse and the salutation to Sri Sri Hara Gauri at their feet. This is indicative of the Shaiva-Shakta influence although practically Rudra Singha was not partisan to any religion. The coins minted by Shiva Singha and his consorts Phuleswari, Ambika and Sarveswari speak of their adherence to Hara and Gauri. The first Ahom coins in the Persian script was struck by Phuleswari (Pramatheswari) and they have striking similarities with those minted by Nurjahan, Queen of the Mughal Emperor of Jahangir. Phuleswari struck coins in two names namely Pramatheswari and Phuleswari.

The coins of Shiva Singha and his queens are significant as they indicate the Shakta influence on the king and the queens. They were initiated by Parvatia Gossain a Shakta Brahmin and all other Ahom kings were initiated to Saktism.

Ahom king Kamaleswar Singha and his successor Chandra Kanta Singha again restored the customary reference to 'Hara Gauri' in their coins. But the coins of Brajanath Singha carry salutations to Sri Sri Radha Krishna as he was a Vaishnava. Jogeswar Singha, protégé of the Burmese struck coins with the customary reference to Hara-Gauri.

The first Ahom coin in Persian script was struck by Pramatheswari, the first queen of Siva Singha. It is a square coin. King Rajeswar Singha also struck coins in Persian script. This shows the growing interactions with the Mughals. The coins of Jayadwaj Singha and Chakradwaj Singha bear the name of Lord Vishnu and Shiva.

This shows that the Ahoms were not influenced by any particular sect of Hinduism. From the reign of Shiva Singha, the adherence of the Ahom Kings to Shakta form of Hinduism is displayed. Pramatta Singha's coins also bear legend signifying adherence to Mother Goddess Gauri. The Ahom Kings used to mint gold as well as silver coins.

The contribution of the Ahoms towards the building of the cities, temples, roads, tanks, bridges and buildings is immense, Assam got a new face during their rule.

The first King Siu-Ka-Pha erected a fort at Charaideo and finally constructed a city true in 1252 A.D. He constructed Langkuri temple (Doul) and Deosal (Place of worship). Siu-Dang-Pha (1397-1407 A.D.) constructed the town Chargua. Siu-Kleng-Mung (1539-1552 A.D.) constructed the city of Gargaon. Siu-Khan-Pha *alias* Khoraraja (1553-1603 A.D.) constructed two towns at Sonapur and Taokak respectively. Siu-Doi-Pha constructed the town at Darika and named it Bokanagar. Rudra Singha constructed the famous Rongpur City. Premier Purnanda Buragohain of Kamaleswar Singha constructed a town at Jorhat. King Udayaditya Singha developed Guwahati as a beautiful city.

The ancient capital city Gargaon has still the four storied royal palace or Kareng-Ghar constructed by Rajeswar Singha. The palace was surrounded by a brick wall and a masonary gate.

Sahabuddin Talish, who visited Assam in 1662 A.D. described the Ahom palace at Gargaon as made of wood. He praised the artistic works.

Rang-ghar, a two storied brick-built structure constructed by Swargadeo Pramatta Singha at Rongpur is a marvel and it is one of the earlier ampi-theatres in the world. The city of Rongpur was developed in a beautiful manner with temples and a large tank which are still in fact. Talatal ghar is an architectural excellence.

Another important work undertaken by the Ahom Kings was the excavation of large tanks called Sagar. Siu-Hung-Mung, (Dihingia Raja) excavated the Kartowa tank in 1454 Saka on the bank of Kartowa river. Of all the tanks excavated during the Ahom rule, Joysagar is the largest. It was excavated during the reign of Rudra Singha. Shiva Singha's first queen constructed Gouri Sagar. The third large tank is Sivasagar constructed by Madambika, the queen of Shiva Singha in 1733.

The stone bridges over Darika, Rahdoi, Dimow, Naduar of Rongpur and Namdang show the ingenuity of the Assamese engineers and workers of the Ahom rule. Gadadhar Singha constructed the stone bridges at Dijoikhana and Rahdoi.

The best stone bridge is of the Namdang river. The three-edged device of controlling water by seven gates is an engineering ingenuity of the period.

The construction of the Hindu temples began before the Ahom Kings embraced Hinduism. Most of the ancient temples of Nagaon and Kamrup were reconstructed.

The architecture of the Ahom period may be broadly classified into two categories, *viz.* the secular and the religious.

The religious monuments and shrines built during the Ahom rule are numerous. Siu-Ka-Pha, the first Ahom King built the Langkuri doul (temple) at Charaideo, Sivasagar, the ruins of which are still visible. Even before their initiation to Hindu religion, the Ahom Kings constructed temples and shrines and reconstructed many ancient temples. Siu-Sen-Pha reconstructed the Nagsankar temple of Sonitpur in 1480 A.D. Siu-Hung-Mung, Dihingia Raja constructed a Shiva temple known as Mahadevar Dol on the bank of the Dihing. Pratap Singha constructed two temples at Debargaon (Dergaon) and Biswanath, Gadadhar Singha constructed four Hindu temples and four Ahom temples. Rudra Singha constructed Joydol or Keshavrai Vishnu Temple, Baidynath Shiva Temple, Devighar (Devi temple), Surya Mandir or Sun Temple, Fakua Temple, Ranganath Temple, etc. on the banks of Jaysagar tank and in its neighbourhood. During the reign of Shiva Singha, Queen Phuleswari constructed Siva Dol, Vishnu Dol and Devidol at Gourisagar.

Her brother Harinath Barpatra constructed the temples of Kalugaon. Queen Madambika constructed the temples of Sivadol, Bisnudol and Devidol during the reign of Shiva Singha. His other queen Sarbeswari constructed Keri-Rajmao temple. In Kamrup, Shiva Singha constructed seven temples, prominent amongst them were Aswaklanta and Siddheswar. Rajeswar Singha also reconstructed some of the temples in Kamrup.

Lakshmi Singha, Gaurinath Singha, Kamaleswar Singha and Chandra Kanta Singha constructed seven temples at different places of Assam. Purananda Buragohain constructed a temple at Kashi (Baranas) in 1812.

The Ahom Kings starting from Jaydwaj Singha with a few exceptions also contributed to the building of the Sattras (monasteries) of Vaishnava pontiffs to a large extent including the grant of revenue free lands. Jaydwaj Singha encouraged Narowa Gossain Damodar with men and money in the discovery of Batradravadham (Bardowa), the birth place of Shrimanta Shankardeva, the great Vaishnava Guru of Assam. He contributed to the re-establishment of this holy place by his grant of revenue free lands and with men and money. He also granted lands and men for the establishment of Narowa Sattra at North Lakhimpur.

Rudra Singha convened a Vaishnava rally at Gargaon and got a list of the Sattras and their chiefs and gave them royal recognition. Pramatta Singha caused a temple to be built at Dakhinpat Sattra.

It is a fact that from the days of Rudra Singha, the Ahom royalty showed their adherence to the Shakta form of Hinduism but pursued a policy of religious tolerance. During the rule of Siu-Khan-Pha *alias* Khora Raja, one Astabhuja image of Durga was brought from Jayantia Kingdom and a Brahmin was appointed for worship of the deity.

The distinguishing feature in the construction of the temples during the Ahom rule was use of bricks in place of stone slabs.

The secular architecture is exhibited by Ghanashyam temple (house) of Joysagar, the palaces at Gargaon and Joysagar and the pavilion building (Rang-ghar). In addition, Moidams (or the burial mounds of the Ahoms) at Charaideo and other places are important from the point that these are comparable to the pyramids. The coffin containing the dead body of a king or a queen or of a noble was taken to burial place where a structure of brick had been kept ready keeping all the amenities including food and the articles of luxury for the use of the dead. The tomb thus constructed for the royalty was called Kareng-Rukdan. Besides these, there were palaces made of wood, bamboo and thatch, the mention of one at Gargaon was made by Shihabuddin Talish. His observation that probably nowhere in the world could wooden houses be built with such decorations and figure curving as by the people of this country is very significant.

Art of Painting

During the Ahom period, there were many works of painting, the most notable of them being the secular branch of painting represented by "Hasti-Vidyaranava" of Dilbar and Dosay. These miniature paintings are of superior skill and workmanship representing various types of elephants and scenes from the Ahom royal court. They depict how the Ahom Kings used to hold their courts and how the game of falconry was played in the presence of the kings and how an Ahom King rode an elephant in a procession. The pictures are in water colours and a large number of them are gold mated.

These paintings show some influences of Mughal painting. Landscapes of the green plains and blue hills, trees, a river flouring down a hill with fish swimming, clouds, etc. are seen. More importantly, the portraits of the author Sukumar Barkath, the painters, Dilbar and Dosay and their royal patrons Shiva Singha and Ambikadevi along with the nobility are seen.

Kaviraja Chakrabarty's *Gita Govinda* depicts some scenes representing the court of King Rudra Singha.

"Sankhachunda Vadha", another work of the period presents beautiful paintings.

In the matter of textiles, the Ahoms brought the art of rearing Muga worms for Muga silk (Khok-Pha) in addition of the already existing practice of rearing Endi worms for Endi clothes (Phok Bun Pha). The dresses introduced by the Ahoms are Pha-sou (shirt), Pha-noi (lungi), Ri Kham (Riha or women's upper garment), Pha Chin (Mekhela or women's upper garment), Pha-Bin-Wai-ram (tongali or waist band) in addition to Khonia Kapar (large shawls), Cheleng Kapar (shawl), Bor Kapar (bigger shawls). The Tai style of bamboo hat (Japi) which has became very popular was also introduced by the Ahoms. The Ahoms introduced the loom as earlier only the loin-loom was used by the tribes.

The Tai residential houses are always built on posts. We have Hang-ren (or Chang-ghar or raised house built on posts), grannary built on posts. The Holong-ghar, i.e. the raised house constructed for the coronation of King was one such raised house. As these were built with timber and bamboo, they did not last the wear and tear of time.

The jewelleries brought in by the Ahoms are Gam-Kharu (ornamental bracelet), Golpota (Pha-lai-leng-Ham kho or necklace) Dugdugi earrings), Joon biri, etc.

The other artificates are Sorai (phun or the raised metalic place made of bell-metal), Bo (or Dola or the palanquin carrying the nobility),

Silver lime pots (Temi), Ning (peera or wooden stool). The cooking utensils are Kanhi (phe), Ban Kanhi, Bera Kanhi, Maihang (all metallic discs with stands) Ban Bati (metellic tumbler with a stand) Hatikhujia Bati (big tumbler), Nam-tao (loota or metallic jar), Bota, Panbota, Barbota (all metallic plates on stands, etc. Sorai (phun or raised metallic disc) Choria (metallic container), Ghagori, Ghoti, Kalah, etc. are some of the utensils introduced by the Ahoms. Long (dheki or wooden husking machine) was introduced by the Ahoms.

There are some of the aspects of culture of the Ahoms.

REFERENCES

Botham, A.W., *Provincial Coin Cabinet*, Shillong.

Buragohain, Dilip Kumar, *Changrung Buranji*, Sivasagar, 1993.

Gait, Sir Edward, *A History of Assam*, Kolkata, United Commercial Press, 1967.

Gogoi, Lila, *Tai Sanskritir Ruprekha*.

Gogoi, Puspa and Bogen Gogoi, *Tai Sanskriti, Purbanchal Tai Sahitya Sabha Dhemaji*, 1994.

Gohain, Dr. B.K., *Tai Ahom Ja Nagosthi Aru Tai Parampara*, Apurupa Publishing House, Dispur Ghty, 2009.

Neog, Maheswar, *Asomiya Sahityar Ruprekha*, New Book Stall, Ghty, 1970.

———, *Cultural Heritage of Assam*, Omsons Publication, New Delhi, 2004.

Sarma, A.C., *Tai Ahom System of Government*, B.R. Publishing Corporation, New Delhi, 1986.

Sarma, Satyendra Nath, *A Socio-economic and Cultural History of Medieval Assam (1200-1800)*, Guwahati, 1989.

7

SANKARDEVA'S PHILOSOPHY OF CULTURE

Jagadish Patgiri

Srimanta Sankardeva (1449-1568) was one of the important proponants of the famous *Bhakti* Movement in eastern India. Sankardeva occupies a significant role in the cultural resurgence of medieval India. The greatest name in early Assamese literature is that of Sankardeva and he has left his stamp on Assamese literature and culture and on Assamese religion and way of life. Sankardeva was a poet, playwright, singer, dancer, actor, preacher and social reformer which introduced Assam to India and India to Assam. Sankardeva's impact on Assamese life is indescribeable. According to Professor Vasudeva, S. Agarwal, "there are poets and composers, there are saints and religious teachers, there are musical masters, there are preachers, but Sankardeva was genius in whom all these qualities were rolled in one. Sankardeva was like the glorious sun under whose warmth of mind Assam blossomed like a lotus of thousand petals (*sahasra dala kamala*). It is difficult to imagine how deep and widespread was the influence of Sankardeva on the cultural renaissance that burst forth in medieval Assam". [Chaliha, Bhaba Prasad (ed.), *Sankardeva Studies in Culture*, 1987, p. 97]. In an age of political distintegration and religious degeneration Sankardeva become a beacon light and cementing force. Throughout his life, Sankardeva waged a relentless crusade against social evils like untouchability, casteism and religious torture and persecution and taught the lesson of unity and brotherhood.

Sankardeva was a prolific writer of Assamese verses and a poet of very high order. In order to popularize his tenets he and his great disciple Madhavadeva turned out a vast religious literature in the current language of the people. Sankardeva also wrote a Sanskrit worked named '*Bhakti-*

ratnakar'. He translated the *Bhagavata* and composed a unique book called '*Kirtan-ghosha*' to be read and chanted by the devotees of all classes. The '*Kirtan-ghosha*' contains quintessence of his creed. He composed popular religious songs upon the life and doings of Srikrishna. He introduced a new feature in his movement by composing dramas (called *Ankiya Nat*) including the cult and depecting life story of Srikrishna, to attract people by dramatic performances, and thus popularize to teachings. *Neo-Vaishnavite* reformers of his time seemed to have done this. The entire life story of Srikrishna was rendered into music, poetry and drama by him and Madhavadeva contributed his share to all these literary performances.

Before Sankardeva, the religious life in Assam appears to have been at very low ebb. The people, Brahmans and the masses, were mostly *Saktas* and their religion was largely an attempt to propitiate the dread mother Goddess by offering sacrifices of animals and sometimes of human beings to her. There was very little of the spiritual in these cults and practices which were based on the *Sakta Tantras*. Sankardeva brought to the people of Assam the message of faith in the one Lord, who was Vishnu. Vishnu is supreme force. Hence, there was no point in offering special worship to the other manifestations of the Divinity which were conceived as the various Gods and Goddesses of Hinduism. He, therefore, propagated the doctrine known as *Ekasarna Namadharma* or *Mahapurusiya* religion (devotion to one Reality).

Unconditional *Bhakti* or devotion to the supreme God Krishna is the essence of this religion. The spiritual philosophy that was born in course of the *Bhakti* Movement, by way of attributing a human interest to the religious texts (*Sastras*) with newer interpretations, liberating religion from shackles of petrified rituals and upholding the rights of the common man in the face of all hindrances put up by authoritarianism, found one of its principle propagators in the personality of Sankardeva.

In the time of Sankardeva a great Vaisnava Renaissance was gaining momentum in the whole of India. So, the new Vaisnavism of Sankardeva can be called a part of the Indian Vaisnavite Movement of the Middle ages. The *Bhakti Dharma* started by the Alvars of South India around the Sixth Century AD had spread all over India taking the shape of a movement. It was Ramanand who transmitted *Bhakti Dharma* from South India to North India and Saints like Kabir, Raidas, Ramanuja, Vallabhacharya, Surdas, Tukaram, Namdev, Gyaneswar, Nanak, Mirabai, Tulsidas, Sankardeva, Chaitanyadeva and others fully popularized the *Dharma* in every part of India.

The *Bhakti* movement was an important landmark in the cultural history of India. The messengers of *Bhakti* movement of these personalities were true bearers of culture since they denounced caste-system, untouchability and preached fundamental equality and unity of man. They were the exponent of *Bhakti* cult, i.e. single minded devotion and love to God. Following Indian tradition, Sankardeva, the great spiritual and cultural leader of Assam contributed immensely to the Medieval cultural renaissance. The seminal ideas of the *Eka-Sarana Dharma* were creatively borrowed from different religious traditions. There is a close relationship between Sankardeva's *Bhakti* Movement and the *Bhakti* Movements in different parts of India. Sankardeva was a saint who widely travelled. For nearly 12 years he toured many holy places in North India. His pilgrimage took him to Puri, Gayam Sitakunda (Mongry), Banaras, Prayag (Allahabad), Ayodhya, Vrindavan, Mathura, Dwaraka, Badarikashram and Varahakunda. His pilgrimage enabled him to discover the soul of India spread over the continent. In this regard Dr. Maheswar Neog writes, "Sankardeva went on Pilgrimage to different holy places outside Assam on two occasions in the year 1481 A.D. at the age of thirty-two and began again in about 1546 at the very ripe old age of about ninety seven (M. Neog Sri Sri Sankardeva, 1948). On the second occasion he did not move beyond Sri Purusottam-Ksetra, where he stayed for three **forth nights** only. In his earlier sojourn, however, he did not turn home for twelve long years. On both occasions his main centre of interest was Sri Purusottam-Ksetra, where most possibly he met all sorts of religious people from Northern and Southern India and came in contact with the currents and cross-currents of the social upheaval that was at that time boiling in the veins of India. These travels to the various centres of learning and of religions importance in Northern and Southern India had not too a little to do with the part he played in bringing about a religious, social and cultural reformation in the country. According to one biographer (*Caritkar*) Sankardeva stayed for four or five months and talked of the greatness of god Jagannath from the *Brahma Purana* to the temple priests.

Vaishnavism in the North received a fresh impetus from the South from the great acharya Ramanuja and his successor's teachings and powerful propaganda. In Northern India Ramananda, Vallabhacharya, Nambaditya, Sankardeva and Chaitanyadeva were the Vaishnava reformers of great repute. Ramananda is said to have been the fifth in apostolic succession from Ramanuja and he lived towards the end of fourteenth century A.D. It is generally said that there are four main *Sampradayas* or sects of Vaishnavism, *viz.*, Ramanuja, Vishnuswami, Madhavacharya and Nimbaditya (Nimbarka). All other current minor sects are said to have been included in these four main *Sampradayas*. It is also said that Lakshmi acknowledged Ramanuja; Brahmana Madhavacharya; Rudra Vishnuswami; and Sanaka, Sanananda, Sanantan and Sanatkumara Nimbaditya respectively.

Jayadeva, the renowned author of the *Gitagovinda* flourished in the twelfth Century Radha and Krishna were his objects of worship. His *Gitagovinda* gave a great impetus to Chaitanya during his life and cult in the beginning of the sixteenth Century. Kabir made spiritual protests against the current Hinduism and Mahomedianism, and wanted to reconcile both the religions like Nanak. A small sect of Vaishnavism originated with Mirabai. She was married to Rana of Udaipur, but as she was a staunch Vaishnava, she could not agree with her husband and his relations, who were Saktas, and had to leave their protection. After roaming over many places she passed the rest of her life, meditating and chanting the name of her *Ista Devata*, Ranchod with the image of Sri Krishna. The founder of the fourth main *Sampradaya* was Nimbaditya or Nimbarka and people belonging to his sect is called Nimat. Krishna with Radha is their God of Worship, and the *Srimad Bhagavata* is their main scripture.

Chaitanya is generally regarded as the founder of *Sampradaya*. His followers not only regarded him as the founder of the faith but also as an incarnation of Krishna and the main object of worship. There had been a bitter controversy between the Brahmin pandits of Bengal and his followers as to his being an incarnation. (Bezbaroa, Lakshmi Nath, *History of Vaishnavism in India, Bezbaroa Granthavalee*, Vol. III). Although the Chaitanya Sampradaya traces its origin to Madhavacharya, the sect of Vallabhacharya has great affinity with this sect. Both Chaitanya and Vallabha flourished about the same time. Chaitanya adopted the worship of Radha-Krishna and there can be little doubt that Jayadeva's *Gitgovinda* and the Maithili Poet Vidyapati's songs played an important part in moulding his thoughts. Some writers ignorant of historical facts have often represented that Sankardeva's School of neo-Vaishnavism in Assam is an off-shoot of the Chaitnaya Movement in Bengal. This is misconstruction and misrepresentation of real historical facts. Lakshmi Nath Bezbaroa writes, "Sankardeva was born in 1449 A.D., whereas Chaitanya was born in 1486 A.D. Chaitanya was not born when Sankara set out on his Pilgrimage. When Chaitanya turned an ascetic in 1510 A.D. Sankara's Vaishnavism was in its full swing. Sankaradeva could not have met Chaitanya during his first Pilgrimage. But during his second pilgrimage from Barpeta he met Chaitanya about 1530 A.D. at Puri. There was no conversation between them as Chaitanya was then observing silence, and, therefore, he pouring water from his Kamandalu Chaitanya indicated that devotion to God is continuous and direct to one channel only like the flow of running water, was his creed. Sankara did not survive long after his return from the second pilgrimage. He died in Cooch-Bihar in the year 1568 A.D. after having attained a very long life of 119 years" (Lakshmi Nath Bezbaroa, *History of Vaishnavism in India, Bezbaroa Granthavalee*, Vol. III, p. 3026).

The idolization of the female element which formed the marked feature of Northern Vaishnavism and of the Chaitanya Movement in Bengal, is conspicuous only by its total absence from Sankardeva's Vaishnavism.

Chaitanya's conception of *madhura rasa* or love relations between the lover and the beloved as the mode of worship of God by His devotee to which he gave prominence, does not find favour in Sankardeva's school of thought. There is neither the combined worship of Radha and Krishna of Chaitanya, nor of Gopi Krishna of Vallabhacharya, nor of Rukmini-Krishna of Namdev, nor of the Sita-Rama of Ramananda. Sankardeva's spiritual relationship with Srikrishna was founded on *Datshya Bhava* (Servility). Sankardeva repeatedly consider himself to be servant of lord Krishna (Krishnar Kinkar).

Vaishnavism of Sankardeva is uncompromising in its attitude against the worship of other gods and goddesss. Sankardeva declared spiritual equality for all men and loudly proclaimed that even a *Chandala* is superior to a Brahmin if the *Chandala* becomes *Hari-Bhakti-Parayana*, i.e. if he becomes devoted to Hari.

There are diverse of opinions regarding the nature of the philosophy of Sankardeva. Some scholars think that Sankardeva is an *advaites* like Sankara, while on the other hand, some other scholars think that he is *Vishistadvaites* like Ramanuja.

Sankardeva's teaching is very relevant to present day society. Sankardeva preached the fundamental equality of all religions. He established a new democratic social order in the society through his philosophy of culture. He constituted a value-based society where different people having different religious faith learn the lessons of humanitarianism from his faith.

Sankardeva's role as a social reformer was immense significance as all aspects of Assamese life, culture, literature, music, dance, painting, sculpture and architecture revived during the Vaisnavite Movement. The cultural region of Sankardeva was definitely golden period in the history of Assam. Sankardeva's Philosophy of Culture has great relevance to the present day problems and needs of the society and the country. The philosopher, poet, playwright, painter, social reformer Sankardeva was the main architect of Assamese society and culture. Although Sankardeva lived and propagated his faith in the fifteenth century his message to mankind in general and India's in particular is of utmost relevance even today as society is replete with all sorts of evils emanating from narrow casteism, domestic communalism, religious fanaticism, greed, jealousy and uncompromising attitudes.

There have been many debates on Sankardeva's literary and cultural (Bhawna, Sattriya dance, etc.), traditions. For instance — the chief disciple of Sankardeva Mahapurush Madhâvadeva's 'Guru-Vatima', 'Nam-Ghosha', other Vaishnava Saints Ram Saraswati, Ram Charan Thakur, Daityari Thakur, Bhattadeva, Vairagi Chakrapani's 'Kathaguru Charit' are remarkable works on Sankardeva's life. In the post Sankardeva period, specially in the colonial period Lakshminath Bezbarua's 'Sankardeva' (1911), 'Mahapurush Sri Sankardev Aru Sri Madhavadeva' (1914) is significant work of Sankardeva's life and works. In the post-colonial period Dr. Maheswar Neog's 'Sankardeva and his Times', 'The Vaisnava Renaissance in Assam'. 'The Creative Force behind the Sankardeva Renaissance' (2011); Dr. S.N. Sarma's 'The Neo-Vaisnavite Movement and the Sattra Institution of Assam' (1966), Kaliram Medhi's 'Studies in the Vaishnava Literature and Culture of Assam' (1975), Harmohan Das's 'Sankardeva: a Study' (1945), Dimeswar Neog's 'Mahapursism: A Universal Religion' (1950), 'Jagat Guru Sankardeva: the Founder of Mahapurusism' (1963), Dr. Birinchi Kumar Barua's 'Sankardeva: Vaisnava Saint of Assam' (1960), Upendra Nath Goswami's 'Vaishnava Bhakti Dhara Aru Santa Katha' (1975), Achayyaria Manoranjan Shastri's 'Asomar Vaishnava Darsanar Ruprekha' (1991), Sonarum Chutia's 'Asomar Vaisnava Darsanar Swarnarekha' (1971), Bhaba Prasad Chaliha's (ed.) 'Sankari Sanskritir Adhyayana' (1978), Dr. Dayananda Pathak's 'Srimanta Sankardeva' (The Great Master), (2009), 'Beautiful Mind of Srimanta Sankardeva' (2012), etc. are remarkable works on Sankardeva. Besides the above noted writers some internationally reputed scholars like Stephen Fakes. Australia, Dr. W.L. Smith Seweedan, Stockholm University, etc. Studies Sankardeva. But the philosophical perspective has not been as critically analyzed as one would hope, apart from a few works that have not been able to capture national and international attention. Inspite of so many work it is a matter of regret that although Sankardeva is worthy of getting an International status, is yet to be explored.

8

IMPACT OF KOCH RULERS ON THE TEMPLE ARCHITECTURE OF ASSAM

Paromita Das

The Koch King Naranarayana and his brother Chilarai were the sons of Vishwa Simha who had laid the foundation of the Koch kingdom in Assam in the sixteenth Century C.E. With the assistance of Chilarai or Sukladhwaj, who acted as Prime Minister, as well as Commander in Chief, the reign of Naranarayana witnessed the rapid rise of Koch power in eastern India. His reign was marked by political expansion as well as the development of literature, religion and the arts. Under the active patronage of Naranarayana and his successors, the rule of the Koch Kings is marked by development in different spheres of life — religion, literature, construction (road building) and art and architecture. Perhaps Naranarayana's greatest contribution towards Assamese society lies in his active patronage of the neo-Vaisnavite saint Sankardeva and the rebuilding of the Kamakhya temple at Guwahati. This chapter focuses on the impact the architecture of this temple had on temple architecture of the succeeding period.

According to the Nilachala Kamakhya Mandir Stone Inscription,[1] during the reign of the King Malla Deva (i.e. Naranarayana) in the Saka year 1487 (i.e. 1565 C.E.) his brother Sukladhwaj (i.e. Chilarai) constructed the Kamakhya temple on the Nila-Salya or Nilachala (Blue Hill). According to the *Darrang Rajvamsavali*, verses 548-55,[2] the king further dedicated seven score or 140 *paiks* (servitors) for service to the temple as recorded in a copper plate charter. These paiks included men of the following castes or professional groups — *Brāhmana* (priests), *Daivajña* (astrologers), *Nat* (dancer), *Bhat* (singer), *Tānti* (weaver), *Māli* (garland maker), *Kamār* (blacksmith), *Kahār* (bell metal worker), *Bārhoi* (carpenter), *Dhobā* (washerman), *Sāloi* (sweetmeat maker), *Teli* (oil presser), *Sonāri* (goldsmith), *Kumār* (potter using wheel), *Hirā* (hand potter), *Kaivarta* (fisherman), *Chamār* (one who skins dead animals), *Muchiyār* (leather worker) and *Hādi* (scavenger). Thus, the king made ample provisions for the daily maintenance of the temple.

The Kamakhya temple is perhaps the most famous monument associated with Assam. As it stands today, the ground plan consists of the components of a typical *Nagara* temple of the post-Gupta period—i.e. a sanctum sanctorum, preceded by three *mandapas*. The best representative of this style is perhaps the Lingaraja temple of Orissa, where the *garbhagriha* or sanctum is preceded by three pillared halls, namely the *Jagmohan, Bhogmandir* and *Nātyamandir*, all on the same axis and having their entrance in a straight line.

In the Kamakhya temple too we have the *garbhagriha*, a connecting vestibule or antechamber — the *antarala*, then the three *mandapas*, popularly called the *calantagriha, pancharatna* and *nātmandapa*. The last was, however, built during the reign of the Ahom king Rajeswar Singha in 1759 C.E.[3] It is the dome or *sikhara* over the *garbhagriha* that marks a departure from other temples of the period as seen from the remains of Madan Kamdev (probably twelfth/thirteenth century C.E.), where monolithic *angasikharas* have been discovered, displaying all the features of a typical *Nagara* temple of the Orissan style. It is not known what the original Kamakhya temple looked like, but the architecture of the temple *bada* points to it being a *Nagara* temple with a *Nagara sikhara* similar to the rock cut *sikharas* found on the western side of the Nilachala itself. The present temple, which was reconstructed during the reign of Naranarayana, is a curious mixture of *Nagara* Hindu and Islamic architecture. Upto the level of the cornice or *verandah*, the *bada* of the temple resembles that of a typical *Nagara* temple of the medieval period — complete with *rathas* or projections, recesses and niches, adorned with sculptured deities, foliage and friezes. Here, however, the resemblance ends. The *sikhara* of the temple, instead of being a four-sided curvilinear tower with *pagas* and *angasikharas*, as common in Orissa and Central India (especially Khajuraho), is a polygonal dome — a unique device unparalleled in contemporary temple architecture. Moreover, the *pancharatha bada* is made of stone while the domical beehive shaped *sikhara* is made of bricks. The *Darrang Rajvamsavali* has an explanation to offer.[4] It records that the task of rebuilding the temple was entrusted to Meghamukdum who used artisans and craftsmen from Koch Behar. The original temple was reportedly destroyed by the renegade iconoclast Kalapahar (in all probability it was destroyed by an earthquake), who accompanied Sulaiman Karanani's invasion of Assam. According to the *Vamsavali*, while trying to reconstruct the *sikhara* out of the stone blocks recovered from the ruins, Meghamukdum failed, the rebuilt *sikhara* twice collapsing. So instead of stone he used bricks and proved successful. This indicates that the masons were more familiar with constructing Islamic type domes of bricks rather than a *Nagara sikhara*. By this time Muslim rule had entrenched itself in North India and the artisans and masons from Koch Behar were probably experienced in building domical structures. The architect Meghamukdum thus evolved a new style — a hemispherical "beehive shaped dome over a *pancharatha bada*. This beehive dome proved to be the model for the temple architecture of the succeeding Ahom period and is aptly called the 'Nilachala type'.[5] According to Pradip Sarma, "the idea of providing isolated *angasikharas* around the main *sikhara* might have also been borrowed from Islamic architecture where minarets and *guldāstas* (turrets) are provided around the dome for decorative purposes".[6]

The *antarāla* of the temple resembles a thatched hut with two slanting roofs or *do-chala* and connects the *garbhagriha* with the square *jagmohan* or *calantagriha*. The roof of the *antarāla* too is duplicated in numerous Ahom temples including those still standing in Guwahati and North Guwahati, *viz*. Dirghesvari, Asvaklanta, Manikarnesvar, Chatrakar, Nabagraha, Ugratara, etc. The roof of the *calantagriha* rests on four pillars and is a four-sided stepped pyramid. Besides the centrally aligned entrance the *calanta* has a second entrance on the north, complete with a *do-chala mukhamandapa*. However, the latter is a later addition and was constructed in the Ahom period along with the *chaitya-hall* shaped *natmandir* in 1759 C.E. as mentioned earlier.

The other noteworthy feature of the architecture of the Kamakhya temple is the roof of the *Bhogmandapa*. Instead of the typical *pida deul* or stepped pyramid we find the flat roof adorned with five domes, all resembling the main *sikhara* beehive dome. The central dome is largest in size and an equal sized smaller dome occupies each of the four corners. Thus, the Kamakhya temple is also the earliest extant *pancharatna* temple in Assam, though differing from contemporary *pancharatna* temples of India where smaller *sikharas* are generally found grouped around the *sikhara* of the *garbhagriha* or sometimes all the roofs have *rekha deuls* as in the Kandariya Mahadeva temple of Khajuraho.

Thus, Naranarayana initiated the development of a new style of temple architecture, which borrowed from Islamic architecture giving rise to a hybrid style, which greatly influenced the temple architecture of the succeeding period. Moreover, he also initiated the system of granting servitors to temples. After him his nephew Raghudeva also actively patronized temple building and like his uncle granted by means of a copper plate charter seven hundred *paiks* or servitors to the Hayagriva Madhava temple at Hajo[7] which he rebuilt (it is, however, dissimilar to the Kamakhya temple in style). The Ahom monarchs, especially Siva Simha, also continued this system. Thus, the Koch King Naranarayana and his brother Chilarai, who is actually recorded to have built the temple at Nilachala, had a great impact upon the temple architecture of Assam.

NOTES AND REFERENCES

1. M. Neog, edited, *Praschya Sasanavali*, Guwahati, 2003, (1974), Texts, p. 2.
2. K.L. Barua, "Human Sacrifice in Assam", in *Journal of the Assam Research Society*, Vol. VI, No. 1, April 1938, pp. 4-11.
3. M. Neog, *op. cit.*, p. 50.
4. *Darrang Rajvamsavali*, pp. 110-11, cited in Pradip Sarma, *Architecture of Assam*, p. 123.
5. Pradip Sarma, *Architecture of Assam*, p. 124.
7. M. Neog, edited, *op. cit.*, pp. 3-4.

9

NEGOTIATING 'CHANGE' AND 'SPACE'
Mamang Dai's *The Legends of Pensam*

Sweta Pegu

A society draws its sustenance from its lived past-immediate and remote. The past colours the memory and finds expression in shared memories. "Memory is a phenomenon that is directly related to the present, our perception of the past is always influenced by the present which means that it is always changing". (http:/en.Wikipedia.org/wiki/cultural-memory). Further, memory as a medium of representation is not limited to individual and private experiences alone, but becomes a "part of the collective domain". This collective memory is then passed on from one generation to the next. It helps forge group identities and unify communities cutting across time and space by creating conscious awareness of the past by a mode of active remembrance. Often, starting with being a private memory, it soon moves into the realm of the collective consciousness as experiences begin to be shared. Based on these collective memories which are handed down from generation to generation, whole histories are constructed and identities shaped.

'Cultural' memory as divined by Jan Assman, draws from the theory of collective memory which thrives on a lot of diverse mediums of representations/expressions such as memorial heads, commemoration days, rituals observed publicly, festivals celebrated and an interest in retro culture. Even mundane activities/articles like food items, songs, and dresses have the ability to spark off these collective memories of a life lived and shared. Interestingly, these ties and memories have also the ability to cement and strengthen communities in these times of conflict where every society is torn asunder with differences of every kind. More and more cultures/societies have markedly begun to go back to their roots to forge their 'community identity'.

"Change is the process by which the future invades our lives, and it is important to look at it closely, not merely from the grand perspectives of history, but also from the vantage point of the living, breathing individuals who experience it" (Toffler, 1971). 'Change' which comes in with the passing of one era into the other is welcomed by some and greeted with an air of resignation by others even as nations are formed, boundaries drawn and redrawn, identities shaped and reshaped and dreams give way to hopes and sometimes to illusions and disappointments. This wheel of 'change' has rolled in earlier in the plains than in the hills of Arunachal Pradesh (earlier known as North-East Frontier Agency or NEFA) located in the far north-east of India.

Inaccessible terrains, dense forests and in no small measure the Inner Line Permit system firmly in force were some of the reasons the region has remained cut off from mainstream India. With the trends of globalization and liberalization setting in, Arunachal Pradesh also opened its borders to progress and development and most importantly, 'change'. The area has become accessible, even hitherto remote areas have become interconnected. The youths of the state now go to the metros in pursuance of higher studies. Nowhere is change more visible than in their mode of dressing, their way of thinking and in their new ways of living. Change has set in everywhere in Arunachal Pradesh. As hamlets give way to towns and towns to cities; old ways also are being abandoned in favour of new modern lifestyles. But, the love of the land remains and it is this bond that pulls the youth back to his homeland, to the familiarity of beautiful landscape, simple, honest and hospitable people and the particular sights, sounds and smells of a land dearly loved.

Mamang Dai, well-known litterateur belonging to the Adi tribe of Arunachal Pradesh traverses along now forgotten trails, reliving old ways, rustling up old memories — of an idyllic life even while recognizing and accepting the momentous changes taking place in her society in her memorable book, *The Legends of Pensam*. 'Pensam' as Dai expostulates, is the 'middle' space/the void. She interprets this 'space' as the hidden services of the heart, home to hidden passions (Dai, 2006). Amidst the bounty of Nature, her people, worshippers of 'Donyi' (Sun) and 'Polo' (moon), live out their lives; the young deftly manoeuvre the old and the new ways and the elderly sit back ruminating over the old, idyllic days and rueing the loss of the old ways. With the passing away of these elderly people, the rich culture of the people reflected in the oral traditions and folk literature in the form of legends, myths, old sayings, folk tales, folk songs, festival songs, lullabies, songs of lamentations, etc. are slowly dying out for lack of documentation and also because, it gets assimilated within a bigger and dominant culture. Caught in the allure of things foreign, the richness of this oral culture also gets enmeshed in the maze of modernity.

The *shamans* (priests) and the elderly are the only ones left to tell the stories of the land. They are the ones who can divine the whisperings carried in the wind, in the rustle of the bamboo groves and in the lashing of the rain. The hills, the rivers — all have a story of their own to tell. The wind carries these stories afar — the stories of the dead, of the valour of their mighty heroes, the origin of the universe, of their world and of the first man on earth. If only the young would deign to pause and listen to these callings!

The elders are apprehensive that with change, the ways of these people would also change — the changes in the physical world would be followed by changes in the thought processes as well. The matters of the heart would take a backseat and the 'secret spaces of the heart' would become crowded. The Adi (the tribe delineated in *The Legends of Pensam*) cannot be separated from his land. The land binds him to his roots — his identity and connect is with his land. When one separates himself from his connect/his identity, alienation creeps in and that is when he loses his bearings. In an effort to forge a strong community feeling, the elders tell and retell stories thus carrying on the legacy of the tribe by indulging in a joint remembrance of a shared past. The dead or those who move away 'beyond the river and down the river' (Dai, 2006, p. 16) are remembered in songs and stories.

In her book, Mamang Dai intricately weaves the history of her people through some remarkable stories and images from their everyday life. These stories are a legacy of the past that her tribe is privy to and have been kept alive in the collective consciousness. Like in Gabriel Garcia Marquez's novel of epic proportions, *One Hundred Years of Solitude*, where memory and myth come together in an explosive interplay while delineating the story of his family spanning four generations, Dai's book also explores the realm of individual and collective memory by tracing the story of her people across time and space.

'Hunting' is an activity passionately indulged in by the community and it has left deep-seated scars on the psyche of the village people who seek and find solace in superstitious explanations after a hunt gone wrong and ritualistic purging thereafter. Stories revolving round this activity abound. In 'The strange case of Kalen, the hunter', Kalen, the hunter also meets with a similar fate as Hoxo's father, Lutor. He is also mistaken for a prey and shot at. In spite of such frequent incidents, life goes on in the villages in its everyday course. People bounce back after tragedies — even monumental ones. Those who go away in fits of anger after some arguments go away for good and never return. They are kept alive in the songs sung and stories told.

In 'The silence of Adela and Kepi', the importance of rituals in the life of the people is stressed upon — showing how rituals are a way of life. When Togum kills a snake, its spirit is thought to have cast a spell on his son, thereby making him ill, unable to speak even. Therefore, the serpent ritual has to be performed on the child; the spirits have to be moved to come and restore the child back to health. While the 'pious' and 'good' spirits come back to do the bidding of the *shamans*, some evil, malevolent ones go away for good leaving the suffering ones to suffer still more. Those whose lives have been touched by pain, choose not to speak of them, taking recourse instead to hide and camouflage their pain while all the time deriving pleasure out of partaking in community activities.

'Si-Ye', the yeast used for fermenting the rice that goes into preparation of rice beer is supposed to possess special powers that may make man hallucinate and lose his bearings. This 'Si-Ye' was handed over to mankind by the 'miti-mili' (a supernatural being) before disappearing overcome by natural visions. Pinyar, the widow who lost her husband in a hunting accident in the forest explains the reason why 'Si-Ye' is forbidden before a hunt or a journey. It supposedly contains a 'bad' spirit which makes man go mad. Therefore, 'Si-Ye' is sprinkled on the eyelids of those people who die unnatural death in the fervent hope that they will not frequent the earth as haunted spirits. The people have a strong belief in family history — the right or wrong kind of life led, a right or wrong act — all can be traced to something in the blood. Failure to observe certain rites or rituals in the past is supposedly the reason behind something going wrong, some mishaps occurring in the present — unexplainable, but quite believable. In 'Travel the Road', through the intermingling of myth and memory where the one merges with the other so deftly that the distinction becomes blurred, the villagers take to telling stories about the coming of the British, the 'migluns' to their home place, and the terrible massacre of 1911 when Noel Williamson, a British political officer, his friend, Dr. Gregorson, forty-seven sepoys and coolies were killed by the angry villagers. The reasons were many and varied— mostly conjectured. The white sahib had come to the village with gifts for the people. But something went wrong somewhere — a kind of misbehaviour on the part of the soldiers accompanying the leader, they had supposedly mocked at the ways of the innocent, simple villagers who had in turn seen red and attacked them all. This incident led to repercussions and a retaliatory attack by the other officers. The village people were forced to raise a memorial stone — a tribute to the memory of the white sahib who had lost his life and the man who had committed the initial 'act' was taken away in chains to an island.

Beside a fire in the night, with the heady brew of 'Apong' (a local rice beer) in hand, it is mesmerizing listening to the recount of these stories — imagined or factual in the songs of the 'ponung' dancers. The 'ponung' (a traditional dance) dancers led by the 'miri', (the *shaman*) narrate their story, and recreate their history through songs and dances. In a daze, the dancers sway and clap their hands and listen to the *shaman* singing of the beginning of the world — how out of 'keyum' (nothingness) was created the world of man and how his world came to be governed by the stars and 'Donyi-Polo'(the sun and the moon). The *Shaman* stresses the importance of understanding their dance and 'why it is important to remember' (Dai, 2006, p. 56).

In 'The Heart of the Insect', the 'miri' recounts the journey of the people to the top of the mountain ridges in search of 'aconitum' — a kind of poisonous root used in the preparation of poison arrows. The journey is arduous and undertaken in terrible conditions. Braving the extreme cold and surviving the journey to and return is a matter of 'chance'. It is the territory of 'Dimi-tayang' — the lonely spirit who wanders about whipping up cold, icy winds and stirring up the lakes. A safe journey back means praying to this spirit to let them go and permit a safe return. They promise to come back bearing more gifts. The men strictly observe all rules pertaining to the mountains and the last man in an attempt to prevent the entry of these spirits into their land — the land of human beings; turns backwards and wipes away all traces of their footprints. Nevertheless, even as they are descending, a swift ball of dust gather speed and follow them, constantly changing in shape and size. In unspeakable terror, the men run down towards their gates shouting at the top of their voices. One of the men fuelled by great anger aims an arrow at the 'object', calling forth his ancestors to guide him. Surprisingly the 'dust — like smoke curled upwards and drifted slowly away' (Dai, 2006, p. 60).Their gods intervene in time to save them.

The evil side of development which wipes off the rich legacy of tradition is also hinted at here wherein the elderly talk about the construction of the great Stillwell Road at the time of the Second World

War. The elderly recall how when the big trees were being cut down to make way for the roads, the 'spirits' guarding them also 'fell with the trees'. They were rendered homeless and so, deserted their village. Since then, the benign shelter of their tradition was destroyed for ever. The craving for more and yet more grows and along with it, their knowledge also grows leading them along hitherto unexplored and untraversed paths. Change is inevitable. What one requires at this point is courage and faith to withstand these buffeting changes.

'Change' comes in with the Road disturbing the old simple innocent ways of the people paving the way for craftiness to creep in. It comes unannounced. Family heirlooms are looted and granaries emptied — incidents which have never happened before. The road promises electricity, schools to the villages, and hence, development. This 'change' is not welcome to some young men who are wary of outsiders and do not want any truck with the government. They would rather be left alone. To stop the road from being constructed, they put fire to the shacks sheltering the labourers and damage the road.

Villages slowly give way to towns and these are being turned into administrative blocks. Young men go off to study in these towns and are absorbed in government jobs. The 'Kebang' (council of village elders who assemble and decide cases) is though operational, not wholeheartedly and fully accepted anymore. The legal judicial system is slowly taking over. The old lifestyle of the villages is fast eroding: "Land was being stolen. Forests were being cut and logs floated away down the river. New fences marked old territory and it seems a curtain had fallen over the old village. What was once sacred, the old sense of joy was being lost" (Dai, 2006, p. 163).

In the market, fish buried in ice packed in crates transported from distant places are sold side-by-side with the local variety — Green leaves with thorny stems, slabs of preserved, moist bamboo shoot, camomile, bitter clerodendrum, wild berries of the belladonna family. . . (Dai, 2006, p. 171) are displayed in the market. Volleyball matches are played by the village teams where one team is disqualified because one player had played with a beer bottle in hand. The long, leisurely gathering of the village elders in 'Kebangs', sitting under trees haranguing every case pondering on its individual merit, its right or wrong in a long drawn exercise of arguments, counter arguments, exploring the human psyche, delving into its very recesses is slowly getting to be a thing of the past. People's unflinching faith in this traditional judicial system is slowly being transferred onto the legal judicial system which fails to treat the local cases in their individual capacities, with little or no understanding of local sentiments and local tradition and culture. The television set makes its entry into households holding the inmates to awestruck ransom at the sight of 'distant world full of bright lights of the plains' (Dai, 2006, p. 182). Change is rampant everywhere. The untrained eye might miss it — untrained as it is to the ways of the hills and its people. But the fact remains that behind the green curtain of the hills, a subtle change has crept in. The young men whizz past in motorcycles, the riversides are full of picnickers in fake fur and woollen caps waving at the passersby. Celebrations in villages now entail cultural programmes where the old traditional lifestyle would be presented alongside the new and the modern: "Yesterday and today would be presented on the same platform; a mingling of old-style presentations and new, modern talent" (Dai, 2006, p. 184). The wave of 'change' that seems manifest in the modern paraphernalia used during these functions like the microphones with wires tapped to boxes floors many. Some like to accept this change even if it leaves them in complete disarray and would like to adjust themselves to the changing times: "It is frightening sometimes. Those deep, booming boxes seem to mock me", he had told me once. "This is what happens when you are out of touch. I must change with the times or shut up and be quiet forever!" (Dai, 2006, p. 187). This gap in the accelerated pace of environmental changes and our delayed response arising out of our inability to keep pace with it is what leads to future shock. Alvin Toffler's *Future Shock* argues convincingly that "unless man quickly learns to control the rate of change in his personal affairs as well as in society at large, we are doomed to a massive adaptational breakdown" (Toffler, 1971, Introduction).

Mamang Dai recognizes that change is inevitable in the general run of life. She effectively traces stages in the gradual shift of outlook in her people. She knows and believes as do her people that so long a person remembers his history and the history of his people, he is and will be. If he forgets, 'he loses his soul'. That is why; Rakut had made "a list of all illustrious sons of the land from British times" (Dai, 2006, p. 188). It is necessary so people do not forget their family line, their clans and their history even while merging with the changing times. Gabriel Garcia's epigraph in Living to tell the tale chooses to say it all: "Life is not what one has lived, but what one remembers and how one remembers it in order to recount it".

Perhaps a new bridge of understanding could be built and a new world created wherein the young would 'never give up on their elders'.

(Dai, 2006, p. 163) and would remember. This remembrance is important to the survival of their people. They — the old and the young would together negotiate 'change' and 'space' over time and there would still be 'moments of magic and laughter' (Dai, 2006, p. 183) in their lives.

REFERENCES

Dai, Mamang, *The Legends of Pensam*, New Delhi, Penguin Books, 2006.
http://en Wikipedia.org/wiki/cultural_memory viewed 8th October, 2012.
Toffler, Alvin, *Future Shock*, London, Pan Books Ltd., 1971.

10

THE PERIPHERAL CINEMAS OF THE NORTH-EAST

Manoj Barpujari

The film fraternity of the north-eastern part of India is often a divided house as and when the question of clubbing all of them in the political entity called the 'North-East' comes up. A film festival-goers hardly could forget an angry outburst from quite a few luminaries from Assam and Manipur at the International Film Festival of India (IFFI) in the mid-1990s when they were asked to address the media through a single press meet; not surprisingly their gesture made the authority cancel the press meet. Just for records: the filmmakers at that press-meet-to-be were Aribam Shyam Sharma, Dr. Bhabendra Nath Saikia, Jahnu Barua and Jwngdao Bodosa.[1] Those who believe that arts can not be judged on the basis of a coterie, they consider the classification of the 'North-East' rather a non-entity, a misnomer; and their logical positivism held the view that every state belonging to the North-East is culturally as diverse as any state in other parts of the country. Although the small states in the region do not really have a significant film-making tradition, they have their own individual experience in it, however, trivial it might appear. They have been making meaningful films over last four decades — except Assam where it all started nearly another four decades earlier — in various indigenous languages spoken by different ethnic groups, braving the onslaught of the Bollywood and, to a lesser extent, Hollywood and East Asian blockbusters. Considering all the pros and cons of regional cinemas of the country, the cinemas made in the north-eastern India can best be described as peripheral cinema: let alone comparing their status with the mainstream Hindi movies that are posing great threat to the very existence and sustenance of the regional cinema. The growing investments in the entertainment industry and the products thereof have a far-reaching market through various outlets in the techno-savvy world nowadays. When it comes to marketing these products, particularly Hindi films, a strictly partisan consolidation of their distribution network has remained a potential threat to all the small cinemas of the north-east.[2]

The Beginning of a Serious Note

Cinema in the north-east began on a serious note when Jyotiprasad Agarwala, the doyen of modern Assamese drama and music, made the first Assamese film *Joymoti.* Released in 1935, the fourth year of Indian talkies, it was a phenomenal film if analyzed in the overall context of contemporary Indian cinema. Its central character *Joymoti*, picked up from a legend of Assam's politically turbulent medieval history, was used as a metaphor of the contemporary tribulations of India's freedom struggle and it made the film distinctively political, a hitherto unknown exploit in Indian cinema.[3] As a freedom fighter he was imprisoned in 1931 and believed to have written the script of the film while in jail. Thus, the realistic depiction of passive resistance against oppression in the storyline had its root in the director's political consciousness and patriotic activism. *Joymoti* actually symbolized the non-violent resistance of people against the tyranny of the ruler making it a film of protest. Another laudable aspect of this masterpiece was its inherent aesthetics, which gave it a character of its own in cinematic terms. Indian filmmakers of the time relied largely on mythologies and leaned heavily towards the theatrical ways, but Jyotiprasad was deeply inspired by the contemporary European movies, thanks to his scholarship in Edinburgh University and a brief stint in the famous UFA studio in Berlin. Moreover, the film can be viewed as the very first attempt by any Indian director to depict the narratives in true feminist colour. The uncompromising resistance shown by Joymoti and other female characters seemed to have overshadowed their menfolk in the narration, unlike the women protagonists in Indian cinema of the thirties who were very passive, always sidelined, hardly out from under the veil.

Jyotiprasad set-up a makeshift studio in Bholaguri tea estate near Gohpur in Assam, where a fairly large number of houses were built to facilitate temporary lodges for his shooting unit while the rehearsals were conducted at the factory of the tea estate. There are other sidelights of making this cinematic tale that could easily be discernible as folklore of film-making. His experience of shooting was no less a formidable task than what a filmmaker usually had to go through in those trying times, particularly in finding out a suitable young lady and convince her to play the role of Joymoti. And during the post-production what he had to face was the most tragic chapter in making a film which was never heard of in other film-making regions of undivided India. He hired cameramen and sound recordists from a Lahore-based studio. But the battery-operated sound-recording system turned out to be quite inadequate, which he found out only at the editing table. With limited money, he could not return back a few thousand kilometers away from north-west India to the far-eastern Assam for re-recording. Finding no other options, Jyotiprasad performed a Herculean task of dubbing about thirty characters with his own voice, including those of the female characters. He admitted later that the film was faulty in the scheme of sounds. When released, people at first turned out in large numbers to witness the film, but soon the audience failed to appreciate its off-beat merits. The ultimate experience with *Joymoti* left Jyotiprasad materially bankrupt. Four years later Jyotiprasad made the second Assamese feature, and his last, *Indramalati* (1939) with the primary intention of restoring financial stability in lieu of artistic qualities.[4] Quite understandably the followers of this visionary failed to tread similar path of film-making. They made films largely with historical or mythological fervour. Yet most of their efforts could not meet with commercial success.

Incidentally, the first film to deal with a major social issue, of communal harmony, was *Siraj* (1948) directed jointly by the revolutionary leftist writer-artist Bishnu Prasad Rabha and versatile actor Phani Sarma and it made significant breakthrough for Assamese cinema at the box office, and immediately it was followed by two films with social theme. Such films may be important in the context of the cinema of Assam, but they are of lesser value in the larger context because they were, in style and content, just as good as photo copies of the popular Hindi cinema.[5] The first film from Assam to receive the President's Certificate of Merit, the best regional film award given by the Government of India (later known as Rajat Kamal), was *Piyoli Phukan* (1955) which was again based on the life and sacrifice made by a freedom fighter of yore. Though this film had the directorial stamp of Phani Sarma, who could easily be acknowledged as the first major filmmaker after Jyotiprasad, it was not free from the melodramatic mood of the mainstream Indian cinema. Even Dr. Bhupen Hazarika, considered as one of the finest film musicians the country produced (who was later conferred with the Dada Saheb Phalke Award in 1992, the highest honour the Government of India gives to an individual for lifetime contribution to cinema), made films mainly to satisfy the viewer's larger demand. Dr. Hazarika debuted with a popular musical *Era Bator Sur* (Tunes of the Abandoned Road, 1956). With a phenomenal success at the box office, it was the first major Assamese film with background score and playback singing utilized as an integral part of the storyline.

Commercial and Aesthetic Breakthroughs

It was, however, Dr. Bezbaroa (1969) directed by Brajen Barua which created an aura of self-confidence in making films in Assamese language. Introducing the mainstream Hindi cinema's formula of melodramatic crime story in Assamese film industry it was the first Assamese feature film entirely shot without help from the studios and technicians of Tollygunge, Kolkata, thereby it stood to be a path-breaker of sort for local filmmakers. An unparalleled commercial success of Dr. Bezbaroa encouraged film producers even from outside the state to come forward. As a result, there was a sudden upsurge in Assamese film production in the seventies that lasted till the early eighties before the video boom and the advent of satellite television. Dr. Bezbaroa was said to be responsible for heralding a so-called golden age of Assamese cinema of that time. Meanwhile Dr. Bhupen Hazarika got the award of the best music director at national level for his work in *Chameli Memsab* (1975) directed by Abdul Mazid which also got Rajat Kamal in regional film category for its poignant tale of inter-racial marriage, of an Anglo-Indian working as a tea estate manager and a girl from the local tea-tribe. Significantly, enough, from the sixties onward the regional film distributors began to exercise control over the cinema-houses and dictate terms for the exhibition of films.[6] They forced the exhibitors to show more profitable Hindi potboilers at the cost of regional films which put hurdles on the path of the rising popularity of Assamese films. In spite of the inauguration of the Jyoti Chitraban film studio by the State government in 1968 to facilitate film production, setting up of the Assam Film Finance and Development Corporation (AFFDC) in 1974 to help local filmmakers, declaration of the State Film Policy and returning of first year's collection of amusement taxes from the cinema-halls to the local film producers, constitution of state-sponsored film awards and so on, the Assamese film industry continued to reel under pressure. Although at first there was a sudden upsurge for making Assamese films, the measures did not prove to be beneficial in the long run and they got irregular and flawed in many accounts.

In his essays on local film industry Jyotiprasad lamented that Assamese language films did not enjoy numerical strength of the ready audience at home.[7] The situation did not turn for the better even after almost eight decades of the birth of the first Assamese film, a bitter truth which prompted a veteran filmmaker like Jahnu Barua tell at a seminar that Darwin's 'Survival of the Fittest Theory' was truly applied in case of Assamese cinema.[8] In spite of all the unfavourable factors, there were filmmakers who looked at things differently and made bold attempts. The first director to revolt against the prevailing norms of film-making after Jyotiprasad was Padum Barua who co-founded the first film society of undivided Assam, the Shillong Film Society, in 1962. In the backdrop of a strong wind of neo-realism in Indian cinema of the seventies, Padum Baruah's *Ganga Chilanir Pakhi* (Wings of the Tern, 1976) announced the arrival of a realistic, humane and quietly revealing film expression, apparently most significant socially meaningful film in forty years after *Joymoti*. It looked at post-independent era in a critical light through a pathetic story of a young widow. Then there arrived Dr. Bhabendra Nath Saikia's *Sandhyaraag* (Cry of Twilight, 1977), a polemical look at the urban-rural divide and middle class character, through which Assam assured its place in the proverbial 'parallel cinema movement' of the country. His films got the stamp of a master storyteller, himself being a celebrated literary figure, with the script leaning heavily towards narratives he would call a style of 'literary film'. His other most notable films like *Agnisnan* (Ordeal, 1985), *Sarothi* (The Shelter, 1992) and *Itihas* (Exploration, 1996) all had a specialty of character-driven dramas, the type of movies that put family politics over state politics. He made seven films in Assamese language and all his films won the Rajat Kamal for best regional film while *Agnisnan*, which examined man-woman equation in a feudal setting, also won the national award for best screenplay.

But to whom contemporary cinema of Assam is indebted to a great extent is Jahnu Barua, an alumnus of the Film and Television Institute of India (FTII), Pune. His films, mainly *Halodhiya Charaye Baodhan Khai* (The Catastrophe, 1987), *Firingoti* (The Spark, 1991) and *Hkhagaraloi Bahu Door* (Its a Long Way to the Sea, 1995) brought most of the laurels at national and international level for Assamese cinema. Yet, after making ten full-length feature films in Assamese language starting from 1982 till 2004, the nine-time national award-winner had to try his hand at making Hindi films notwithstanding his public announcement of a possible sabbatical from film-making. That a filmmaker of Barua's stature has been continuously discouraged by poor response to his otherwise powerful cinematic endeavors tells the pathetic situation the regional film industry is going through.[9] *Halodhiya Charaye Baodhan Khai* was a milestone film in the history of Assamese cinema, which had won the national award for best film, besides several international recognition. The best actor award won by Indra Bania at Locarno for excellently portraying a crisis-ridden peasant protagonist in the film was the first time an actor of Assamese cinema won the coveted award in an international competition. A striking feature of Jahnu Barua's cinematic tales is dwelling on the rural characters with compulsions and conflicts against pastoral backdrop of the Assamese society. The strength and appeal of his narrative style of works lie in a consistent exploration of expression in simplicity with powerful backing of irony, satire and a rustic charm. In 2012, however, Barua ended his sabbatical by making a comeback to Assamese filmmaking with a poignant tale of an aged couple traumatized by the infamous 26/11 terrorist attack in Mumbai. The film titled as *Baandhon* (Waves of Silence, 2012) was selected as the inaugural film of the Indian Panorama of the IFFI and later it won the best film award at the Bengaluru International Film Festival, Rajat Kamal of best regional film in Assamese and it also marked the revival of state financing of local films by the AFFDC.

Promises and a New Law

Assam is a State of multilingual identities; but a film in other than Assamese was first made only in mid-eighties marking a gap of five decades between the release of the first Assamese language film and making of a film in another indigenous language of the state. This film was *Alayaron* (*The Dawn*, 1986), in Bodo language, directed by Jwngdao Bodosa which was a national award winner among non-scheduled languages of the country at that time. Bodosa, an alumnus of the FTII, develops a character in the film to show how love can transform a hardworking but exploited young man to a self-reliant entrepreneur with the backdrop of the Muga silk cultivation. Bodosa's more acclaimed film *Hagramayao Jinahari* (Rape in the Virgin Forest, 1995) swoops down heavily on the nexus between influential people in the administration and unscrupulous timber merchants. The story has a middle-aged man whose daughter is raped by the timber smugglers and the name of the girl is Mithinga which in Bodo language means the nature thereby suggesting an allegory of the rape of the nature. It is pleasantly surprising how the director used an old-fashioned Bolex Camera, a pack of ignored Fuji-colour film to shoot the entire script in only ten days, with an unbelievably low budget and yet won a national award for best film on environment issue.

Among the most important films there was *Wosobipo* (The Cuckoo's Call, 1990) made in another indigenous language of Assam, the Karbi. It was directed by Gautam Bora who was trained at the Konrad Wolf Institute in erstwhile East Germany. The film won two national awards: best first film of a director and the best music director (for ace musician Sher Chowdhury). It told the story of a tribal community on the verge of disintegration because of the modes of change in agricultural pattern from shifting to settled cultivation and land-grabbing tactics adopted by merchants in a distinctly metaphorical film language. Then there was *Haladhar* (The Yeoman, 1992) by Sanjeev Hazarika that also won the Swarna Kamal for best first film of a director award. It is about the poor and the dispossessed of the Assamese village and their realization of the sense of dignity. Though made as a simple narrative, it has a distinct freshness in approach to the subject matter originally penned by renowned writer, film critic Apurba Sarma (whose book on Assamese cinema won Swarna Kamal for best book on cinema in 2001) and it focused on the land relation in a semi-feudal society. Next came Bidyut Chakraborty's first film *Raag Birag* (Vacation of a Sanyasi, 1996) that won three major national awards: best first film of a director, best editing and best cinematography. It was sheer beauty of technique and innovative camera work which was originally shot in 16 mm and later blown up to 35 mm; and the cameraman of the film was Mrinal Kanti Das, a product of the FTII, who earlier left his job of forester in the State government for pure love of cinema and whose work apparently earned the rare distinction of being the first from Assam to win a technical award at national level. *Raag Birag* deals with a well-off middle class family facing identity crisis and uncertainty involving its young male members coming to terms with contradictory social forces. The film also got the rare distinction of the inaugural film of the Indian panorama of the IFFI. At the same time Dr. Santwana Bordoloi's debut feature *Adajya* (The Flight, 1996) made a strong statement against the situation of widowhood in a conservative Brahmin family of pre-independence era. Based on a novel by the Jnanpith Award winner Mamoni Roisom Goswami, the film won important national and international recognitions.

A writer-turned director Manju Bora's directorial debut *Baibhav* (A Scam in Verse, 1998), the best film in Dhaka International Film Festival in 2000, revolves around a young man desparately in search of his roots and retribution against troubles in the family and public life. Her more acclaimed film is her third feature called *Akashitorar Kathare* (A Tale told a Thousand Times, 2003) that won national awards for best regional film and best female playback singer for its music director Torali Sarma. This film centered around the theme of gender bias portrayed through the eyes of a young lady with her research on the status of women through the folklore of Assam and then in her real life. A prolific filmmaker of the age, Manju Bora's new film *Ko:Yad* (A Silent Way, 2012) in the indigenous Mishing language gave a vivid picture of the riverine community's struggle for livelihood and the film received awards for best regional film in a non-scheduled language and best cinematography at the national level, besides best Indian film at Bengaluru International Film Festival.

There are other gifted filmmakers like Hemanta Das, Ranjit Das, Sanjib Sabhapandit, Arup Manna, Moirangthem Maniram, Jadumani Dutta and Bobby Sarma Barua, to name a few. It is painful to note that quite a few filmmakers after their impressive debuts could not make their next film due to the marketing limitations. This is where the government must lend a hand and provide outlets, which has been a popular demand among India's off-beat filmmakers from Satyajit Ray of yesteryear to Onir Dhar of present times who continue to be at the forefront of the cause of the serious or parallel or indie cinema. Ray said: "The biggest boost for a filmmaker comes not from critical praise or the praise of a small coterie or from a festival prize; it comes from the acceptance of the film by the public for whom it was made".[10] The national awards have been coming in almost regularly, but commercial success to nurture an industry or guarantee returns on investments have always eluded the filmmakers of Assam. The situation makes the artists and technicians of the regional cinema in Assam, and elsewhere in the north-east, to look for livelihood in commercially viable mobile theatre groups, VCD films, the TV channels and government sponsored or commissioned programmes in the Doordarshan Kendras of the region. An out-and-out commercial pot-boiler in the mid-nineties enthused the scene with new hopes and another golden era of Assamese cinema was claimed to have arrived when one film (*Jauwane Amoni Kore* directed by Ashok Kumar Bishaya) hit the box office and its success encouraged even theatre activist, cine journalist, photographer and established musician to join the bandwagon as new filmmakers. The euphoria did not last long though. Now, it is well-nigh impossible to imagine houseful shows of Assamese cinema at urban theatres unlike the sixties and seventies when truck and bus loads of rural people came to see a Nip Barua, Siva Prasad Thakur or Pulak Gogoi film much to the relief of the film producer. Even some media hypes created around a new release are failing to draw satisfactory crowds. The end of the nineties and beyond 2010 have seen a disconcerting trend in Assamese cinema when some meaningless films with love stories, filled with songs, so-called 'item numbers', stunts and actions began to sideline even good and healthy entertainment-oriented cinema. It gives a picture of pathetic struggle for survival, although there has been no dearth of occasional creative upsurge in cinema of the infra-structurally backward and ethnically and linguistically diverse state of Assam.

Cinemas of Other North-Eastern States

The most important film-making State in the north-east, after Assam, is Manipur where all the theatres were converted to video screens following threats by the secessionist outfits against screening of mainstream Indian (Hindi) films in the year 2000.[11] And what a flamboyant development hereafter: Manipur earned the reputation of being the first State in India to grow a fully digital film industry; and the young filmmakers from the state, through a petition in the Guwahati High Court, got the Central Information and Broadcasting Ministry change the rules to make digital films eligible for the national film awards and Indian Panorama. Today Manipur is producing around 50 digital feature films a year in as unbelievably low budget as ₹ 6 to 15 lakh. The industry earned a nickname Imphalwood by the enormous *diktats* the filmmakers have to abide by, shunning everything that is not akin to Meitei culture. However, after a gap of a dozen year, a film is now made in celluloid, which is *Japan Landa Imphal* (Imphal in Japan War, 2012). Narrating the story of a local girl in love with a Japanese soldier during the Second World War as Manipur is turned a battle-ground between advancing Japanese troops and Allied Forces, the film is the fourth by the producer-director couple Chandam Shyamacharan and Chandam Manorama Devi. When the film was released at a new auditorium of the Manipur Film Development Corporation, it rekindled a hope of revival of local celluloid films.

The first attempt to make a film in Manipur was made in 1949. But it was in Hindi language as the script based on a Manipuri play written by Ayekpam Shyamsunder Singh was translated to Hindi purely for commercial viability. Its shooting was initially done at a studio in Kolkata, direction was by Jyoti Das and the cast included Bengali and Manipuri artists. Unfortunately, the film could not be completed due to financial difficulties. In a last ditch attempt to revive the production work, the Maharaja of Manipur was approached; although he showed clear interests, the political situation over Manipur's future status as a part of the Indian

Union, the rise of wide-scale resentment, often violent, could not allow any further negotiation and the film remained incomplete.[12] It was quite long after that the first film was successfully made in Manipur, the title being *Matamgi Manipur* (Today's Manipur, 1972) directed by Deb Kumar Bose: its music was scored by Aribam Syam Sharma, the man who later on put Manipuri films on the global map. Sharma made his directorial debut in 1974 and stole national limelight with his second and third films in 1979-80. His following film *Imagi Ningthem* (My Son My Precious, 1981) based on a short radio play by the acclaimed Manipuri writer M.K. Binodini is the first Indian film to have won the Grand Prix in the Festival of Three Continents, Nantes in 1982.[13] It has a strong underline of human bondage dealing with a motherless child and its emotional depiction has made this exceptionally low-budget cinematography with an outdated Bolex camera even more stunning. Sharma's *Ishanou* (The Chosen One, 1990) is another masterpiece that won jury's special mention for its actress at the Cannes Film Festival. The story of the film delving deep into the Maibi mysticism and sacrifical custom of the females is such a beauty that it could hardly be discarded as a celebration of Hindu revivalism. His next film *Sanabi* (The Grey Mare, 1995) is also replete with rich cinematic vocabulary and poetic expression. It was made as a love story, but in the vein of an impossible love between a wayward man and a young divorcee, with the grey mare symbolizing the lost and endangered human relations. Though music was his first love, and although he studied Philosophy in Santiniketan, Sharma pursued other art forms like theatre and dance and the acquiring knowledge in all these art forms made him a true follower of a composite art called cinema in later years which he vividly described in his beautiful autobiography '*Living Shadows*'. Sharma just proved to the world that with sincerity towards humanity and belonging to the roots could do wonders to the images created in various shots of a film. There lie the spirits of cinema.[14] Following footsteps of the master filmmaker who has received eleven national awards for features and non-features are a host of talented young directors making their presence felt at the national level as well as international circuit.

In Meghalaya, noted historian-educationist-writer Dr. Hamlet Bareh Ngapkynta was the maker of the first ever Khasi film, *Ka Synjuk Ri ki Laiphew Syiem* (The Alliance of Thirty Kings, 1981). The first coloured film in Khasi language was *Manik Raitong* (Manik the Miserable, 1984) directed by Ardhendu Bhattacharya. An Indian Panorama selection and the only film ever to win a National Award (in 1985) from Meghalaya, it relates an ancient and popular legend about a woman forced into marriage with the Syiem (or chief) and finally choosing the funeral pyre of her lover Manik, the flautist, over the material bliss of the palace. In Mizoram, a digital feature made with a paltry sum of ₹ 11 lakh is termed the state's first big budget film. Titled *Khawnlung Run* (The Plunder of Khawnlung, 2012) and produced-directed-shot-edited by Mapuia Chawngthu, the film is hailed as the first made in Dulian dialect, the lingua franca of the Mizos. It is set in the 1856 backdrop of the raid of Khawnlung village by rival chieftains marking the bloodiest attack in the entire history of the Mizos. Employing ballads, folk music and a layer of a story of a desperate man in search of his sweetheart carried off from the plundered village as a slave by a warrior, the film was shot in a specially created village near the original one which was burnt down while portraying the harsh realities of tribal warfare. The way various actions are enacted in the film in long sequences is really praiseworthy and usually rare in low budget films.[15]

In Tripura, a film has proved that cinema could play an important role in raising issues of concern for the region. *Yarwng* (Roots, 2008), made in Tripura's tribal language Kokborok, opened the Indian Panorama's feature film section at the IFFI, won the first national award for the state and special jury mention at the 3rd Eye Asian Film Festival of Mumbai. Directed by Joseph Pulinthanath, the film tells the story of large-scale displacement of tribal people that took place in Tripura when a hydroelectric power project was set up in the late 1970s. When it was screened at the IFFI, the story centering around a couple, caught the eyes of an international gathering and the director's speech made the central minister to assure that he would do something for the 60,000-strong displaced people![16]

In Arunachal Pradesh, Dr. Bhupen Hazarika made a Hindi film in the backdrop of the border state getting status of statehood and the local populace going through a period of transition. The film's title was *Mera Dharam Meri Maa* (1976) produced by the Department of Information and Public Relations, Government of Arunachal Pradesh. However, the first ever film made in a local dialect of the state is *Sonam* (The Fortunate One, 2006) directed by Ahsan Mazid. It was shot at high altitude Himalayan foothills depicting life of the Brokpas, the Yak shepherds, and their custom of polyandry using Monpa dialect and a poignant tale that caught world-wide attention. Thereafter, another film in native Shertukpen dialect was made by an alumnus of the Satyajit Ray Film and Television Institute of Kolkata named Sange Dorjee. He is the first native of Arunachal Pradesh to make a full-length feature film (as both

Bhupen Hazarika and Ahsan Mazid hailed from Assam). Titled as *Crossing Bridges* (2012) that already has done the rounds at the festival circuit around the country, it tells the story of yearning for the roots told through the experience of a Mumbai-returned youth in his remote village, shot entirely in a hilly village and with participation of local non-actors in the cast.

Sometimes, making films look easy in this hilly region, but making profits out of it is an Herculean task. Among all, Nagaland is the only state which is yet to see the birth of a feature-length celluloid film made in any of its own spoken languages or dialects, though it has been going through a change-over after a long insinuating period of insurgency, the longest of its kind in Independent India. In fact, the paradoxes of existence in the region are getting proper ventilation in politics and literature, but they are yet to find unassailable aesthetic reflection in cinema. The inability to absorb and avail the film culture by the general people has deprived many talented filmmakers of fulfilling their dreams and aspirations. The lack of inter-cultural interaction among film fraternity and passive outlook of the state governments have further alienated the respective states, particularly the less privileged states.[17] But the documentary film genre in the region has something to celebrate always. Perhaps there lie another reality, another dichotomy of cinema(s) of the North-East.

NOTES AND REFERENCES

1. The bizarre episode in the prestigious IFFI was widely publicized in the national media and I wrote a piece taking a cue from a report in a Kolkata based newspaper. Manoj Barpujari, "Chalachitrar Satabarsa, Anweshan Aru 'Itihaas'", *Dainik Agradoot*, Vol. 1, No. 125, 1996, p. 5.
2. Gautam Bora, "The Regional Cinema: The Dilemma and the Perspective" in Kulada Bhattacharjee (ed.), *Should North-East Cinema Exist*, Guwahati, NEFTPDA Publication, 2006, pp. 31-32.
3. The realistic treatment and the subtle suggestion of a message of protest interwoven into the story were quite uncharacteristic and conspicuously absent in the contemporary Indian cinema. Apurba Sarma, *Jyotiprasad as a Filmmaker (and the Forsaken Frontier)*, Guwahati, ADI Publication, 2005, pp. 26-28.
4. Manoj Barpujari, "Assamese Cinema: Dreams, Reality and Dichotomies" in K. Moti Gokulsing and Wimal Dissanayake (eds.), *Routledge Handbook of Indian Cinemas*, London and New York, Routledge, 2013, pp. 52-53.
5. Apurba Sarma, "The Assamese Cinema: Changes Through the Twentieth Century" in Manoj Barpujari and Dr. Garima Kalita (eds.), *Perspectives on Cinema of Assam*, Guwahati, Gauhati Cine Club, 2007, pp. 8-9.
6. *Ibid.*, p. 9.

7. Jyotiprasad Agarwala, "Asomor Film Silpa Gorhat Asomiya Darshokar Dayitwa" in Dr. Hiren Gohain (ed.), *Jyotiprasad Rachanavali*, Guwahati, Assam Publication Board, 2007, p. 538.
8. Jahnu Barua, "Small Cinema: A Question of Survival", in Bhattacharjee (ed.), *Should North-East Cinema Exist*, Guwahati, NEFTPDA Publication, 2006, p. 53.
9. Manoj Barpujari, "Against Odds", *Frontline*, Vol. 30, No. 20, 2013, p. 95.
10. The situation is not peculiar to the north-east. As Satyajit Ray once pointed out: "Where the vast majority of films bypass reality altogether and pander to the lowest common denominator, any effort that spurns these tendencies comes as a radical departure, and is to be applauded. Unfortunately such films are apt to run into trouble when the question of bringing them to market arises". Satyajit Ray, "The New Cinema and I", in Sandip Ray (ed.), *Deep Focus: Reflections on Cinema*, Noida, Harper Collins Publishers India, [2011 (1980)], pp. 59-60.
11. R. Nithya, *Culture of Censorship in Manipuri Cinema*, 2013, http://newsclick.in/india/culture-censorship-manipuri-cinema (accessed on 27 January 2014).
12. See http://indpaedia.com/ind/index.php/Manipuri_Cinema (accessed on 27 January 2014).
13. Renowned critics and festival programmers were seen praising the film in spite of its technical deficiencies. In *Films and Filming* (March 1982), noted critic John Warrington wrote: "A discovery was from Manipur. Technically, the film was a mess: a postage old stock, badly printed and shot on an aging 16mm Bolex with sound equipment that would be a BBC technician's nightmare. An amateur but . . . the direction and performances are so closely observed that they glow through all the imperfections . . . I am glad to say that it will be appearing as my Critics Choice at the next London Film Festival". Aribam Syam Sharma, *Living Shadows*, Guwahati, Gauhati Cine Club, 2006, p. 98.
14. Here I am tempted to quote from Andrei Tarkovsky: "when you realize, quite consciously, that what you see in the frame is not limited to the visual depiction, but is a pointer to something stretching out beyond the frame and to infinity; a pointer to life". Those films which are truthful to life have permanent value. The spirit of images depicted in the most regional cinema is thus most universal. For further reading: Gabrielle A. Hezekiah, *Phenomenology's Material Presence: Video, Vision and Experience*, Bristol & Chicago, Intellect, 2010, pp. 61-74.
15. Bitopan Borborah, *Mapuia Chawngthu: The Pioneer in India's Hinterland*, 2013, http://www.filmfocusindia.com/e-cineindia-july-2013.html (accessed on 27 January 2014).
16. See http://www.navhindtimes.com/story.php?story=2008112418 (accessed on 27 January 2014).
17. Raphael Warjri, "Meghalaya Film Frame: Freeze in Time" in Bhattacharjee (ed.), *Should North-East Cinema Exist*, Guwahati, NEFTPDA Publication, 2006, p. 75.

11

WOMEN IN EARLY NINETEENTH CENTURY ASSAM

Manjula Phukan

The nineteenth century is of great importance in the history of India. It was an age of contrary pulls in the realm of politics, economics, intellectual ideas and attitudes towards women. The establishment of the British rule set in motion certain progressive forces. The introduction of modern means of transport and communication, the introduction of modern Western system of education and the adoption of the British legal system in India, though understandably to facilitate the exploitative colonial machinery, had far reaching effects on the entire socio-cultural fabric of India. That these structural changes had ushered in new and progressive ideas from the West had not been denied even by the Nationalist School of Indian Scholars.[1] In the social sphere, the resultant inevitable clash between the two radically different structures of the East and the West led to a number of social reform movements in India in the nineteenth century.

It is in the backdrop of this clash in the social sphere, that the chapter would seek to review in brief the place or the condition of Assamese women in the early decades of the nineteenth century. The work is mostly confined to the Brahmaputra Valley.

Pre-colonial traditional Assamese society possessed a few distinctive features. The status of the Assamese women varied according to caste, class and religion. Although their position was relatively better when compared to most of their other Indian counterparts, there remained many social obstacles for the Assamese women. The social norms for the upper caste women differed from those of the rest. They had similarities with those of their counterparts in the rest of the country. They were bound by age-old customs, setting dual standards of power, status and morality for the male and the female due to the existence of a patriarchal society. Existence of several social evils like polygamy, early marriage, prohibition of widow — remarriage, especially among the upper caste Hindus, had greatly lowered the position of women. Though, '*Kulinism*', '*Sati*' or self-immolation of widows, and infanticide were not practiced in Assam, yet it cannot be overlooked that women especially during the decadence of the Ahom rule were regarded as 'private property', subjected to a secluded life and denied education. Spaces were sharply divided into private and public. The home space was identified with the women and public space or that of the outside world with men.

That some of the contemptible Hindu practices like *Sati*, infanticide and the dowry system could not strike roots in Assam, was perhaps the net effect of the composition of the Assamese society, consisting of a predominantly tribal population along with a non-tribal one and the consequent intermixing of culture. Hence, it possessed certain characteristics which were peculiar to itself. While modern Assamese historians, taking note of the absence of inhuman practices like '*Kulinism*' and '*Sati*' in Assam, have also to take note of the fact that Assamese women too led a life of denial.

Despite limited sources for reconstructing the structure of the society in the pre-Ahom days, it could be assessed from the general mode of cultivation practiced in the tribal areas of Assam that the Assamese society was predominantly a semi-tribal one before the establishment of the Ahom rule in the region.[2] Thus, with the exception of the lands gifted to the Brahmins and religious institutions by the Ahoms and the pre-Ahom rulers, the main mode of cultivation was shifting cultivation.[3] A redeeming feature of the tribal culture of Assam was the position of importance occupied by women. Many suggest that the important social position occupied by women in the tribal culture of Assam had roots in the worshipping of Mother Goddess in various forms.

The coming of the Ahoms, however, led to significant changes in the whole socio-economic structure of the Assamese society. The Ahoms practiced wet-rice cultivation instead of shifting cultivation in Assam. The new mode of cultivation had tremendous impact on the social life of the people for it required permanent places of residence and possession of cultivable land. The growing profitability of this mode of cultivation and the increasing royal patronage given to it must have led to the accumulation of some amount of wealth in the hands of the '*Khels*'.[4] The increase of wealth inevitably led to the overthrow of female supremacy in the Assamese society and the establishment of patriarchy.[5] Under the conditions, women were soon relegated to the position of private property especially during the period of decay of the Ahom rule. There were instances when Ahom rulers had gifted away women, which also included royal princess to other rulers to forge an alliance with or as a part of tribute to a foreign ruler. For, e.g. Romoni Gabharu, an Ahom princess was gifted away to Aurangzeb to persuade Mir Jumla to leave Assam. Chandrakanta Singha in order to conclude alliance with the Burmese ruler also gave away an Ahom princess.[6] Although the colonial state formally abolished slavery through Act V of the (Bengal) Regulation of 1843, and the Indian Penal Code of 1860 made it an offence to engage in trafficking or keeping slaves, yet, there were instances of its practice in early colonial Assam. The *Orunnodoi* in Vol. 1, No. V, 1846, recorded the news of a sale of a woman by her opium edict husband to a Muslim man.

The elimination of Assamese women from positions of importance in the society was also affected by the great *Vaishnavite* Saint, Sri Sankardeva. Sankardeva, had made no distinction of people while accepting disciples, but in case of women, he displayed an attitude of strange intolerance. The same attitude of chauvinism was also witnessed in the *Sattras* established by the followers of Sankardeva, where women were excluded from all aspects of the religious and cultural life. Petty duties like wiping the floor of the prayer-hall were denied to them.[7] Even up to this day, women are denied entrance to most of the important *Vaishnava* shrines of Assam. The example of the *Barpeta Kirtan-Ghar* could be cited in this context.

Moreover, during the reign of Ahom King Rudra Singha, the influence of Bengali customs and prejudices began to be felt in Assam. The customs of child-marriage, prohibition of widow re-marriage, seclusion of women, which had become the bane of the Bengali Hindu society found easy acceptability amongst the Brahmins and upper castes of Assam who subjected their women to a secluded life and denied them modern education.[8] If at all they were given any education, it was very limited and mostly related to household work and responsibilities.

The social reform movement of the late eighteenth century in India exercised little influence in Assam in the first two decades of the nineteenth century, when Assam was still nominally under the Ahom rule. But even after the British annexation of Assam partly in 1828 and fully in 1838, the response to progressive Western ideas that permeated in through Bengal was not initially too encouraging. The causes for this belated response could be traced to the educational backwardness of the region and also to some deeply embedded features in the structure of the Assamese society.

Many of the society's ill could be traced to the oppressed condition of women. As already mentioned there prevailed the practice of early marriage of girls especially among the upper-caste Hindus. B.C. Allen in *Assam District Gazeteers, Nowgong*, 1905, writes that except in Goalpara, in all other districts of the Brahmaputra Valley, the practice of early marriage was not so common other than among the upper class which also included some *Kalitas* as well.[9] Parents seldom took into consideration the consent of their daughters for marriage. The common consideration was that the women had to be younger than men. Marriage was almost a compulsory proposition for the girl's as well as the boys.

The early marriage of girls was also a major cause of early widowhood as the age between the bride and the groom often happened to be disproportionate. It also contributed to the practice of polygamy among the higher castes, especially among the Brahmins, as they were forbidden to marry off their girls to someone from the lower caste.

Among the many disabilities of women, the condition of the Hindu widow was pathetic. The American Baptist Missionaries were also keen observers of the problems of Assamese widows. Their writings and sermons had some usual elements of exaggeration, yet, there was hardly any doubt that the Assamese widows had also to lead a very miserable life. Miles Bronson, a missionary, writes about widowhood as, "The *sastras* forbid their ever marrying a second time. On the death of a husband, the ornaments were stripped off and their head shaved. They became the drudge and servant of family where they dwell. How cheerless is life to such!"[10] It must, however, be noted here, that in Assam it is not the general practice that the widows had to shave their head.

Neelkanta Barua, who through his novel, '*Mem*', serially published in Assamese news magazine *Bijuli* from Calcutta in Vol. II, 1891, depicted the plight of the Assamese widows, especially the higher caste Hindus. It was perhaps the first novel in Assamese which advocated widow re-marriage. Similarly, Lakshminath Bezbarua, a new generation Assamese writer, who was directly exposed to the literary and political influences of post 1857 Bengal, was strongly in favour of widow re-marriage, but ridicules the whole idea of equality between the sexes as demanded by the supporters of the western form of women's emancipation.[11]

Besides, there were issues of *purdah* or seclusion of women, imposed by the customs and practices of the society. Among the upper class families, the women were shielded from public view as well as from other males who were not relations. The women of the lower class were relatively free from such seclusion as elsewhere in India. Noted Assamese poet, Nalinibala Devi (1898-1976), a woman from upper class family in her autobiography, *Eri Aha Dinbor* (The Bygone Days)[12] mentions the practice of *purdah* among the higher class women and the restrictions imposed on their movements. Social mixing of girls was disapproved.

Amidst such a distressing social situation for the women of Assam, the entry of the British into the province in 1826, initiated far reaching changes in the socio-political life of the state. Against this changing background, efforts to lift womanhood to a higher social level among people began with the advent of the missionaries into Assam. Further, their presence in the region was considered necessary by the East India Company for consolidating its commercial empire in the East.

The arrival of the American Baptist missionaries cut an outlet for the flow of certain Christian ideas into the socio-cultural life of the Assamese society. It was, however, no secret that their works of charity, philanthropy and humanitarian were also methods of influencing people and attracting converts.[13] Hence, working for the education of the natives was, therefore, a part of the proselytisation job of the missionary and hence women's education was a special task. But the upper class Hindu and Muslim women of the plains were under *Purdah* and it proved difficult for the men to gain access to the interior of their homes to influence them spiritually. It was here that the gender of women missionaries were utilized by the church to gain access to the interiors of the elite and influence the girls of the lower echelons to come to school meant for education them. The missionaries soon realized that for a large section of girls the custom of early marriage was a formidable obstacle to formal education in schools. To counteract this, attempts were made by mission ladies to impart instruction to females of higher castes in *Zenana* or 'private apartments' as was done by Women's Missionary Society in Calcutta, "for ladies of rank seldom left their homes, if they did, they travelled in such a way that none but their household should see them".[14]

With devotion and sacrifice, the missionaries pioneered women's education and co-education in Assam. They began work among women by setting up schools. But as parents were reluctant to commit their children to the care of a Christian teacher, the missionaries picked up even '*bazaar girls*' or abandoned and destitute girls for initiation to learning. A missionary wife, Mrs. Brown in a letter written in 1851 had expressed, "The women are so stupid after having grown up in their ignorance, that they are fully impressed with the belief that they cannot learn, besides the ridicule to which they are subjected makes it very difficult to induce them to continue. Our old Brahmin pundit often comes along by the little room and laugh at the idea of my spending time teaching women to read. I have had a few very promising girls given to me by their parents and guardians, whom I hope to keep in good degree separate from heathen influence".[15]

Many were critical of missionary activities and the impact of western influence, which they argued resulted in the erosion of traditional values. The spirit of hostility against women's education was strong among large sections. Even advocates of female education abhored the very idea of girls becoming doctors and lawyers after taking higher degrees in the University. The utmost they desired was that they should have knowledge of the three R's and a little knowledge of history and geography.[16] Even as late as 1874, the Deputy Inspector of Schools, Nagaon, reports, "skill in weaving, cooking and paddy husking is considered a greater accomplishment in a girl than all her knowledge in reading, writing and arithmetic. Besides a girl is a great help to her mother in attending to little babies, including other domestic works, ...but if she attends school, a servant is necessary to accompany her to and from the school".[17] Being a patriarchal society, women were totally dependent on males, be it father, husband or sons for support. Further, the female child spent her youth preparing for marriage. Thus, in such a social environment, the pursuing of knowledge was almost equal to suicide. In the words of Keeler, a woman missionary, who worked for women's education in Assam, "the indifference we find among them to any personal responsibility concerning their souls' welfare, is but the result of their spiritual guide, adoration and obedience to their husbands and 'gohains' (priests) is all that is required of them to fit them for this life or the life to come. This idea is more deeply instilled into minds of those of the higher castes".[18] Thus, owing to the prejudices of the higher classes and the degeneration of the female sex, the difficulties of promoting their education was great.

Even educated women like Padmavoti Devi Phukanani, who published *Sudharmar Upakhyan* (1884), argued that women have three *dharmas, viz., bhakti* towards God, the *dharma* of '*Patibrata*' and '*Satidharma*'. The wife who can satisfy her husband through love and service, who in the absences of her husband, never thinks of other men, who, however, bad her husband might be, always tries to bring him to the right path with patience and who maintains her relations with her in-laws and parents, is the most ideal woman.[19] There is a total submission of the wife to the husband in her writings and it defines the home as the women's proper sphere.

Prejudice and other cultural imperative discouraged women from making use of their intellectual talents. Educational expectation for men and women remained unequal largely because marriage was considered as the ideal career for women, whereas the necessity of earning a livelihood was drummed into males from an early stage. Curricula, text books were all on the basis of sex and an unwritten code of conduct all worked against women. A little arithmetic for girls, but science and mathematics for boys, placed girls and boys on an unequal footing at least as far as educational attainments were concerned.

The social reform movement in Assam was a limited success. It was almost impossible for the women to dislodge the imposed cultural pressures and raise their independent voices. Further, the ideal Assamese family during the period of study remained joint families, which in most cases acted as a preserver of tradition. However, simultaneously, the period was also marked by a growing tendency to critically analyse the evils within the Assamese society and also of the evils introduced by foreign rule. Thus, the status of women and the question of evolving a meaningful change in them was an issue of great concern to the nineteenth century reformers in Assam, as elsewhere in India. Lack of formal education, early marriage, prohibition of widow remarriage, segregation, seclusion and restrictions on movement were identified as the evils or problems to overcome.

NOTES AND REFERENCES

1. Tilottama Misra, *Literature and Society in Assam*, Omsons Publications, Guwahati, N. Delhi, 1987, p. 2.
2. Amalendu Guha, "Samantajugar Asamar Bhumi Byavastha Aru Samajik Shreni", *Natun Prithivi*, Guwahati, 1972, pp. 126-47, cited from Tilottama Misra, *op. cit.*, p. 105.
3. *Ibid.*
4. Tilottama Misra, *op. cit.*, p. 106.
5. W.W. Hunter, *A Statistical Account of Assam*, Vol. I, Sanskarak Prakashak, Delhi, 1975, p. 129.
6. Kasinath Tamuli Phukan, *Assam Buranji Sara*, Calcutta, 1906, DHAS, Assam, Guwahati 1964, pp. 39, 66.
7. Tilottama Misra, *op. cit.*, p. 108.
8. H.K. Barpujari, ed., *The Comprehensive History of Assam*, Vol. V, Publication Board Assam, Guwahati, 2007, p. 307.

9. B.C. Allen, *Assam District Gazetteers, Nowgong*, Caledonian Steam Printing Works, Calcutta, 1905, p. 69.
10. H.K. Barpujari, *The American Missionaries and North-East India (1836-1900 AD): A Documentary Study*, Spectrum Publishers, Guwahati, 1986, p. 177.
11. Tillotoma Misra, *op. cit.*, p. 127.
12. Nalinibala Devi, *Eri Aha Dinbor*, Lawyers Book Stall, Guwahati, 1976.
13. Rev. M.C. Mason, "Methods of Mission Work", in *The Assam Mission of the American Baptist Missionary Union*, Baptist Mission Press, Calcutta, 1887, reprint by Spectrum Publishers, Guwahati, Delhi, 1992, pp. 96-112.
14. H.K. Barpujari, ed., *The Comprehensive History of Assam*, Vol. V, Publication Board Assam, Guwahati, 2007, pp. 201-02.
15. H.K. Barpujari, *The American Missionaries and North-East India*, Guwahati, 1986, pp. 107-08.
16. Priyam Goswami, "Tradition and Modernity: Nineteenth Century Discourse on Assamese Women", *Guwahati University Journal of Arts*, Vol. XLI, Guwahati University, Guwahati, 2010, p. 202.
17. Report of Public Instruction in Assam, 1874-75, Chapter on Female Education, Shillong, 1876.
18. Orell Keeler, "Women's Work Among the Assamese", in *The Assam Mission of the American Baptist Missionary Union*, Guwahati, 1992, p. 188.
19. Prafulla Dutta Goswami, *Padmavati Devi Phukonani Rachanavali*, Asom Prakashan Parishad, Guwahati, 1994, pp. 18-19.

12

QUIT INDIA MOVEMENT IN NAGAON DISTRICT
Some Observations

Akunthita Borthakur

After the Non-Cooperation and Civil-Disobedience movement, the Quit India movement has usually been regarded as the next great struggle of the people of India for freedom. Indeed, the struggle beginning on 9th August, 1942 was a mass upsurge of unprecedented dimensions which expedited the liberation of the country. During the Quit India movement, the people of Assam like that of other parts of India offered a positive response to the call of Gandhiji's 'Do or Die'. Irrespective of caste, creed, religion, gender and community people from all districts came forward to participation a few were martyred and thousands faced police atrocities and thus contributed to the success of this mass movement. During this struggle, the district of Nagaon played a prominent role. Public meetings and prayer meetings were organized and *santi-sena* (peace corps) organizations were established at different places in Nagaon. Though the British authorities adopted suppressive measures to crush the movement they could not break its spirit. In the present chapter an effort has been made to portray the participation of the people of Nagaon in the Quit India movement with an objective of rereading the role of Nagaon district in the said movement from a local perspective.

The encouragement provided by the leaders of Assam Provincial Congress Committee to participate in the programmes of the Quit India movement drew a large number of people towards it. Their programmes mainly included self-*satyagraha*, boycott of courts, schools and government services, picketing of shops selling foreign cloths and liquor and non-payment of tax, etc. The people also tried to disrupt communications, burnt police stations, attacked railway carriages and also destroyed military vehicles and made the authorities main target of attack. Even the students demonstrated among the peasants to get full cooperation from them. The establishment of emergency sub-committees in the provincial and the primary level by the Assam Provincial Congress Committee to activate the *santi-sena* organization and to launch a village organization scheme accelerated the pace of the movement.[1] The village panchayats which were organized to exercise executive and judicial functions at the local level also became active. Even in interior villages like Bahjani, Balijan, Hatisung, Raha, Jamuguri, Dhakuakhana and Sootea such panchayats worked actively.[2] It was the encouragement of the APCC leaders that people from all parts came forward to join in the movement.

In the 1942 Movement the Nagaon district played a prominent role. It is said that the Quit India movement at Nagaon was started through a public meeting at Barhampur on August 9, 1942, under the initiative of Haladhar Bhuyan, Purna Chandra Sharma, Islam Khan, Bimala Kanta Bora, Ganesh Borthakur, etc.[3] They played an important part in arousing anti-British sentiment among the general masses by establishing *santi-sena* organizations, public meetings and prayer meeting at different places in Nagaon.

The movement became very intense and widespread in the district and most of the revolutionaries tried to uproot the railway lines, destroying of bridges, etc. They derailed a goods train on 24th August near Bebejia.[4] On 25th another one was derailed at Kampur.[5] The district portions of tract between Kamrup and Jamunamukh and at Puranigudam were removed on the night of 24/25 August, 1942.[6] On 25th August, 1942 the people of Kampur while carrying out a procession to defy prohibitory orders of the Government attacked the local post office and the circle office and also damaged the railway station.[7] They forced the police Officer in Charge and railway officials including one constable to wear Gandhi-caps and shout *bande mataram*. At Phulaguri a group of people after damaging the railway station and setting fire on railway-shade and staff-quarters proceeded to the post office at Jajori. An inspection bungalow at Kathiatoli, a circle office at Raha, several excise shops and some cattle-pounds and school buildings at Puranigudam, Bebejia and Kaliabor were also damaged by them.[8] The revolutionaries cut off telegraph lines and damaged some road-bridges at several places. A few road-bridges on the Amluckie and Laokhowa were damaged. On night of 25/26 August the mob burnt a bridge at Bebejia, three miles west of Nagaon and when the Public Works Department party arrived there next day to repair the damages, they were attacked and driven away by the revolutionaries.[9] The same day in the morning the police patrol-party found another group of people engaged in digging one side of the approach-road to the Dighaliati Bridge at Jungalbalahugarh.[10] Although the British authorities deputed police and the military resorted to firing in some of the places to suppress the movement they could not break its spirit.[11] On the night of 28th August Tilak Deka, a volunteer of the *santi-sena* organization was killed by the police while warning the villagers by blowing on a buffalo-horn about the approach of the police patrol-party in the villages.

On 16th September, 1942 while the people of Nagoan were observing Panchabir Dibas (An event to commemorate five heroes) in memory of Kalai Koch, Hemoram Borah, Hemoram Patar, Gunabhiram Bordoloi and Tilak Deka (who laid down their lives for independence) with *prabhata pheri, nam-prasanga*, prayer meetings and felicitation of the relatives of the martyrs[12] they came into clash with the police at several places. At Kampur, a person tried to snatch away a rifle from the sentry of the inspection bungalow.[13] On 18th Sept, at Barhampur a public meeting was organized where the people were celebrating the Panchabir Dibas by holding a community feast but suddenly Mr. H. Rose and commander Mr. Finch along with armed troops and two Magistrate entered the name and the Magistrate ordered for immediate demolition of the camp constructed by the people and dispersal of the crowd.[14] Although a local Congress leader tried to persuade the Magistrate not to take such a drastic action but instead of paying any attention to him the Magistrate ordered to him to be arrested along with other Congress leaders.[15] Immediately thereafter the police troops went into action forced the people to demolish the camp. They also kicked and beat the people. Lakhi Kanta Hazarika, Thagiram Sut and Balaram Sut were martyred.[16] But it could not break their spirit and the harsh measures of the authorities aroused the common people to fight for the cause of freedom.

The Quit India movement brought the womenfolk of Nagaon to the vortex of the freedom struggle. Many women were found to be holding Congress flags and shouting Congress slogans in different parts of Nagaon.[17] They even faced severe police atrocities. At Barhampur while the military officers were trying to snatch away the Congress flags form the hands of a young girl Ratna, her aged mother Bhogeswari Phukanani intervened and hit one of the officers with the small flag-staff.[18] She was immediately shot dead. Jaimati Saikia of Chakalaghat village helped with the revolutionaries to burn the Bebejia Road Bridge.[19] Girls like Pitrani Saikia, Kali Saikia, Punimai Saikia and Dagati Bora worked for the security of underground male workers.[20] Guneswari Devi and her associates made remarkable contribution in this phase.[21] A few women were also involved in underground activities. Abali Phukan was charged with setting fire to the Government Inspection Bungalow at Monoha and received imprisonment where she died in 1942.[22] Inspite of the inhuman police atrocities most of the women participated wholeheartedly. This indicates that not only men were associated with the struggle, but women also came to the forefront to actively participate to make their country free from the bondage of the foreign domination.

To suppress the movement the Government arrested most of the Assam Provincial Congress Committee members. People rose in protest by taking out huge processions, resulting to hartals (strikes) and organized several meetings at different places of Assam. Taking up the cause of the Congress leaders some British authors and journalists addressed a letter to Mr. Amery, Secretary of State for India.[23] In which they urged for the release of the Congress leaders who had been arrested by the authority.[24] The Government released Gopinath Bordoloi, the leader of the Congress Party in Assam on 26th January, 1944. It also released the Congress Members of the Assam Legislative Assembly and they attended the Assembly session headed by Bordoloi in November, 1944 after being freed from imprisonment.[25] In Nagaon, Purna Chandra Sharma was released under restrictive orders along with Puspalata Das.[26] In view of this development, the Government of Assam through a notification dated 31 May, 1945 removed the ban on the leaders of the Assam Provincial Congress Committee and all District Congress Committees.[27] In the meantime, the Government released Congress leaders to participate in the proposed Simla Conference in June, 1945 and with it the struggle that had started since August, 1942 came to an end.[28]

In conclusion it can be observed that in response to Gandhi's call of 'Do or Die' a large section of people of Nagaon came forward to participate in the struggle and a few of them even became martyrs for the cause. The harsh treatment of the Government failed to break their spirit and ironically it drew a large number of people to the cause. Irrespective of caste and creed both men and women came forward to the national call. In the present scenario in India characterized with separatist movements it has become essential to reread, reinterpret and restate the role of the people of each and every locality of India in different phases of the freedom struggle with a view to restoring a new spirit and enthusiasm in the minds of Indians and reconstructing emotional integration among people of different parts of the country, to make them feel as oneness and be proud Indian with their own story of contribution to the freedom of their country.

NOTES AND REFERENCES

1. A.C. Bhuyan (ed.), *Political History of Assam (hereafter PHA)*, Publication Board of Assam, 1999, Vol. III, p. 61.
2. *Ibid.*
3. L. Keot, *Katha Mukti Sangramat Nagaon*, Sri Panchami Publication Society, Nagaon, Assam, 1995, p. 186.
4. *PHA, op. cit.*, p. 78.
5. *Ibid.*
6. *Ibid.*, p. 77.
7. *Ibid.*, p. 78.
8. *Ibid.*, p. 69.
9. *Ibid.*
10. *Ibid.*
11. Confidential B, File No. C. 251/1942, *Subject: Congress Movement 1942—Progress of Movement in Assam*, n. 25.
12. *PHA, op. cit.*, p. 70.
13. *Ibid.*
14. *Ibid.*
15. *Ibid.*
16. *Ibid.*, p. 71.
17. *Ibid.*
18. *Ibid.*
19. A.C. Bhuyan (ed.), *Nationalist Upsurge in Assam*, Guwahati, Assam, 2000, p. 174.
20. *Ibid.*
21. A.C. Bhuyan (ed.), *op. cit.*, p. 248.
22. *Ibid.*, p. 250.
23. A.K. Sharma, *Quit India Movement in Assam*, Mittal Publication, 2007, p. 141.
24. *Ibid.*
25. A. Sharma, *op. cit.*, p. 141.
26. *Ibid.*
27. *Ibid.*, p. 142.
28. Bipan Chandra and Others, *India's Struggle for Independence*, Penguin Books India (P) Ltd., p. 470.

13

SOCIO-CULTURAL ASPECTS OF BAJALI

Kanan Medhi

A part of Barpeta district in Assam, Bajali is an ancient region. It covers a large area which includes numerous rivers and brooks, lakes and ponds, farms and villages of distinct tribes, their cultures, beliefs, rituals, practices, culinary habits and colourful attires. Bajali, which covers an area of 280 sq. miles, is seen as a cultural hub of Assam.

The origin of the term Bajali is not very clear. According to Dr. Surya Kumar Bhuya someone named Bajalian Konwar ruled and inhabited this land and hence the name Bajali was coined.[1] However, any evidence of the existence of Bajalian Konwar is hard to find. Two kilometers north from Patacharkuchi in Bajali is the River Kaldia and on the banks of this river is the village Kunwara. The geographical location of this village hint towards a historical area, yet no clear connection has been found between this place and Bajalian Konwar.

Bajali being a tantric dominated area, a few experienced people want to say that the term *bejali* is the root of the word Bajali.[2] From primordial times many village *ojhas* and *bejas* (village medicine men) performed *bejali mantras* and treated the villagers. And thus in time the name Bajali might have come from the word *bejali*.

Since, Bajali has been a part of ancient Kamrupa, various groups like Austrics, Kiratas, Dravidians, Aryans, etc. inhabited this land since historical times. In addition to them, the Mongoloids also lived in Bajali since historical ages. Moreover, Bajali is taken as the habitat of the Australoids by the scholars.[3]

Though the original tribes of Assam have Mongoloid origins yet it also comprises a mixture of various Caucasian elements because the Caucasians emerged before the Mongoloids. The Mongoloids living in the plains of Bajali came in contact with the Caucasians with time.[3]

Sometimes, this mixture of the Mongoloids and Caucasians has been so deep that it has become difficult to find its original roots. Most of the ancient Australoid traits were absorbed by the Mongoloids and the Caucasians in due course of time. It is very difficult to say who came first between the Mongoloids and the Caucasians but in physical appearance they have both retained their identities as separate groups.[4]

The Bodos of Bajali (Kacharis, Rabhas) have come in such deep contact with the Caucasians that many of them have lost their Mongoloid characteristics.[5] The primary landscape of Bajali consists of three Aryan origin tribes — Austrics, Dravidians and Caucasians who together comprise the term Koch-Koch Hindus.[6] Muslims, too, reside in Bajali. When Mirjumlah invaded Assam, some *yaban* warriors were attracted to the land of Bajali and thus, established their residence here. Apart from the fact that they are of different religion, no other difference is found between them and the Assamese Hindus. The Brahmins and Kayasthas followed next.

Bajali's density of population from distinct culture and religion can be classified in the following ways — (i) Assamese Hindus, (ii) Bodo Kacharis, (iii) Bengali Hindus, (iv) Assamese Muslims, and (v) Migrated Muslims. The structure of Bajali's population indicates that most of the people are of Assamese origin. Yet people of various other religions and speaking languages other than Assamese like Bodo, Bengali, Rabha, Nepali and other local languages are also there. Among the Assamese speaking people exist the Bodos, Koch, Brahmins, Kayasthas, Kalitas, Kaibartas, Keots, Potters, Washermen, Barbers, Ironsmiths, Goldsmiths and Muslims. Though towns like Pathsala has witnessed the arrival of Marwaris and other Hindu trade communities, they too have become mixed with the Assamese language and culture.

The impact of Hinduism on Bajali's distinct communities is indivisible. Most of Bajali's populations have converted to Hinduism severing ties with their previous religion. Their beliefs and practices are similar to other Hindus. Hinduism here is reflected in the forms of Sakti, Vaishnava, Saivism, Tantricism, etc. All Hindus whether tribals or non-tribals follow one of the above mentioned path to practice their religion.[7] People of Bajali, through their paths of Saivism, Sakti, Tantricism, Vaishnavism, Islam, etc. have successfully established their existence in the contemporary times. Though a wide variety of religions are followed by people, in reality their impact is not that immense on an individual's everyday life. More than belief and faith on these religious organizations, one can see that the importance of other spheres is far greater. The villagers of Bajali follow a whole array of cultural norms, rituals, beliefs, deities and *mantras*. The present day Bajali's most areas comprise the followers of Mahapurush Sankardeva who developed and propagated *Eka-sarana-namadharma*, a faith of allegiance to one God. Impact of Damodardeva is also visible.

Bajali's population is mostly agrarian based. Agriculture is their livelihood. Modern irrigation has reached one or two places here yet most of them practice traditional ways of agriculture. Whole of Bajali's land is rich in nutrients due to the presence of rivers Kaldia and Pasumara. These two rivers along with their territories and agricultural fields play a huge role in Bajali's demography, economy, culture and their progress.

Bajali is mainly a rural area. Pathsala, termed as a town in 1968, is the only town here, with all other areas being mostly rural. Pathsala is located in the juncture of National Highway number 31 and the railway line of North-East India. However, places like Patacharkuchi, Nityananda, etc. have transformed into small towns at present times. The names of the places here are often after a situation or personality or reflect any story or some fact, for instance, Bamakhata, Kenduguri, Bhogpur, Ratnanpur, Bamunpara, Bamunkuchi, Choudhurypara, Kothalmuri, Bhootpuabari, etc.

Located in the north-eastern part of Barpeta district, Bajali and its people's sentiments are expressed through various religious festivals, cultural fares and feasts, etc. Farmers, peasants and other agricultural people of different class and caste participate in various social events during their recreational times, especially in the months of *Magh* and *Phagun*. These social events and festivals help in bringing up the feelings of unity and integrity among the people. Through these festivals and events, the people of the concerned villages celebrate them in the memory of their ancestors. Some major festive gatherings (*sabhas*) include *Ranasabha* (Rana burha's sabha), *Majer Sabha* (Majiu burha's sabha), *Kaithether Sabha* (Kaeth burha's sabha), *Gangather Sabha* (Ganga burha's sabha), *Bangaonor Sabha*, etc.

In these festivals, people celebrate with various performing arts like *ojapali*, *yatraparti, dholiya*, etc. People participate and celebrate them with pomp and show irrespective of their caste and class.

Since, ancient times, the wondrous performances of the *dholiyas* inspired a sense of pride to Kamrup. Undivided Kamrup had many teams and groups of *dholiyas* in various small and big villages. Different shows in different parts of Kamrup district had one thing in common — performances of *dholiyas*. Instruments, gestures, wrestling, circus, aerobatics, facial behaviours, etc. were used effectively by them to perform their act. They have a few similarities with *sattriya* dance, *gayan-bayan* and *ankiya naat*. The clowns and their pure, pristine and funny jokes and gestures provide entertainment to the villagers. Their numerous majestic instruments like *bordhol, guridhol, taal* and their sounds, different aerobatic fits, etc. mesmerize their audience. The changes of the contemporary world have sadly lowered their importance and interest significantly.

Dubi, in Bajali, with its Parihareshwar Temple has followers of both Sakti and Saivism. *Pari*, an Assamese term, means Goddess Parvati and *Hareshwar* means Lord Siva. The contribution of this temple to the cultural field is the dance form of *Devadasi*. This dance has a tradition of worshipping Lord Siva and is performed to satisfy him. The Ahom king Siva Singha brought in *devadasis* from Gorgaon and hence popularized this dance form. These *devadasis* remain mostly unmarried and fully surrender their lives to the Lord severing all times with any luxury. The *Devadasi* dance traditions could not, however, sustain and gradually it degenerated and lost its glory and identity. It has been a matter of pride, though, that the recovery of this beautiful and historic dance form has taken place. Inquisitive and culturally devoted Pathsala's Ratnakanta Talukdar and Kalaguru Bishnu Prasad Rabha led this endeavour by taking inspiration from *devadasis* Kaushalyabala, Royabala and *kholbadak* Becharam Bayan and taking it to a new level by mixing the tradition with the modern, thus popularizing it at both regional and national levels. It is also noteworthy that the *Devadasi* dance form was also performed in the temples of Da Parbatiya, the Biswanath Siva Temple, the Hatakasulin Siva Temple, Dergaon Siva Temple, Hajo's Haygribh Temple, Sonitpur, etc.

Historically, rich Bajali is known for its dramatics. Since, 1888 when Bhogiram Kakati of Bhalukguri directed his *yatraparti*, a whole new range of *yatraparties* started to come up. These *yatraparties*, however, performed only in Bengali in its initial days. Later with the passage of time, they were translated in Assamese. Some of the noteworthy *yatraparties* of that time were *Bamunkuchi Yatradal, Ganagaon Beenapani Opera, Sri Sri Sankardev Opera, Dubi Parihareshwar Yatraparti, Medhikuchi Yatradal, Helena Yatraparti*, Bamakhata and Kenduguri's *Bholanath Opera*, etc. These *yatraparties* became immensely popular thanks to the many known and unknown artists. Numerous actors, organizers, experts and their indescribable hard work built the foundation for these *yatraparties*.

The above mentioned *yatraparties* also led to the coming up of novel theatre groups. This was possible because of the unending efforts of two brothers — Sada Lahakar and Sri Achyut Lahakar. Sada Lahakar's Natraj Opera, established in 1959 showed a new way to Assamese drama. Through this drama team, the popular artist Achyut Lahakar gave birth to a dynamic form of mobile theatre group named Natraj Theatre in the year 1963 in Pathsala.[8] Taking inspiration from this, numerous other mobile theatre groups have come up in Pathsala over the years. Mancharupa Theatre, Aaradhana Theatre, Assam Star Theatre, Anirban Theatre, Kohinoor Theatre, Aabahan Theatre, Pallavi Theatre, Devadasi Theatre, Parihareshwar Theatre, etc. are some of the noteworthy theatre groups of Bajali.

Mahapurusha Sankardeva's inspiration and principles led to the establishment of *sattras* and *sattra* culture all over Assam and the case was no different in Bajali. Gobindapur village in eastern Bajali has the famous *Gobindapur Sattra*. Damodardeva's favourite student Bhagawandeva established this *sattra*. The deity worshiped here is Shyamray (Lord Krishna). According to the name of the deity, this *sattra* was named as *Samragher Ghara* (Shyamray deity's home) among the locals. Orally, this place was named Nimisha. Later, Damodardeva coined the term Gobindapur. Festivals related to Lord Krishna like *Doul, Pasati, Astami*, etc. are celebrated here. During Bohag Bihu, the festival of *Paora-toola* is celebrated here with great pomp and show. In this *sattra*, the *Sivalinga* is represented by a long bamboo stick, lust laden Parvati is represented by a red cloth, a garland made of red flowers, deer skin, etc. Siva-Parvati as a couple is shown respect in the very first *bihu* of the year. And it is believed that moving around the symbols that represent them in the field with instruments prevents various diseases and the harvest is good. The word *paora*, according to few, has been derived from the word Parvati. Association with tantrics of the *sattras* has resulted in a change in the consequent belief system.[9]

Akaya Sattra in Manikpur block follows the *nika samhati*. Though it was established according to Damodardeva's principles, it later shifted to Harideva's principles. It is one of the most developed *sattras* of Bajali. The *namghar, manikut, doulghar, baatsora*, etc. of this *sattra* are still arranged in the most disciplined way. The festivals celebrated here are *Doul, Krishna astami, Pasati* and Shankardeva and Madhavadeva's birth and death anniversaries.

Mahapurusha Madhavadeva's nephew Ramacharan Thakur's great grandson Purnananda Thakur founded the *Bamakhata Sattra*. This *sattra* idolizes the deity Madanmohan and follows the *nika samhati*. Mahapurusha Shankardeva, Madhavadeva and Mathuradas Burha's death anniversaries are celebrated here. In addition to them, *Magh Bihu, Bohag Bihu, Doul, Astami, Pasati* and other festivals are also celebrated here.

Some of the other *sattras* are *Pata Sattra, Haripur Sattra, Kuroobaha Sattra, Kaaljeerapara Sattra, Bhabanipur Sattra, Anandpur Sattra, Bhaluki Sattra, Bejkuchi Sattra*, etc. These *sattras* form the heart of Bajali's rich culture and tradition. In addition to these *sattras*, every village has its own *namghar*. These *namghars* are a kind of replica and enactment of the *sattras*. These organizations not only have developed the spiritual aspect of people but also have created a cultural atmosphere. They have led to unity and integration among the various groups of people and have further strengthened our democratic norms. According to Maheswar Neog, the *sattra* is the village club and theatre. It exercised a close spiritual control over all members of the community. In fact it can also be called the village parliament.[10]

With the dawn of the contemporary world, modernity has arrived in the historically rich Bajali. Imitations of the modern way of life and the consequent attraction towards Western ways have considerably increased and have drastically changed the mindset of the masses. Once, tradition is distanced, it becomes hard to go back to the traditionally rich past. Changing times and modern education have changed the interests and the values of the people, especially the youth, and a mechanical mindset is resultantly growing. This is not just the case of Bajali, but the whole of Assam is brimming with changes because of industrialization and globalization, thus distancing us further and further away from the rich traditions.

NOTES AND REFERENCES

1. Bhuya, S.K. (ed.), *Kamrupar Buranji*, 1930, p. 33.
2. Sarma, Munindra Nath, "Bajalir Aitihasik Patabhumi", in Sarma, Bhupendra Nath (ed.), *Bajali Darpana*, Assam Sahitya Sabha, 1987, p. 7.
3. Das, B.M., *Tribes of North-East India*, Shillong, 1984.
4. Raatan, T., *History, Religion and Culture of North-East India*, Isha Publications, 2011, p. 81.
5. Patra, Jiban Krishna, *Bajali Darpana*, 1987, p. 38.
6. *Ibid.*, p. 38.
7. Dutta, Narayan, *Bajali Darpana*, 1987, p. 29.
8. Patgiri, Jagadish, *Natya Aru Chetana*, p. 4.
9. Dutta, Narayan, *Dharmar Satot Bajali*, p. 28.
10. Neog, Maheshwar, *Maheshwar Neog Rachanawali*, Vol. VIII, 2012, p. 723.

14

TOURISM AND ITS SOCIO-CULTURAL ASPECTS OF THE NORTH-EASTERN REGION

Tulika Chowdhury

Tourism — a service oriented industry has emerged to be a revolutionizing phenomenon, especially in the second half of the present century. Tourism is important and in some cases, vital for many countries. Today, it is one of the largest and dynamically developing sectors. According to a recent study, tourism provides about 10 per cent of the World's income and employs almost one tenth of the World's workforce. In the Manila Declaration on World Tourism of 1980 the tourism was recognized as "an activity essential to the life of national because of its direct effects on its social, cultural, educational and economic sectors of national societies and on their international relations". In 1941, Hunzikar and Kreps defined — tourism as people who travel, "the sum of the phenomena and relationships arising from the travel and stay of non-residents, in so far as do not lead to permanent residence and are not connected with any earning activity".

In 1976, the Tourism Society of England defined the concept as follows: "Tourism is a temporary short-term movement of people to destinations outside the places where they normally live and work and their activities during the stay at each destination. It include movement for all purposes". Thus, tourism we can define as a travel for business purposes or for recreation or leisure. Now-a-days, it has become a popular global leisure activity.

India, an Asian country, where population is more than a billion (2000) and an area of 32,87,263 sq.km. is known for its natural resources, deserts, forests, beaches, mountains, rivers, sea, etc. India is spiritually and traditionally a rich country. It has a rich culture which is more than 5000 years old. All these make India a tourism gold-mine. Since, Independence, tourism industry was very neglected. It was considered to be a luxury industry.

But, today's picture is a totally changed one and now tourism industry in India is growing speedily. According to Provisional Statistics, 6.29 million foreign tourists arrived in India in 2011, which was 5.78 million in 2010. This ranks India as the 38th country in the world in terms of foreign tourist arrival. Delhi, Maharashtra, and Tamil Nadu are the most popular states for foreign tourists.

North-East India is the eastern — most region of India bordering by Bhutan and Tibet, Myanmar and Bangladesh. The North-eastern region consists of eight states — Assam, Arunachal Pradesh, Manipur, Meghalaya, Mizoram, Nagaland, Tripura and Sikkim. The region is very rich in natural resources. The natural beauty, dense forests, wild-life, hills and mountains, water-falls, fragrant tea-gardens, the rich cultural heritage have always been a source of attraction to people from other parts of the country and abroad. Assam has a number of famous wildlife reserves — The Kaziranga National Park, which is the home to one-horned Rhinoceros, Nameri National Park, Pobitora Wild Life Sanctuary, Dibru-Saikhowa National Park, etc. Sivasagar is famous for the Rangghar, Karengghar, Sivadol, etc. These are ancient monuments of Assam. The numerous temples including Kamakhya temple, Madhab-mandir, Gopeswar mandit, Umananda, Doul Gobinda, etc. are also places of pilgrimage. The Ambubasi fair at Kamakhya temple attracts large number of tourists.

Sherra (Cherrapunji) is the wettest place on earth. It is a popular and beautiful hill station. In Meghalaya, the natural attractions include water-falls, lakes, caves, peaks, and dense forests. Meghalaya is also known as the Scotland of India. And there is the place Mawsynram, which experiences the highest rainfall place in the world.

Manipur is a hilly State. The Imphal, capital of Manipur is surrounded by hills and lakes. The important tourist spots are Logtak lake, Lamjace Deer Sanctuary, Keibul. Manipur has begun taking steps to develop its tourist potential. But the tourism infrastructure is not developed adequately in the State.

Arunachal Pradesh is a beautiful State which is also known as the land of 'rising sun'. In Arunachal Pradesh, the tourist spots are Twang, Zero, Bomdila, Parasuram Kund, Namdopha Sanctuary, etc. The state is also famous for its rich arts and crafts. Arunachal Pradesh has the highest Buddhist monastery located at Twang.

Though Nagaland is new to tourism, the people of Nagaland are open to tourism. There are tourist lodges in Nagaland which presents cultural programmes.

Mizoram holds a great deal of appeal for nature lovers because the landscape is rich with dense bamboo jungles, rivers, paddy fields, etc.

Sikkim is one of the loveliest hilly places in India and the State is getting consistently as the third best tourist State in India.

Therefore, we can easily say that the entire north-eastern region is endowed with diverse tourist attraction. Art and cultural media too have always constituted an important motivation for travel and the north-eastern states produce attractive handicrafts which are one of the main attractions of tourists. Weaving is a traditional art in all the States. Mainly tribal women are very efficient in weaving.

Tourism has wide impact on the socio-economic life of the region. It seems to be an ideal tool for economic development of the country. Tourism promotes peace and cooperation among nations. Through tourism people from different States or countries can learn our rich culture and customs. It can help to preserve the local traditions and handicrafts. It is widely accepted that tourism development can contribute to the protection and enhancement of traditions, customs, and heritage, which would otherwise disappear through the waves of modernization.

The entire north-eastern region is suffering from unemployment problem. Attached to it, terrorism is also a burning problem of the region. Tourism is a labour-intensive industry. It requires less investment. Therefore, local people or unemployed youths can easily find employment opportunities in the industry. They can open-up restaurants or hotels, which can help promote local indigenous delicacies, fabric, etc. Employment opportunities increase incomes and create better standard of living for and reduce poverty of the people. Tourism may also create opportunities for local craftsman, weavers, artisans, and create marketing avenues for their products. By doing so, they can earn more income.

The income generated through tourist encourages investment on infrastructure like hotels and resorts, roads, water and sewage system, airlines and entertainment venues such as amusement parks, shopping mall; music venues, etc. Developed infrastructure can improve the region. It also contributes to tax-revenue. Not only it helps to earn tax-revenue, but it can also generate foreign exchange and improving the position of the State in the world map.

In spite of having all potential for the development of tourism, the industry is yet to be developed to its full potential. Various factors are responsible for this. Important among them are — poor infrastructural facilities, lack of proper tourism policy, insurgency, lack of communication, lack of entrepreneurial motivation, etc. On the other hand the cost is high in the region because of the isolation from the mainstream of India. The whole north-eastern region is largely covered by hills which increase mainly the transportation cost and take more time to travel.

Here, I want to mention that tourism has negative affect also. Tourists often negatively affect the ecology by deforestation and culture of the area they visit. Tourists may fail to respect the local tradition and customs, etc. But negative impacts must be minimized and positive impact must be maximized.

Therefore, for the sake of the economic and social development of the north-eastern region, we should develop the tourism industry. Keeping in view the benefits of the industry, steps should be taken for the development of the industry. To increase the inflow of tourist, government should develop infrastructural facilities, (such as transportation and communication facilities, banking facilities, hotels and restaurants, etc.). Proper plans and policies and a marketing strategy to diffuse information must be prepared. Local NGOs can also take steps for the development of the industry. Financial assistance should be provided for the development of tourism industry both by the Central and the State government, so that the State will develop with respect to the tourism industry.

REFERENCES

Batra, G.S. and Dangwal, *Tourism Promotion and Development New Advances*, Deep and Deep Publications Pvt. Ltd.

Bhatia, A.K., *Tourism Development — Principles and Practices*, 1982, Sterling Publishers Pvt. Ltd., New Delhi.

Chutia Ranjan Hemanga and Saikia Samaran, *Tourism in North-East India*, Purbanchal Prakash, Guwahati.

Dayal, Shambhu, *Hand Book of Tourism Ethics*, Akanksha Publishing House, New Delhi.

Goswami, R.K., *Tourism and Environment*, Cyber Tech Publications, New Delhi.

Krishna, G. Radha, *Promotional Perspective and Issues*, Icfai Books, The Icfai University Press.

Makan, Dileep, *Tourism as an Economic Enterprise*, Adhyayan Publishers and Distributors, New Delhi.

Negi, Jogmohan and Monohar Gaurav, *Rural Tourism: Planning and Promotion*, Authors Press.

Sethi Praveen, *Handbook of Modern Tourism*, Anmol Publications Pvt. Ltd., New Delhi.

Sharma, K.K., *Tourism and Development*, Sarup and Sons, New Delhi.

Internet.

15

TRIBAL CULTURE AND ITS RELEVANCE IN PLANNING IN NORTH-EAST INDIA

Nivedita Brahma

Introduction

The north-eastern region of India enjoys a very vital, strategic and sensitive location in the country. Flanked by Bhutan, China, Burma and Bangladesh this region today attracts all eyes towards it. These strategic characteristics assumed much more significance during the Second World War when the Japanese started knocking at this corner. The partition of the country and the creation of Bangladesh as an independent nation, have added many problems to this region. In past, there has not been a year which has not witnessed a turmoil, clash, uprising, disturbance, riot and alike in one or other part of the region. The latest had been the Assam and Mizoram problems, disturbance in Meghalaya, insurgency in Manipur and Tripura, etc. This vulnerable part of India with continuous occurrence of violence and reports of secessionists activities in past had created a potentially explosive situation in north-eastern India. The gravely disturbing situation in this part of the country had posed several challenges. It is often said that the hypersensitive people of this region who have been for a fairly long time harbouring anger against the 'aliens', are anxious to retain and strengthen their 'distinct identity' as well as 'cultural traditions'. Every socio-economic problem believed to have its roots in history as well as ebb and flow of cultural traits. The problems of this region are no exception. Further, the development divorced from the real needs of the people and totally alien to their cultural landscape, is liable to create more problems than it is going to solve. The consequences of some such steps have already become vividly clear to sociologists, economists and planners. Thus, it is the need of the day to have an appreciation of the cultural fabric of this region. Here, an attempt has been made to present in brief some aspects of the socio-cultural heritage of the region which has great relevance not only in understanding the socio-economic problems of the region, but also to find solutions to the complex problems of the region.

Tribals of the North-East

In the north-eastern India, there are more than 100 tribes and sub-tribes. Of them 55 are considered to be major tribes. The tribals of the region are its oldest inhabitants. There have been references to these people in old literature and in the epics as 'Kiratas'. These people crossed into the region at different points of time and the waves of migration continued for fairly long period. In course of time, the 'Aryans' who migrated into the area much later and who happened to be a relatively superior group, dislodged these aboriginals who, for survival, sought refuge in the high hills and the thick forests of the region. The entire Sub-Himalayan belt and other sides of the Patkai range along the Naga hills running through Manipur and Tripura up to Chittagong hill tracts where it merges into the Arakan range is inhabited by tribal people belonging to a number of groups and sub-groups.

Ethnic Groups and Races

Ethnologically, north-eastern region is a very interesting as well as fascinating part of the country where people of different castes, clan and ethnographic groups live together. The region has a long history of migration of people of varying races at different points of time. The migrants entered the region, fought against and conquered the different native groups and later on settled here and became the native of this soil. Traces of migrants Nigritos or Negrolike people have been found in Angami Nagas of the Naga hills. They entered India from Africa through Arabia and Iran in pre-historic times. After Nigritos, the people who migrated to north-eastern India were Proto-Austroloids. The Mongoloids, *viz.*, Tibeto-Burman groups and the Ahoms belonging to Siamese group were probably the next to enter north-eastern India. The Tibeto-Burman tribes, who from their center of dispersal occupied the eastern Himalayas bordering Assam, are the Akas, Abors, Nishis, and Mishings. The most important Indo-Mongoloid people in the region are the Bodos. They formed a solid block in the north-eastern India covering the major part of Southern Assam, North Cachar hills, Garo hills and south of Tripura.

Of the other Tibeto-Burman groups, Nagas are the most important, inhabiting the entire Naga Hills and extending to the neighbouring hills of Manipur in the South and the Karbi hills to the west. Being secluded in their mountain fastness, they were spilt-up into a number of mutually exclusive tribes who do not understand each others' speech. Of the Assam-Burma section of the Tibeto-Burmans, the Kuki-Chin tribes formed an important branch and are found in south eastern Assam and Burma. Leaving their kinsmen in Burma, they appear to have settled in fairly ancient times in Manipur as the Meities, in Mizoram as well as in the Chittagong hill tracts. From Manipur and Mizoram they infiltrated in large number into Tripura hills where they form an important section of the people. Of the Kuki-Chins, the Karbis are one of the groups which are concentrated in the Karbi Anglong district of Assam.

Another important group in the region is the Khasis who mainly inhabit the Khasi-Jayantia hills in Meghalaya. An authoritative and extensive description on the history and culture of the Khasi people has been given by Bareh, and according to him the Khasis came from the east than from any other direction. There is a tradition that the Amwi-Khasis reached their present land from the East and that their ancestors were originally connected with the Mekong river. In Amwi, Cambodia means clever and indigenous. This gives a clue that the ancient Khasis were immigrants some where from the Cambodia region and from the bank of the Mekong river. Further, it is interesting to note that there is a matriarchal tribe called Khasi in Laos which is associated with the Moi and Rade Jarai groups of clans. Further, there is a tradition amongst Khasis that they originally came into Assam *via* Patkai range. Gurdon states that many affinities can be traced among the Khasis and the people of the Far East, and on the grounds of such resemblance he came to the conclusion that the Khasis came from the East. In support of the above view, he observes that the Khasi branch of the Mon-Anam family had possibly used the same route of migration which was in the direction commonly followed by the other immigrants from Burma as was the case with the Ahoms *via* Patkai range and similarly the movements of the Khamptis and again the Singphos from the country to the east of Hukong.

Apart from the racial elements mentioned that go to form population of the region (Assam) — The Nigritos, the Proto-Austroloids and the Indo-Mongoloids, there were Dravidian elements who have been absorbed in the various strata of the population. There had again been intrusion of the Aryan elements particularly the Alpine Dinaric who have also become part of the people of the region (Assam). In fact, all the racial elements that go to build up the people of north-east India with the difference that while in other parts of the country, elements like Aryans and Dravidians are pre-pondering. The former Governor of Assam and Meghalaya rightly called the north-eastern region, the mini India and the most beautiful part of the country.

Social and Cultural Life

The north-eastern region can be divided into two cultural zones. First, the tribal and non-tribal divide and second, a movement away from the folk loric stage. The division of the zone into tribal and non-tribal in terms of cultural growth (folk loric and non-folk loric) is actually linked with the general sequence of development. The cultures of the State of Arunachal Pradesh, Meghalaya, Mizoram and Nagaland belong to the tribal category. This also includes the culture of some parts of Assam, Manipur and Tripura where there are tribal concentrations. Culture in this category is essentially folk loric although new literature and culture have also emerged in recent times. In the non-tribal category are the dominant cultures of Assam, Manipur and Tripura characterized as non-tribal and recognized by their folk-loric temper.

Thus, the distinctive factor is actually the mobility in terms of social development following growth in the material base of culture. The folk loric aesthetic expressions are generally need-based and a direct outcome of the collective social consciousness and therefore, the tribal culture is a collective and participatory with total psychic involvement of all the individuals as members of a composite group. The cultures of the first culture zone of north-east region belongs to this category. The second category culture — the non-tribal culture has developed in Assam, Manipur and Tripura under a feudal order and thus, passed through various social, administrative and economic compulsions. In the process, the tribal way of life faced gradual dissolution and a new situation was created when new cultural expressions were available.

Social and Cultural Life in Assam

In Assam, the major tribal groups are:

1. *The Bodos*

The Bodo tribe is one of the Major and largest plain tribes of Assam. They are found predominantly in the district of Kokrajhar, besides Kamrup, Nalbari and Darrang districts. The Bodo society was divided in to certain groups or clans based mainly on the principle of labour, such as Basumatary (land owners), Gayari (in charge of arcanut cultivation), Tamular (in charge of betel leaf cultivation), etc. The traditional social division, however, have lost their original significance and in the present day Bodo society, these divisions only represent their surnames and clan names.

Usually, the Bodo family structure is patriarchal. The family property passes to the male member of the society. But, the position of womenfolk is at par with man. The village priest looks after the proceedings of several rituals that mark their social and religious calendars. The most important community institution of the Bodos is the village. The village council decision in all matters is accepted by the people.

The Bodos are known for agriculture and they go for improved agriculture with irrigated land. Rice is the staple food like other non-tribal neighbours. The art of fishing and hunting and preserving dehydrated meat and fish are part of Bodo culture. The Bodo people are festival loving people. Three main categories of festivals are seasonal, religious, ritualistic and ceremonial. Baisago festival is an occasion of merry making and dance is a part of this festival. Bagrumba is the most attractive group dance of the Bodos. For good harvesting they perform Kherai festival. They worship a tree — Shiju — personified to Hindu Siva, in the similar way as the Assamese worship Tulsi.

The Bodo language is currently an associate language in Assam. It has been introduced as the medium of instruction in the schools and colleges in Bodo dominated areas.

2. *The Karbis*

There is a hill district of Assam known as Karbi Anglong District located to the north of NC Hills and south of Jorhat and Golaghat District where inhabits the Karbi Tribe. Unlike other Mongoloid tribes, the Karbis are not fair complexioned and bear a light yellow brown complexion. They are patriarchal tribe having five exogamous clans which are — Terang, Teron, Enghee, Engti and Timung. Their principal crop is rice which they cultivate by primitive Jhum system. Piggery and poultry is common amongst them. Rearing of silk worm, spinning and weaving is in their culture. They also have tradition of cane and bamboo work, carpentry and blacksmith works.

The traditional religion of Karbis is Hindu and they believe in one supreme being. The sacrifice of pigs and fowls are associated with their rituals. The Karbis are colourful tribe in their traditional dresses, ornaments, dances, music and folk songs. Even their death ceremony is associated with dances and music which is rare amongst others. Karbi folk dances are very colourful. They dance with perfect rhythm associated with drum beating and songs.

The village Council is the pivot in Karbi village. All the male householders are its members. The head of the Council is elected. Matters serious in nature are decided by this apex body.

3. *The Mishings*

The Misings are mostly based on the riverine areas of Lakhimpur, Dibrugarh, Sibsagar, Jorhat and Sonitpur districts. Joint family is the basis of their social system. They are divided into many clans and sub-clans and marriage within the same clan is impossible. The clan is called Aprin. They believe that their clans are originated from their forefathers and they give divine status to the originators. The Gam is the village headman and each important matter can be taken up after due debate at the Kobang, village assembly. A Banokobang is consisted of few Kobangs. The Gam is not hereditary and his decision can be cancelled by the Kobang. All the public works are done by the Mumbrir — Yame, the organization of the unmarried boys and girls and this organization itself sprung from the Murung — the bachelor's dormitory. The Mishings perform the Ali-Aye-Ligang festival before the summer cultivation and Porag after harvesting. They perform Dubur ceremony having sacrificed a young female pig and hen for the betterment of cultivation. Symbolically, this is a tribal fertility rite and it shows how such rites are done by all the human races from Indus civilization to the present days. The priest of the Mishing is called Mriri and from the Mriri they came to be called as Miri by the non-Mishing people.

4. *The Dimasas*

The North Cachar hills, presently known as Dima Hasao district is inhabited by the Dimasa people.

Agriculture is the principal occupation and main source of livelihood of the Dimasa. They practice jhuming or shifting cultivation, but the Dimasa settled around Maibong go for wet land system by irrigating their fields from nearby rivers. Rice is their main crop, but they also cultivate maize, sesame, cotton, chilly, pumpkin, gourd, ginger, etc.

In Dimasa, the village system is called Nablai meaning a cluster of houses and whole village with population is called Raji. The traditional village headman has both executive and judicial powers. No community function in a Dimasa village can be performed without the prior approval of the village headman.

The Dimasas consider themselves to be Hindus although they have traditional gods and goddesses. The dress reflects culture of the people. A Dimasa man wears a *dhoti* green in colour. He uses a *chadar* and a turban as a head dress. A Dimasa woman puts on a skirt like Assamese Mekhela and a *chadar* to cover the upper part of her body. Both men and women are fond of ornaments.

Music is part of Dimasa life. They have a number of musical instruments to add spices to their culture. They are generally peace loving, but can be dangerous if provoked. They accept modern technology or ideas if convinced and can adopt very quickly.

There are other tribes in Assam like The Rabhas, Deoris, Ahoms, Tiwas, Tea-tribes, Sonowal Kacharis, Khamtis, Singphos and many more. Each tribe has their own cultural identity. They made Assam their home and became part of greater Assamese society.

Religious Beliefs and Festivals in Assam

Assam today is the home of Hindus, Muslims, Christians, Vaishnavites and Shaktas and thus people profess different faiths and celebrate different festivals. The Shakta cult is said to have begun with the establishment of the Kamakhya temple. The Shakta cult presents a modified form of tantric faith and hinges upon blood and sacrifice. The cruel practice of sacrifice are now losing ground with increased awakening and outside contact.

Sixteenth century AD is known as the period of religious uplift, social emancipation and general awakening of Assam. The major credit for this goes to Shankar Deva who brought about a revolution in the field of religion and literature. Through his compositions and preachings he waged a battle against superstitious belief, sacrifices and undesirable rituals. The form of religion he preached was universal in nature and cosmopolitan in content. He fought tooth and nail against high and low and persuaded people of all shades, categories and ages to sit under one roof and worship the Almighty. He preached the Vaishnava cult of Hinduism and helped people to shun orthodoxy and dogmatism and persuaded to come under the umbrella of wide awakening and spiritual enlightenment.

The major festivals of Assam are the three Bihus — Rongali Bihu, Bhogali Bihu and Kongali Bihu; Holi, and Diwali. The Muslims and the

Christians celebrate Id and Christmas respectively. The Rongali Bihu has special significance in Assam. Assamese new year starts in April and the occasion is celebrated through this festival. It is marked by cultural activities like singing and dancing called Hunsori.

Social and Cultural Life in Manipur

The State of Manipur falls in two broad divisions — hill tracts and valley belts. These two distinct divisions are by and large inhabited by two distinct people — tribals and Meiteis respectively. Meiteis are Hindus and they dominate all other sections of the populations. There are seven major clans of Meiteis, *viz.* Ningthouja, Luwang, Khuman, Angam, Khaba-Nagania and Chinglei. About Meiteis, it is believed that they are the progeny of inter-racial marriages between Aryans and the Chinese. Meiteis constitute the highly civilized section of the Kuki people and at present they form politically and economically a dominant group.

Among the Meiteis, polygamy is allowed, but polyandry is disapproved socially. At present, the trend is mostly to have one wedded wife. Divorce in Meiteis is very uncommon. Men and women actively take part in social life. Women are treated with high respect.

Singing, dancing and fishing are indispensable part of the easy going Meiteis. They have a homogenous society and it can be felt at different ceremonies like marriage, child birth, *Sasthi Puja*, temple ceremonies and festivals. The uniformity in the dress of men and women is the best proof of homogenous character. The dress of men is the white *kurta*, *dhoti* and *pagri* (old men). The dresses are distinct and specific for ceremonial occasions. The women wear a choli to cover the upper part of their body, and a skirt type garment called Fanek is wrapped around the waist upto the ankles. A cotton chador is wrapped around the upper body.

The main profession of Meiteis is agriculture and fishing in rural areas. Weaving and basket making is practiced as sparetime activities both in rural and urban areas. Paddy is the main crop of Manipur and practically all types of vegetables are grown. Agriculturally, Manipur is the most advanced State in the region.

Another major tribe of Manipur, the Kukis are spread over southern part of Manipur. The men are short as well as medium sized. Their face is broad and round and complexion is fair. Their hair is dark and rarely turn grey by age. The ladies wrap their body by two pieces of cloth, one for the upper portion and the other for the lower portion. Kuki women are fond of ornaments.

Kukis observe exogamy as regards the family and endogamy as regards the clan. In the Kukis, polygamy is not a system. Widow remarriage solely depends upon the will of the widow. The bride price is paid by the groom's side and is bases on the bride's beauty, dowry value and the clan she belongs to. Divorce is not so common but easy to settle if the couple so decides. Adultery is punishable and rape is regarded as a crime. The eldest son inherits the property but this depends upon the will of the father.

In some parts of Manipur there is a system of bachelor's dormitories called Morung. Here, the young males get the trainings in jhuming, singing, dancing and community service.

Religious Beliefs and Festivals in Manipur

Hinduism was the principal religion of Manipur. With the arrival of the Britishers, Christianity also made successful inroads — specially among the different tribes living in the hills. Further, with the migration of people from Bengal, Islam also made its entry in Manipur. Today's demographic set-up of Manipur is characterized by the people who profess different religions and cults.

In ancient past, Manipur was the abode of Shaktas. The *Devdasis*, i.e. the maids given to the service of deities used to worship and propitiate Lord Shiva through their dancing musics. It has been a welcome attribute of the Manipuri culture that it never became static in form, but adapted itself to the variations of time and space. Dancing is the most exquisite form of Manipuri culture. The dances of valley carry religious overtones, while those of hills, i.e. tribal dances are expressive of joy and entertainment and resound with chivalrous expressions of wars and hunting campaigns.

Manipuri dance, known as Jagoi is the greatest exponent of Manipuri culture. The dance has variations and the main background tale is mainly based on Radha and Krishna. The costumes of the dance is very attractive and the participants are attired in only specified dresses.

Manipuri is a recognized language by the Sahitya Academi. In old times, Manipuri language had its own script, but the historical compulsions made to lose much of its ground. Unless serious efforts are made to revive and rejuvenate this script. It is feared that it may die forever.

The main festivals of Manipur are Rath Yatra (Performed in July on the pattern of Puri festival of Orissa), and Chalinrity, the most popular dance is performed on this occasion. Thabal Changba — a fortnight long festival held in February-March is an old folk dance, performed by young boys and girls and in a way help them in choosing their life partners. Yaoshang festival is similar to Holi festival of north India. Baruni festival is associated with the closing of the year and festival Cheiroba is associated with the welcome of the new year.

The Manipuri society on the whole, is dominated by both tribals and non-tribals. The scenic beauty and rich cultural heritage of Manipur had perhaps prompted Pandit Nehru to call it the "Jewel of India".

Social and Cultural Life in Meghalaya

Meghalaya is mainly inhabited by the Khasi, Jayantia and Garo tribes. Their descendency is counted from mother's side. But the society is administered by the male. No one can take decision on the inheritance of property without the consent of maternal uncle. The husband is like a guest, because he does not belong to the clan of his wife's mother. Here, the husband is to live with his wife's family, not the wife with her husband's family. The power and function of a married man is limited within his family. Even after his death his remains never find place with that of his wife and children is to be sent to his own mother's graveyard. Marriage within the same clan is impossible. For a Garo, he is to marry his mother-in-law at the death of her husband. But at the absence of any son-in-law, a widow can not marry without prior permission from the family of his dead husband. But unlike the other tribes, for whom land is a common property, the Garo village headman is the sole occupant of land. A Jayantia man never lives with his wife; he always leaves for his wife's house at sunset and returns to his mother's house at the morning. His earnings always go to his mother's house and not to his wife and children. But in the administrative matter, they are always male. Khasi clan is ruled by the Chiyems but unlike the Mizos, Khasi Chiyem have no *de-facto* power. He has to discuss all the important matters with the Council. At the death of a Chiyem, his elder sister's son is selected by the Durbar (eleted body) to the Chiyem's post. To the Garos, their land belongs to their great Mother. Their all clan heads can take part in the executive body of their tribes and vote. If any individual of a clan is killed by an individual of an another clan, the revenge is never forgotten and to be taken by killing the murderer or any relative of the murderer. In their social customs, like some other tribes of Assam, a long round stone pillar is posted at the burial of male and a flat stone pillar at the female's burial. This custom is prevalent among all the primitive tribes of the world.

Boiled rice and cooked dried fish are major food items of Meghalaya tribes and they relish practically all types of meat; beef and pork are, however, more popular. Hunting, fishing and jhooming are practiced both on community basis as well as on individual basis in rural areas. The folk songs and dances of Meghalaya are related to the ceremonies of birth, matrimony, heroism, love and festive occasions. The dances in the Khasi and Garo hills are performed in the open. Both men and women dance in different circles. The female dancers move to and fro on their toes and shake their bodies in different ways. Many instrumental musicians accompany the dance. Married as well as unmarried males, in colourful attire, participate in the dance. Nongkrem, a festival of dances and songs, is regarded as a religious occasion — the famous thanks giving ceremony to the Almighty Father for bestowing agricultural prosperity. Despite the spread of Christianity and intrusion of Western culture, this festival is celebrated for five days in Meghalaya.

Christianity entered Meghalaya in the early nineteenth century when the Serampore Baptist Mission established between 1812 and 1938. The Christianity has made social transformation and spread education in the area and brought the impact of western culture. The capital city of Shillong at present gives a cosmopolitan look where people of all tribes, castes, religion and creed co-exist. It is the place where all the major festivals of India are celebrated with equal pomp, gaiety and communal harmony.

Social and Cultural Life in Mizoram

Mizoram is mainly inhabited by the Mizos who were also known as Lushais. The Mizo tribe is the combination of five major tribes like Lushai, Ralte, Hmar, Paitee and Pawi and eleven minor tribes known under common name Awzia. While the five major tribes retained their respective dialects, the eleven minor tribes either lost their distinctive dialects as a result of association with larger tribes. What is known as Mizo language today is synonymous with the Lushai dialect and the correct name of the language is Duhlian-twang. In Mizos and other tribes free mixing of boys and girls is allowed and the marriage is by consent. Pre-marital sex is not looked down upon in Mizos, the dating system between boys and girls is called 'Nula rim' and is very common. Divorce and marriage are allowed among Mizos.

The village administration in Mizos is headed by a chief, who is assisted by a council of elders. In addition, the chief do have an advisory committee known as 'La Ilpa'. The chief is given certain fixed share of income but have no right to levy any tax he liked. The cases of theft, rape, etc. is almost unknown to Mizos. An wonderful institution in Mizo life was Zawlbuk, a dormitory for bachelors who stayed there at night. To construct Zawlbuk, whole village contributed free labour. The dormitory also served the purpose of village guest house. These institutions have now died out.

The Mizos like pork, beef and fowl's meat. Rice and maize form their staple food. Their local rice beer, 'Zu' is very popular. The Mizos have strong social customs. They have customs to contribute for community work and to render help to the distressed person. Mizos are fond of dance. their most popular dance is 'Cheraw' or bamboo dance performed by girls. The dance has fast rhythm and symbolizes the pulsating youth. Khual-lam is another popular dance of the Mizo boys. Solakia dance is performed after hunting. Men and animal dance around the hunted animal to the accompaniment of drum beats.

The supreme god of Mizos is pathian. The Mizos believe in two worlds after death, i.e. *Piaral* (Heaven) and *Mitthi Khua* (Hell). The Christianity in the north-east India has influenced the Mizos and as such they are the most westernized society and forward looking. However, many of the old traditions, customs and beliefs are followed by them.

Social and Cultural Life in Tripura

At present, there are 18 tribes in Tripura. The Mundas, Oraons, Santhals, Bhils, Lepchas, Bhutias who migrated to Tripura in the past for employment are numerically insignificant, politically unorganized and socio-culturally isolated from other tribes The latter two tribes came from northern Bengal, while others have come from the area around Chotanagpur. The Tipra tribe dominates all other tribes of the State. The Jamatias, Reangs, Chakmas and Mughas are the other important tribes of Tripura. Tripura is basically a Hindu dominated State. Bengali Hindus migrated to Tripura since time unknown. Part of the population follow Buddhist religion also.

Thus, Tripura is inhabited by two distinct groups — tribals and non-tribals. The tribals prefer highlands and practice *jhum* cultivation. The non-tribals, now the majority group, practice settled cultivation on relatively flat lands and valley basins. Tea, coffee and rubber plantations are promoted to replace the primitive cultivation. The traditions and customs of Tripura are similar to those of Bengali Hindus. Some of the tribal groups retain their traditional rites, rituals and faiths. In old days, the bride's parents used to dictate terms and conditions of marriage and extorted bride's price whereas today the daughters are considered as a burden. There are strange beliefs in Tripura. They believe that the earth rests on the back of a tortoise. The milky way is described as the path on which the spirits of deceased persons proceed to the heaven. The rainbow is said to be a huge snake that appears on the horizon to drink water. The hailstorm is explained as the shower of fried articles by gods and goddesses above. Lightning is shown as hide and seek appearance of a woman, who in a bid to save her honour flew from this world and took refuge in the sky. Cyclone occurrence is linked with the uncleared debts. Only those persons who failed to pay their debts in their life are said to be punished during those cyclonic storms.

The folk-lore of Tripura has been enriched by legends, folk Rales, folk songs, etc. They deal with variety of themes like love, courtship, jhooming, myths and rituals, nature, flora, fauna, etc.

The various cults persued by the people had influenced art and architecture of the State Idols of Lord Shiva and Parvati found in various parts of Tripura indicate influence of Shakta cult. The famous temple of Tripuri Sundari goddess Of Radha Kishorepur points towards the probability of naming the State after the deity. The Tripuri Sundari also symbolizes Shakta cult. The idols of Lord Vishnu and Ganesh found in the state indicate prevalence of Vaishnavite cult. Buddhist Viharas and image of Lord Buddha found in the state testify prevalence of Buddhism. Thus, Tripura was a State where religious toleration was at the climax in the past.

Social and Cultural Life in Arunachal Pradesh

There are about 82 tribes and sub-tribes living in different parts of Arunachal Pradesh. Of them the major tribes are, the Nishis or Daflas, Gallongs, Tagins, Wanchos, Monpas, Mishimis, Noctes, Apatanis, Akas, Sherdukpens, Abors or Adis, Tangas, etc. The natural environment has resulted into multiplicity of dialects and variations in customs of these tribal groups. Here, is a brief sketch of some of these tribes.

Monpas and Sherdukpens

These two tribal groups inhabit the western district of Kameng. They profess Buddhism and are strongly influenced by the culture and tradition of the Tibetans and the Bhutias. The Monpas largely concentrate around Tawang where one of the biggest monasteries in India was built. It was at Tawang where the sixth Dalai Lama of Tibet was born. The Monpas practice settled cultivation on terraced land and rear animals. On the other hand, the Sherdukpens are keen traders who migrate to foothills during winter and, therefore, their agriculture is neglected. The Monpas are expert in carpet weaving and the Sherdukpens are good carpenters, blacksmiths and silversmiths. The family structure of these tribes is patriarchal and the sons inherit the father's property. Monogamy is the prevailing form of marriage Divorce and widow remarriage are permitted. The Sherdukpens have village councils locally called Jung. This system has now been accepted by the government as Village Panchayat. The Concil dispenses all individual disputes, theft, adultery and all other socially repugnant offences.

The Apatanis and Nishis

These two tribes are mainly concentrated in the Subansiri District. The Apatanis lead a well organized life based on communal cooperation. They are good farmers. On the other hand, the Nishis, once called Daflas by the Assamese, are turbulent, tough and are rated as born hunters. They are polygamous and marriage with the daughter of maternal uncle is very popular. The social status of a Nishi depends on the number of wives, mithuns and Tibetan bells. In Apatanis, premarital relations are in vogue. The child born to an unmarried mother is known as Hipa and is not a problem as the man marrying the girl would regard him as his own clan.

Abors or Adis

The Abors or Adis live in the Siang district. They are good weavers and have adopted modern methods of agriculture instead of shifting cultivation. Their village council known as 'Kevangs' runs the day-to-day administration and dispenses justice. Their matrimonial relations are like that of the Nishis. They believe in Buddhist religion.

The Mishmis, Nocte, Wanchos, Tangas, Khamptis and Shingphos

The Mishmis live in the Mishmi hills in Lohit district. They are considered as the most attractive people of Arunachal Pradesh. Young Mishmi girls look like fairies and are fond of ornaments. The Mishmis are highly individualistic and village community has no meaning to them. The Mishmi women are expert in handicrafts and particularly in weaving handloom fabrics. The Mishmis find their reference in '*Bhagavata Purana*' where their king Bishmark's daughter Rukmini married Lord

Krishna. In Tirap district, the Nocte, the Wancho and the Tanga tribes are found. Among the Noctes and the Wanchos, the 'Chief System' prevails and the villagers are required to pay tributes to their chiefs who rule them. The Wanchos have little contact with the outside world. They are good in weaving, cane and bamboo work and wood curving. The Tangas are a hunting race and being close to Indo-Burma border, their habits, customs, traditions, dress, etc. resemble to Burmese neighbours. In eastern part of the Lohit district the Buddhist tribes of the Khamptis and the Singphos are found. Khamptis are the only tribe in the State who have their own script. They are good traders and agriculturists as well. Because of their constant touch with the plains, they are more sophisticated and advanced than the other tribes.

Arunachal Pradesh thus, can be divided into three lateral belts exhibiting distinct cultural patterns, *viz.* the northern belt close to China and having influence of Tibetan culture, the southern belt having contact with Assam plains and having influence of Assamese language, culture and traditions, the central belt is the most backward area and tribes living here have little contact with the outside world. Some of them still live in primitive conditions.

Social and Cultural Life in Nagaland

Nagaland with its capital in Kohima is the home of Angami, Chakhasanga, Zemi and Rengma tribal groups. The Aos, the Lothas and the Sema tribes live in Mokokchung district. The Konyaks, the Changs, the Sangtams, the Phoms and the Yimchungi tribes live in Tuensang district.

Nearly two thirds of Naga tribe profess Christian religion. Inspite of being Christians, some of the Nagas follow superstitions, sacrifices and other features of animistic religion. The organizational set-up of Naga villages differ from tribe to tribe. The Angamis, the Aos, the Lothas, the Rengmas and the Zemis follow democratic set-up in their village councils. In the Semas, the institution of village council is hetreditary and, therefore, the chief is more powerful and authoritative. The Changs follow a local self-government system similar to the Semas. The Konyak chiefs are only *de-juro* heads.

Rice and meat are staple food of Nagas. The common meat items are beef, pork and chicken. They also eat mithun, dog, cat, fish, spider, birds, crabs, snakes — in fact all living things that they can lay their hands on. Agriculture, animal rearing and poultry are the main occupations in the rural areas. Cane and bamboo work, spear making, weaving are the traditional side occupations of the Nagas The Naga tribes being the turbulent race, practiced head hunting in the past. This practice, however, disappeared with the spread of Christianity.

Among the Nagas, Shawl is an important part of their traditional costumes. The pattern of Shawls differ from tribe to tribe. Apart from Shawl, kilt is another important costume. It is of black colour. The common ornament of Nagas is the bead-necklace. Tufts of cotton and red paper are used for decorating ears. Rings of cane around the legs and armlets of ivory are also worn. The ceremonial dresses and ornaments are extremely colourful.

Nagaland has number of festivals and these are related to agricultural operations, such as clearing of *jhum* land, sowing, harvesting, etc. These festivals are celebrated differently by different tribes, but they have some common features, *viz.* It is obligatory on the part of the villagers not to cohabit during the festive season, the whole village is given a new look by cleaning streets, ponds, wells, etc. departed souls are remembered, feasts are thrown by the well-to-do people and rejoicings continue for 3 to 6 days, participation of all households in rejoicings is compulsory, participation of children is a significant feature of the Naga festivals and it is a part of Naga tradition of grooming their children for future responsibilities. Many of the Naga festivals are confined to a particular region.

Imperatives of Tribal Development

The foregoing discussion brings out certain special socio-cultural features which need to be taken into account in development plans. The first and foremost feature is that the region is dominated by the tribal population with large number of relatively small tribes. Many of the tribes cut across not merely State boundaries, but also international boundaries. Thus, there is great deal of heterogeneity of population within the area. The multi-caste problems that existed in other parts of the country do not find place in the tribal areas, as there is a great deal of equality within the tribals

The second important feature that emerges is that the tribal communities of north-eastern region differ significantly from the tribal communities in the rest of the country. They are educationally more advanced and, therefore, the ability of the tribal community to benefit from the job opportunities generated through development process is substantially greater in the north-east as compared to the other tribal areas of the country.

The historical perspective reveals that the tribal societies of the north-east have lived in isolation for a very long period of time and as such traditional attitudes are still prevalent. One such example is the non-competitiveness of the tribal society where each person has a certain way of living and a standard of life which he is not prepared to change at the expense of other members in the group. Production for self-consumption and subsistence is the basis for economic activity and production on the basis of market value is rare. In such a situation, when the system is opened to the market forces, the local tribals, even though they are well educated, may not benefit. Further a substantial portion of non-agricultural enterprises in hill and town areas, particularly in the towns, are controlled by non-tribals. The nominal ownership may rest with a tribal, if nothing else because of the exemption from income tax this would entail. But the bulk of the profit would accrue to the real owner. This situation obtains not merely in industry but also in trade, transport and other services. One reason for this is the inability of tribal entrepreneur to cope with the superior business acumen and enterprise of the non-tribal. The educated tribals who could perhaps enter these areas of self-employment, tend to prefer the more secure avenues of salaried employment open to him. Thus, the process of development in non-agricultural sector does not always benefit the tribals in the north-east.

Coming back to the market economy, it is true that the growth of such economy has progressed very much and many communities who live by barter have been exposed to cash nexus. It has been found that the trading intermediaries in the market economy are generally non-tribals and thus there exists a social gulf between the trader and customer which opens up possibilities of exploitation. Traditional crafts are under pressure as the cost of factory made articles is less. Indebtedness to moneylenders increases as the cash requirements of the households rise with the decline in traditional crafts and shift away from the subsistence cultivation. There are some tribal groups which have had long tradition of contact with the market economy and they are in a better position to cope with the opening up of their economies There are, however, many other groups which had lived a more isolated existence who may lose out if they are exposed to uncontrolled market forces. These variations in the ability of different tribal communities to cope with a new economy have to be taken into account in development strategy.

The land tenure system in the tribal areas of the north-east has special features and is governed to a large extent by the social customs and traditions besides, the prevailing primitive agricultural practices. Apart from village lands and lands under individual ownership in certain cases, there are clan lands used for land tenure system in jhum areas characterized by communal ownership, but operational management is separately done by households. The absence of land ownership rights by the individual causes serious hurdles for investment in land and thereby raising agricultural production. An individual finds difficulty in getting financial support or loan, etc. from the financial institution because the mortgaging of land in favour of security of loans is practically impossible under such a situation. It has also been noticed in many cases that acquisition of land for development projects in the region suffered a great deal on account of individual ownership. Further, programmes of replacement of *jhum* cultivation by settled cultivation has also suffered due to the typical land tenure system in the region.

Another important characteristic of the tribals is the environment or the nature, which has been their real ruler. They have accepted the natural settings as the child accepts its cradle. They love nature, obey her laws and learn from her. The nature's beauty has given them a strong sense of colour and love for rhythm. Their dances, tunes, dresses, etc. are the testimony of nature's tremendous influence on them. Further, self-help, self-reliance, strong social and democratic institutions and community spirit which sustained them through centuries in hostile surroundings, are important positive virtues of these people, and these should find place in development policies.

The matriarchal system of inheritance prevalent in some tribes of the north-east, *viz.* Khasis, Jaintias and Garos has special significance. Generally, the system involves passing all property through female branch and in such cases, it is possible that the men who work, property may not have a significance incentive to undertake improvements and innovations. This hypothesis, however, needs to be tested.

As each tribe in this region has a distinct identity and a way of life, they present a scene of fantastic diversity and a unique colourful cultural mosaic. The tribes have a rich cultural heritage of which they are rightly proud of. However, this cultural heritage is facing the problem of preservation. During the last few decades the tribal society has been exposed to modern conditions and has experienced the impact of external influences. As a result, perceptible changes have come about in their way of life and their traditional cultural patterns. The traditional culture has started decaying and over a period of time, it may get diluted and start loosing originality and vigour. Ultimately, it may face extinction. Thus, while accent on development of tribal areas is essential for improving their standard of living as well as for generation of natural resources, it is equally important to take certain positive measures for retention of the cultural identities of various tribal groups in the north-east region.

Thus, the situation in the north-east region on face of it appears to be paradoxical, i.e. whether economic and industrial growth that brings about radical changes in the social structure due to new production relations would not disturb the rich folk cultural traditions. At the same time there would be compulsion of moving away from folk tradition in order to accelerate economic growth by galvanizing the process of development.

Thus, in the face of this paradox, the challenge is twofold — first, retaining the cultural tradition and second a perspective planning for the future. But no separate plan for cultural growth is possible. Culture emanates from social growth based on material development. Culture will assume an autonomous character with all signs of modernity, assimilating tradition in the process, only when the economy and society are modernized. But nothing can be imposed. The growth must take place from within by a rational exploitation of resources, both material and human. The plan push must rely on unfolding. Culture will then unfold itself for a movement to the next historical phase.

REFERENCES

Bareh, Hemlet, *The History and Culture of the Khasi People.*

Bhattacharya, K.K., *North-East India.*

Brahma, Nivedita, *The Tribals of the Brahmaputra Valley.*

Dutta, M.R., *Early Assam.*

Ghose, G.K., *Tribals and Their Culture.*

Yogi, Anand Kumar, *Development of the North-East Region.*

16

ENGLISH LANGUAGE TEACHING IN ASSAM IN SECONDARY SCHOOL

Manoj Kumar Choudhury

English has become an international language rather than the language of only the English speaking countries such as the UK and the USA because the number of the people who use English as a means of communication exceeds much more than the number of the people who speak it as their mother tongue. Knowledge of English is essential for establishing intellectual, cultural, economic, commercial and political relations with the rest of the world. It has been almost 66 years that we have attained Independence and instead of diminishing the importance of English, it has increased far beyond anybody envisaged at the time of Independence. Hence, we find that English still occupies and will continue to occupy an important place in our educational system and curriculums at different levels. Unfortunately, despite repeated recommendations by different Education Commissions constituted by the Government of India, the position of English in the curriculums and methods of teaching have always been in a state of flux. The standard of achievement in the subject has been falling day-by-day. In most cases the teacher of English has no idea of the goal he/she is to achieve and the old traditional method still reigns supreme. The so-called Functional Communicative Approach associated with "Learning English" series of text books has not helped either. We are yet to evolve a uniform method of teaching English as a second language keeping its socio-economic set-up, available resources and existing infrastructure without importing it from any other country.

Language learning is only producing some grammatically well-formed disjointed sentences; it should enable the learners to use these sentences in real life situation to achieve the 'communicative purpose'. Hence, importance should be laid on the acquisition of language proficiency, rather say competence. But the present system of examination prevalent in the secondary schools of Assam directly or indirectly inspires the learners to be well-trained in producing memorized important answers in the answer-sheets and secure good marks. English learning has become similar to learning other subjects in the curriculum. Though the prescribed course in English should concentrate on improving the language proficiency and literary competence of the learners, it rather trains learners only in mastering the literary content of the syllabus. No efforts have been taken to improve their Listening, Speaking, Reading and Writing (LSRW) skills, Study skills and Dictionary skills and to strengthen their critical sensibilities.

Teacher enters the classroom, 'transmits' the content knowledge by means of giving word meaning and paraphrasing the lessons, provides answers to the crammed questions and washes hands off with great satisfaction that he/she has completed the prescribed course in the stipulated time to the contentment of the learners, administrators and parents. Now, it is the only avowed duty of the learners to take down those answers often incorrectly and subsequently memorize them like 'parrot' so that they can 'chew the cud' during examinations and come out with flying colours (!). They always depend on their teachers and expect 'spoon feeding' in the form of notes and ready-made answers. The worst facet of this condition is well reflected when they request their teachers to provide important and probable questions for the examinations. They are not even ready to learn all the answers to questions provided in the exercise at the end of each prescribed lesson. Interestingly, enough if any teacher studies some question papers of previous examinations, he/she can easily 'guess' the probable questions. Hence, the prevalent examination system compels the teacher to be a 'crammer' rather than a 'facilitator of learning' or 'manager', and so on in the classroom as visualized by many modern methods of English language teaching. Surprisingly, their 'performance' in the language is also evaluated in terms of marks they score in the tests/examinations. Only motivating factor that works is securing good marks, thereby facilitating admission in reputed colleges. Aims and objectives of teaching-learning English language, various approaches and methods, techniques, etc. have proved only to be a resource for library enrichment; rather confined within the four walls of the reading room. This examination-oriented approach vehemently hinders the process of 'real' English language teaching-learning in the secondary schools of Assam. It does allow our teachers to translate the goals of English teaching-learning into a reality. One more acid truth that adds fuel to the fire is that many teachers lack adequate training in language teaching, while some others are even unaware of any modern teaching methods. And the one who is well-equipped with all the requisites of teaching English language is either reluctant or cannot implement the programme in the practical field for various other detrimental factors — Socio-economic background, huge number of students in one classroom, lack of adequate infrastructure, lack of exposure to the target language, and so on.

We have, in general, urban, semi-urban and rural students. And even among them, we have learners, who have all along studied through English medium and learners who have studied through the regional medium with English as one of the subjects. In addition, we have the learners from varied socio-economic, linguistic and complex cultural backgrounds. This situation stands to testify that we have an awesome number of learners, an amazing variety among them and varying kinds of competence in English language among the learners. Environment and family background play vital role in success of learning process. In Assam, where majority of the people are farmers, have a poor background in education. Moreover, the income of majority of the families is not adequate. Hence, the parents are not interested in giving good education background to their children. In contrast, they are willing to engage the children in some jobs in order to earn money. This is one of the basic reasons and the affecting factor in teaching in rural areas. Apart from that, our parents/guardians still adhere to the age-old notion of securing good marks in examinations. They do not initiate any step and inspire rather dislike introduction of any innovative tactics in the classroom. They are reluctant to come out breaking the shackles of the 'so-long harboured straightjacket' of prevailing education process. This may be because of lack of education on their part or an orthodox view about the teaching-learning process. Recently, in a field study among teachers of English, they were asked what the learners, parents and school administration expect from them. To this question, 85.71 per cent teacher respondents replied that the learners, parents and school administration want them to prepare the learners for examinations. Only 14.29 per cent replied that they want the teachers to help the learners develop the ability to use English in speaking and writing. They further add that any deviation from the prescribed textbook bring a negative impression on the teachers. This is because of the fact that English teaching is directly related with the overall result of the learners. This analysis clearly shows that the prevailing system of English learning is guided by the evaluation system.

Hence, it is a well-accepted fact that students will be more interested in learning those items, which may tested in the examinations. The students will not naturally show any interest on items which do not form a part of examinations. Keeping in view the need based notion of English language teaching-learning, adoption of a proper evaluation system is the need of the hour.

The role of the teacher has been envisioned as a facilitator in a learner-centred classroom in the prescribed textbooks of secondary schools. But it is found that 82.14 per cent teachers act as a transmitter of knowledge, where the learners act as passive recipients. Most of the teachers think that for successful teaching-learning, the teacher must be able to dominate the classroom environment. Only 17.86 per cent project the ideal role of a language teacher as a role model for the students. Again, regarding the prevalent classroom scenario, 91.37 per cent students say that their teachers teach, explain, and give notes and students take down the same (based on a field survey conducted in twenty high schools). Only 8.64 per cent students replied that teachers ask them to read aloud, indulge in pair-group work, find out answers through discussion. This analysis clearly shows that the role of teachers is still traditional one as in the 'banking system of education', where learners are considered to be similar to bank accounts (Freire, 1982). Of course, it is a well acknowledged fact that it is very difficult for a teacher to play the innovative role of a facilitator, since the prevailing education system is strictly syllabus-oriented and examination-driven.

Regarding the proficiency of teachers of English, 46.82 per cent students say that their teachers can speak as well as can teach English well, 33.64 per cent say they can teach well, but cannot speak fluently. But 67.92 per cent students studying in vernacular schools say that their teachers can teach English well, but cannot speak fluently, whereas only 19.82 per cent say their teacher can speak as well as teach English well. The horrifying scenario is well reflected when 5.66 per cent say that their teachers can neither speak fluently nor teach English effectively (110 students from 10 vernacular schools were interviewed). This analysis categorically indicates that most of the teachers, especially in vernacular schools, lack the skill of speaking.

Application of appropriate teaching methods results in effective teaching-learning process. In order to attain 'communicative competence' of the students, it is quintessential to use modern methods like Communicative Language Teaching, Task-based Language Learning, etc. But the prevalent scenario inside the English classroom is quite contrary. 100 per cent students from vernacular medium schools say that their teachers translate the content into mother tongue. At the same time, 100 per cent students from English medium schools say that their teachers illustrate the meaning of the content in English. Irrespective of vernacular or English medium schools, 100 per cent students say that their teachers give word-meaning and question answer, and assign homework. But only 30 per cent students of vernacular medium schools say that their teachers ask learners to read aloud, whereas the percentage is very high in English medium schools — 84.21 per cent. Again, only 3.77 per cent students of vernacular medium schools say that their teachers relate the content into real life, whereas 63.16 per cent students of the second category agree to that point.

On adopted methods for teaching English, 60.71 per cent teachers opine that instead of following a particular method of teaching English, they prefer to teach their students using their own method as per their convenience. Only 7.14 per cent teachers say that they are well aware of various methods of teaching English and use the same as per need in their teaching, while 17.86 per cent find it difficult in using those methods; therefore, they teach in the traditional way.

From the responses discussed above, it has become clear that most teachers of English in the schools adopt translation or traditional method while teaching English. The teachers in vernacular medium schools explain the content of the text by giving meaning of the difficult words, translating it into the vernacular language, and finally by giving notes, which are prepared by them. In English medium schools, the scenario is slightly different, where instead of translating the content of the textbook; they explain the same in English language. Quite naturally, the learners in an English classroom are passive listeners who hardly contribute anything to the classroom teaching. Students are not provided with any opportunity to expose themselves to the target language. This is thoroughly against the objectives of modern methods like Communicative Language Teaching. Thus, it is evident that the basic objective of teaching English as a second language, i.e., developing learners' proficiency in the language is largely ignored. As a result, the majority of the learners are poor users of English. In fact, most of the teachers do not have idea about any method; hence, teaching takes place in a very unmethodical way. But this scenario is slightly better in English medium schools where students are provided with the opportunity of developing their speaking, reading skills and above all, teachers try to bring the real world to the English classroom. After all, language learning is not only producing some grammatically well-formed disjointed sentences; it should enable the learners to use these sentences in real life situation to achieve the 'communicative purpose'.

The pronunciation, stress and intonation pattern of English language is different from that of Bengali, Hindi or Manipuri language. In the syllabi of Class IX and X, ten marks have been separately allotted for oral English. It aims at developing the learners' speech skills so that they can acquire the strategies for interpersonal communication in English. It demands learner-centred activities having frequent and lively interaction among teachers and students, and among students in pair work and group work. During the survey, 67.86 per cent teachers feel that they should teach the learners how to speak English with proper pronunciation, stress and intonation; whereas 17.86 per cent say that it is not possible to teach such pattern in the traditional classroom without requisite aids/ infrastructure. But only 38.64 per cent student respondents say that their teacher teach them to speak English using proper pronunciation, stress and intonation; whereas 37.27 per cent disclose that they are never taught such aspects of the language in their classroom. One important factor to note here is that 68.42 per cent students from English medium schools say that these are frequently taught in their classroom; whereas only 6.6 per cent students from vernacular schools agree to this point. Again, 77.36 per cent students from vernacular medium schools opine that these are never practiced in their classroom, and surprisingly enough, no students from English medium schools ticked this item. This proves the fact that even the practice of teaching oral English, i.e., listening and speaking is far better in the English medium schools than that of the vernacular medium schools. The students of English medium schools get ample scope for developing their oral skills, where the students of vernacular medium schools lag behind remarkably. During interview with the students studying in vernacular medium schools, it was learnt that they are not taught 'oral English'; rather marks for such units are simply added with the total mark. Hence, it becomes clear that the goals envisaged by the curriculum designers are never practised by the teachers inside the classroom.

Effective teaching-learning demands proper utilization of time and systematic presentation of the teaching materials. To cover the syllabus within the stipulated time, teacher has to make a proper lesson plan before the classroom teaching starts. But 85.71 per cent teachers fail to realize its importance and rather opine on the contrary saying that following a lesson plan they cannot complete the content in a given time or they feel that lesson plan makes teaching mechanical. Only 14.29 per cent prepare a lesson plan before starting a new lesson and regard it as part and parcel for an effective teaching-learning situation.

In order to improve the prevalent dismal scenario of English teaching-learning in the high schools of Assam, the following steps may prove fruitful:

- English language teaching should be incorporated from Nursery, even in vernacular medium schools.
- The time allotted to teaching English and the number of English class need to be increased.
- Almost all the students from vernacular schools opine that they face difficulties in English speaking; they need a congenial, friendly and 'fear proficiency free' atmosphere to learn this skill.
- Many teachers, particularly in vernacular medium, don't turn up in time and skip classes. In the name of teaching a language like English, many teachers are content only with giving notes to the important questions so far as the examination is concerned. Such practices should be eschewed under any circumstances.
- Students need extra classes, remedial classes to practise and learn English and acquire mastery over the four skills — listening, speaking, reading, and writing.
- Oral practice and listening skill, though included in the syllabus are not given due importance by the teachers. In order to communicate in day-to-day life, it is necessary to have more classes on oral practice.
- All the interviewed teachers (100%) opine that they should be provided with in-service training, seminar, workshop, etc. where they can equip themselves with suitable methods as well as techniques of teaching English language. Thus, the concerned authority should help them improve teachers' skills and equip them with various innovations and developments in relation to methods, techniques, etc
- More space should be provided in the syllabus to cultivate the speaking skill.
- The examination system demands a drastic change.
- Parents should encourage their children to read English newspapers, magazines, watch English news, etc. so that they can get exposure to English language even outside the four walls of the classroom.
- Teaching English as a second language may be more effective if it started by teaching the spoken form which comprises listening and

speaking skills. Common observation indicates that learners in English medium schools, who start with the spoken form of English, eventually end up almost mastering all the four language skills. On the contrary, learners in vernacular medium schools, who start with reading and writing, end up with a mastery (sometimes partial) of only these two skills.

- As far as teaching methods are concerned, it is evident from the study that teachers still use traditional methods like Grammar Translation Method or Direct Method, etc. which do not allow the teachers to act as 'a facilitator to stimulate learners' response', as envisaged in the prescribed textbook. The main focus, as cited in 'A Note to the Teacher' in the textbook, will be on presentation by the teacher, performance by the learners and consolidation through pair work and group work. But the scenario observed inside the classroom presents a fully opposite picture. It is felt that lack of trained teachers with ELT background and more importantly, the prevailing evaluation system are accountable for this appalling condition. Teachers should be trained and encouraged to apply methods like structural-situational, communicative language teaching, etc., so that, the said problem can be solved to a great extent. Oral practice/oral drill suggested by the structural approach is highly recommended for effective teaching-learning of English in the high schools, especially in the vernacular medium schools. The learner should be able to apply the language learned inside the classroom in real life situations, as recommended by the situational approach, which is the need of the hour.
- In a fast changing world — a world of internet and technology, robots and exciting media presentations — the classroom teaching of English is still traditional, dull with 'chalk and talk', uninteresting and irrelevant; the learning culture has changed tremendously but the teaching culture is still 'stagnant without any innovation'. English teaching needs to be entertaining and interactional in addition to being instructive as well as informative. Here, lies the inculcation of various teaching techniques such as role play, pair work and group work, information exchange, interaction through discussion, conversation and so on. Learners should be engaged in debate, extempore speech, etc. thereby making them ready to communicate in real life situations which is authentic and unpredictable.

- It is directed to the concerned teachers in the prescribed textbooks of English by SEBA that "audio cassettes providing speech practice will be used as and when practicable" in order to train the learners adequately in the spoken form of the language. But the irony of the fact that has come to light during the visit to the schools is that classrooms are adorned with only desk-bench and chalk-blackboard; and are bereft of any teaching aids. Hence, it is the ardent call of the time to realize the printed objectives of the textbooks inside the classroom so that teaching takes place in its true form. It is the avowed duty of the concerned authority to equip the English teaching classroom with the minimum requisite paraphernalia; let's not talk on modern innovative interactive devices like Computer-Assisted Learning or Computer-Assisted Language Learning.
- Alongwith these, learners should be encouraged, if possible facilitated, to listen to watch English news, movies, and other programmes telecast in English. Reading English newspapers, magazines and so on can be an added advantage for the learners in mastering the skills of English language. Low cost audio materials like radio, tape-recorder, audio discs; audio-visual materials such as television, printed materials with recorded sound, etc.; and visual materials like pictures, flash cards, charts, posters, models, etc. should be supplied in order to make English teaching-learning a pleasant and fruitful experience. With the help of such materials learners can easily comprehend what they listen, speak, read and write; resultantly they help the learners to be proficient in using the language in day-to-day social context. It is worthwhile to mention here that teachers should be trained to use such aids in the classroom to acquire maximum benefit from such use. At the same time, the concerned authority should encourage the teacher folk to use their own innovations in order to make English learning an enjoyable experience.
- During interviews with students as well as teachers, the researcher could realize the absence of any remedial measures being carried out for the learners during the normal teaching periods. The teaching inside the classroom mostly confine to reading, explaining and paraphrasing the prescribed content, dictating notes and giving occasional homework to the students. Such 'teacher-textbook-traditional classroom affair' activities are not sufficient enough in improving the learners' competence and proficiency in the target language.

- Teaching of English should not aim at teaching only about the language; rather it should involve presentation and practice of such linguistic items which are closely related with real life situation. At the same time, teachers should be well-aware of their role and internalize the fact that learning is a bidirectional process. "Silence" inside the classroom should not be regarded as a positive sign; rather it should be treated as an indicator of failure of teaching-learning process. Teachers, as a counsellor or a manager in the process of teaching-learning, should create a congenial atmosphere wherein students feel at ease to open up their mouth. At the same time, teacher — as a role model — should possess enough proficiency in the language, and use proper pronunciation, stress and intonation so that learners can inherit those qualities from him/her easily.
- It is observed that in vernacular schools, the mother tongue of the learners occupies the classroom teaching. As a result, such students lag behind in the sphere of spoken skills of English language, hindering the very process of teaching-learning English. Hence, the use of the mother tongue should be judicious and purposive and teachers should encourage their students to use English. They may struggle and commit mistake; but communicative competence develops in the process of struggling to communicate. The students should be encouraged to communicate in English with friends, if possible with parents and other members of their family and society. Over emphasis on only written skills in such schools should be discouraged under any circumstances. Here, lies the need of reformation of the prevailing evaluation system. The examination system should encompass different units that evaluate equally all the skills of English language.
- Vocabulary items should not be taught in isolation. Mere translating them into the mother tongue or explaining them in easy comprehensible way is not sufficient. Students should be encouraged to use them in real contexts.
- The class-size should be smaller and the number of English periods should be increased.

Of course, teachers are hard pressed for time to cover the syllabus and cannot spare much time to handle the language items. And students will also make complaints that the teacher has not taught the lessons. In such conservative situations, the teacher can spare at least ten minutes in each class to train the students in language items. The students can learn and acquire the language under the 'able' guidance of the teacher. The remaining time can be utilized for teaching the students in the conventional or expected manner. It is vital, therefore, that every teacher should aim at directing every classroom to equip the students with the basic language skills they really need. What is important is to motivate the students, by creating awareness amongst them regarding the importance of English and then gradually helping the student to attain his goal. The basic objective should thus be, to make the student independent. It has rightly been said, "If you give an individual a fish you feed him for a day, but, if you teach him to fish you feed him for life" (Sindkhedkar, 2012). It is up to the teacher to make the student realize that gaining competence in English he/she shall hold the master-key to success in the contemporary world. Now let us not sit 'idle' expecting our governments, policy-makers, and curriculum planners to annihilate the 'loopholes' in the English language classroom; rather set out emblazoned with a zeal for innovative teaching in order that we can help our learners pave a 'golden path' in near future to be 'efficient communicators'. Let us stop them from becoming 'bookworms' or 'linguistic robots'.

REFERENCES

Nagaraj, G., *English Language Teaching — Approaches, Methods, Techniques*, Hyderabad: Orient Longman Private Limited, 2008.

Saraswathi, V., *English Language Teaching: Principles and Practice*, Orient Longman Private Limited, Chennai, 2005.

Sindkhedkar, S.D., "Objectives of Teaching and Learning English in India", in *Researchers World — Journal of Arts, Science & Commerce*, 2012, Vol. III, Issue 1, Jan. 2012 [191]. Retrieved 4th November, 2013 from www..researchersworlld..com.

Tickoo, M.L., *Teaching and Learning English*. New Delhi: Orient Longman Private Limited, 2003.

17

HIGHER AND TECHNICAL EDUCATION IN NORTH-EAST INDIA

Daisy Nath Choudhury

"If India was the Jewel in the Crown of the British Empire, the remote North-East of that country is its Hidden Jewel". — *Tony Howard*

Introduction

North-East of India is the land of Blue Mountains, Green Valleys and Red River. Nestled in the Eastern Himalayas this region is abundant in Natural Beauty, Wildlife, Flora & Fauna and its Colourful people. A blend of all these makes it the most beautiful Eco-Tourism area in the Country besides being identified as a Bio Diversity hot spot.

The region comprises of eight States of Assam, Arunachal Pradesh, Meghalaya, Nagaland, Manipur, Mizoram, Tripura and the latest inclusion Sikkim.

Fact file of these states are presented in Table 17.1.

Table 17.1: Fact File of North-East States of India

Name of the State	*Capital*	*Area (sq.km.)*	*Date of Attaining Statehood*	*Population*	*Literacy Rate*	*Approx. No. of Institutions for Higher Education*
Arunachal Pradesh	Itanagar	83,743	20/02/1987	10,91,117	66.95	17
Assam	Dispur	78,438	15/08/1947	2,66,38,407	76.30	396
Manipur	Imphal	22,327	21/01/1972	23,88,634	79.85	72
Meghalaya	Shillong	22,429	21/01/1972	23,06,069	72.10	72
Mizoram	Aizawl	21,081	20/02/1987	8,91,058	89.90	31
Nagaland	Kohima	16,579	01/12/1963	19,88,636	63.70	47
Sikkim	Gangtok	7,299	26/04/1975	4,06,457	76.60	9
Tripura	Agartala	10,492	21/01/1972	31,91,168	87.75	24

In the above presented data sheet, Higher Education Institutions refers to all such institutions which offers UG programme (e.g. B.A., B.Com., B.Sc., B.E., B.Tech., MBBS, BAMS, BHMS, BBA, BAJM, etc.) onwards to PG (M.A., M.Com., M.Sc., M.E., M.Tech., MD, MS, MBA, MCA, etc.) and Doctoral studies (PhD).

The momentum of development of higher and technical institutions in the North-Eastern States of India has rather been sluggish. The manpower generated has fallen short of the requirement. One of the main reasons appears to be the slow development of the industrial environment and the isolated existence of industry and academia. Mainly due to this reason, existing institutions have not been able to emerging areas or thrust areas specified by AICTE from time-to-time. Moreover, the different Ministries/Departments controlling the different sectors of technical education from certificate to post-graduate level and almost zero coordination of the departments in State level has prevented the North-East from having a rational development in technical education. For the same reason, the existing institutions could not fulfil the requirement of necessary inputs for many local problems and development.

The Preamble of Act of 1857 by which the first three Universities of Calcutta, Bombay and Madras were established stated "*for the better encouragement of her majesty's subjects of all class and denominations within the Presidency of Fort William in Bengal and other parts of India in the pursuit of a regular and liberal course of education it has been determined to establish a University at Calcutta for the purpose of ascertaining by examination the persons acquired proficiency in different branches of Literature, Science and Art and of rewarding by awarding degrees as evidence of their respective attainments and marks of honours proportioned there unto*" highlights the first step in modern higher educational system in India and its purpose.

Consequently, the Indian Universities Education Commission 1902 recommended, "*We think it desirable that there should be uniformity in the nomenclature of the examinations and degrees in Arts and Sciences at the different Universities*" thus, leading to the naming of three apparent examinations namely the Matriculation Examination, the Intermediate Examination and the Degree of B.A. or B.Sc.

Thereafter, the Indian Universities Act, 1904 gave the Universities the right of teaching along with the right of conducting examinations which earmarked the grant of autonomy to the institution of University.

The University Education Commission 1948-49 observed "*the standard of admission to University courses should correspond to that of the intermediate examination, etc. after the completion of 12 years of study at a school and an intermediate college*".

The Three-year Degree Estimates Committee of UGC, 1956 recommended that the three-year degree courses should be introduced in as many Universities as possible.

Further, on the recommendations of the Education Commission 1964-66, the National Policy on Education called upon to have uniform pattern of Education 10 + 2 + 3 (3 year Degree Course), which is still prevalent in India, with the first 10 years of schooling at the Secondary Level, 2 years at the Senior Secondary/Higher Secondary/Intermediate Level and 3 years at the first Degree level of non-professional Education. The duration of Degree for professional courses varied from 4 years for Engineering Subjects, 4½ years for Medical courses and 5 years for Architecture courses after the Senior Secondary/Higher Secondary/ Intermediate level.

The growth and shape of technical education in India can mainly be attributed to Sargent Report of 1944 followed by N.R. Sarkar Commission Report, 1946 and Radhakrishnan Commission's Report of 1948-49, Thacker Committee Report, 1959, Kothari Commission's Report of 1964, etc. Due to inadequate infrastructure in the NE States, the recommendation of the commission could not be implemented properly, resulting in slippage from original principles regarding locations, curricula and programme.

Current Scenario

Due to limited number of colleges and consequently less number of seats available for the students, they try their luck in colleges outside the states. In the North-East, only Assam and Arunachal Pradesh till the turn up of twentyfirst century had a few Technical Institutions of repute, of which 4 were in Assam and one in Arunachal Pradesh. As a result the students moved outside the region in search of careers in technology, engineering and management. Instances were there where at times such students ended up in sub-standard educational institutions in various parts of India, thereby resulting in huge loss of prospective Human Capital of the region as well as both time and money of those deprived. This situation is likely to continue developing till facilitation of establishing good colleges of Technology and Management of high academic standards are made.

A total of 13 numbers of Universities are available catering to the technical and higher educational requirements of the region in all the eight states. There are in all 18 colleges for Engineering Education apart from one IIT at Guwahati and one IIM at Shillong. Medical Colleges in the region are eight apart from few Homoeopathic Colleges and one Ayurvedic College. A recent surge in establishing institutions for higher education is witnessed in this region with more private participation in the field of Technical and Management Education. In the recent years (post 2006) a total of seven Engineering Colleges and three Management Institutions came up with private investments.

Table 17.2 provides a State-wise break-up of Technical and Higher Education of the region.

Table 17.2: State-wise Break-up of Technical and Higher Education in North-East

Name of the State	*Name of Universities*	*Year of Establishment*	*No. of Colleges Affiliated/ No. of Constituent Colleges*	*No. of Technical Institutions*	*No. of Medical Colleges*	*No. of other Institutions, viz. Teacher Education, Management Education, Hotel Mgt, etc.*
Arunachal Pradesh	Rajiv Gandhi University	1984	17	1	—	4
Assam	Gauhati University*	1948	183	7*	2*	49
	Dibrugarh University	1965	153	2*	2*	23
	Tezpur University	1994	NA	1	—	—
	Assam University	1994	51	1	1*	—
	Assam Agricultural University	1969	5	—	—	—
Manipur	Manipur University	1980	72	1	1	NA
	Central Agricultural University	1992-93	NA	—	—	—
Meghalaya	North-Eastern Hill University	1974	72	3	1	NA
Mizoram	Mizoram (Pacchunga) University	2001	31	1	—	NA
Nagaland	Nagaland University	1994	47	1	—	NA
Sikkim	Sikkim Manipal University of Health, Medical and Technological Science	1995	NA	1	1	1
Tripura	Tripura University	1987	24	1	1	3

* Engineering and Medical Colleges in Assam has come under the purview of Assam Science and Technical University and Srimanta Sankardev University of Health Sciences.

(i) *Rajiv Gandhi University (RGU):* This is a Central University under the Ministry of Human Resource Development, Government of India. The University has been converted into a Central University by an Act of Parliament with effect from 9th April, 2007. It was formerly known as Arunachal Pradesh University. It is located at Rono Hills in Papumpare District, 12 kilometers away from Itanagar, the capital city of Arunachal Pradesh.

(ii) *Dibrugarh University (DU):* It is the eastern most university of India, which was set-up in 1965 under the provisions of University Act, 1965 enacted by the Assam Legislative Assembly. The University is located at Rajabheta at a distance of 5 kms. from the town of Dibrugarh, in the eastern part of Assam.

(iii) *Gauhati University (GU):* It is the first university in North-East India. It was established in 1948 under the GU Act, 1947. The University is located at Jalukbari within the Guwahati City area.

(iv) *Assam University (AU):* Assam University came into existence through Assam (Central) University Act, 1989. It was established in 1994. The University is located at Dorgakona, 20 kms. away from Silchar, a major town in south Assam.

(v) *Tezpur University (TU):* Tezpur University was established in 1994. The campus is located at Napaam about 15 kms. away from Tezpur the headquarters of Sonitpur district of Assam.

(vi) *Manipur University (MU):* Manipur University was established in 1947. It was earlier a State University but of late it has been converted into a Central University.

(vii) *North-East Hill University (NEHU):* This university was established by an Act of Parliament and was notified in 19th July, 1973. It is located in Meghalaya, 12 kms. away from the Capital city of Shillong.

(viii) *Mizoram University (MZU):* The university was established on 2nd July, 2001 by the MZU Act which appeared in the Gazette of India on 25th April, 2000 as a Central University.

(ix) *Tripura University (TRU):* Tripura University was established in 1987, but was converted into a Central University in 2nd July, 2007 by Tripura University Act, 2006. The university was located at Suryamani Nagar, near the Capital City of Agartala.

(x) *Sikkim Manipal University of Health, Medical and Technological Science (SMUHMTS)* happens to be one of its kind in the region, established in 1995, at Tadong, Gangtok in the State of Sikkim. It is the first government-private initiative in the region. SMU is recognized by the University Grants Commission and approved by the Government of India. Sikkim Manipal University offers quality education to the students from North and North-Eastern parts of India.

(xi) *Nagaland University (NU)* is a Central University established by the Government in India in the State of Nagaland. It was established in 1994 with campuses at Kohima, Lumami and Medziphema. There are 47 colleges affiliated to it, with a total student enrollment of about 18, 000.

(xii) *Assam Agriculture University (AAU)* was established in 1969 under the Assam Agricultural University Act, 1968 January 2, 1969. The jurisdiction of the University extends to the entire State of Assam with regard to teaching, research and extension education in the field of agriculture and allied sciences. Presently, it has 5 constituent colleges under it.

(xiii) *Central Agriculture University, Manipur (CAU):* Central Agricultural University was established in Manipur in 1992 with a specific objective to groom agricultural researchers and students in the region. Since, its inception, Central Agricultural University has been functioning as a proactive research in the field of agricultural sciences for the six States namely, Manipur, Mizoram, Meghalaya, Tripura, Nagaland and Arunachal Pradesh, situated in the north-east of India.

Apart from the details mentioned above, the following Open Universities have also started functioning, thereby catering to the educational needs of the students in the open and distance mode.

(a) The Krishna Kanta Handique State Open University, first of its kind in the entire North-East and fourteenth amongst the Open Universities in India was established by the Assam Legislative Assembly by an *Act (XXXVII of 2005)* in 1995. The Act received the assent from the Governor on 7th September, 2005. The University formally started functioning from December 11, 2006.

(b) The Global Open University, Nagaland has been established under the provisions of The Global Open University Act, 2006 (Act 3 of 2006) of the Government of Nagaland with a view to introducing vocational, job oriented and employment centric education in the North-East in general and in the State of Nagaland in particular. The State Government of Nagaland has taken bold steps in strengthening the activities of The Global

Open University, Nagaland for enabling the World Institution Building Programme (WIBP) to develop adequate infrastructure in Nagaland in general and at Wokha, Kohima and Dimapur in particular.

Also several Private Universities are on the offing and about to commence their Academic Activities very soon in the region, namely —

1. University of Science and Technology, Meghalaya
2. Don Bosco University, Guwahati
3. Assam Down Town University, Guwahati
4. Martin Luther University, Shillong
5. University of Technology and Management, Shillong
6. ICFAI University, Tripura

Following are few Institutions of National Importance set-up in the region, namely —

1. Indian Institute of Technology, Guwahati
2. Indian Institute of Management, Shillong
3. National Institute of Technology, Silchar
4. Central Institute of Plastic Engineering and Technology
5. National Institute of Pharmacy Education and Research
6. Indian Institute of Entrepreneurship
7. North-East Institute of Science and Technology, formerly RRL, Jorhat, etc.

Challenges Ahead

Three basic requirements for any modern educational institution to flourish in today's context are:

1. Finance/Funding
2. Infrastructure
3. Human Resource Capital or Trained Faculties.

In the North-Eastern States of India, along with the rest of the Country, there is acute shortage of trained, qualified and dedicated faculty. Earlier, when teachers' jobs were almost only jobs available (in Colleges and Universities), only the best qualified for the same. But, with rapid strides in Industrialization and Liberalization of the State's economy in the country as a whole, many more high paying jobs were created, which, drew the best talent and teaching as a profession took the back seat with only the left overs opting for the same.

As George Bernard Shaw has said "*Those who can, do; those who can't, teach*" highlights the magnitude of the problem in hand.

To attract good teachers, salaries will have to be good, comparable to those in the industry. An environment will have to be created, where a teacher's job is considered socially acceptable in more senses than one and also be respectable. This is where finance comes in. In the NE, there is serious lack of capital for industrialization, which causes lack of jobs in the region which again in-turn leads to less or no investment in other areas including education.

Infrastructure includes both the academic as well as those facilities which are of utmost importance to draw the best to the field, such as the general — travel/transport, residence facilities, etc.

Higher Education in India, in general, suffers from several systemic deficiencies and the same is much more felt in the North-Eastern part of India, the area being industrially/economically backward as compared to the rest of India, which in-turn adds to the lack of employment opportunities. Whatever, higher educational set-up exists, they mainly catered to the award of degree, which in-turn resulted in producing Graduates who were not employable. Public expenditure in this regard was also not encouraging until the late part of twentieth century and start of twentyfirst century, which saw establishment of few Central Universities, Technical Institutions, etc. in the region.

Statistics reveals that India on an average produces 1000 PhD's as compared to an annual average of 5,000 in China, 20,000 Master Degree's and over 2,30,000 graduates in the technical education. And ironically only 20 per cent of such graduates are deemed fit for employment. Such a situation is quite alarming, more so, with respect to the already disturbed areas of the North-East. Industry reports suggest shortage of technical/ skilled manpower. This in-turn exemplifies the fact that at present majority of the higher educational set-up in the country is nothing better than factories producing non-performing human capital. Either this has resulted due to the shortage of qualified teachers or due to the lack of flexibility in our University Education system which are burdened with more of administrative hassles in managing their endless list of affiliated colleges rather than primarily focusing in research and development oriented teaching learning process.

Another statistics reveals that roughly 8 per cent of our eligible have an opportunity to enter the higher education and the number ought to be closer to 16-20 per cent. Which in-turn signifies the requirement for more colleges, more Technical Institutions, more Universities, more research Programmes, more teachers and more facilities? On one hand expansion of such magnitude requires massive public expenditure and on the other hand this becomes an opportunity for the private investments. This has resulted in the education system being suspended between over-regulation by the state on the one hand, and a discretionary privatization that is unable to mobilize private capital in productive ways. The result is a sub-optimal structuring of higher education. The most potent consequence of this is a secession of the middle class — ironically the very class whose interests these institutions were supposed to serve — from a stake in public institutions.

North-East India too saw the upsurge in private participation in the field of higher and technical education, with as much as 9 private managed Engineering Institutions being already set-up in the past 2-3 years. Also the MHRD, Government of India in its recent declaration have come up with plans to add 6 more NIT's in the region apart from one Central University in each State and several polytechnic. What remains to be seen is how such quantum leap in establishing Institutions of Higher Learning is supplemented by the required number of qualified trained teachers, adequate infrastructure build up, facilities created, etc. More so when the Higher Educational system in India is already facing acute shortage of technically qualified manpower in terms of Professors, Readers, and Lecturers, etc.

Hence, *the need of the hour* is to strike a judicious balance between the regulatory framework and the requirements for an atmosphere which shall draw in adequate Private Investments which may call for a paradigm shift from being regulatory in nature towards being that of a facilitator without compromising the quality of education delivery mechanism. And, to ensure the quality and standard of education a strong and a rapid accreditation system should be brought in place. This maybe done by expanding the authority of NAAC creating several regional/zonal Directorates, such that, the span of control is brought within reach. Such step shall be beneficial to pool in private investments in a more fruitful way, more so when the vital resources to build up a strong higher educational system is very scarce at the moment.

Scalability within the present system for example:

1. If the engineering admissions are made during both semester, then optimum utilization of scarce resource can be made possible utilizing the same infrastructure at place and attracting double the admissions within the single academic year.

2. As per AICTE guidelines the desired student faculty ratio is 15:1 which may be made more considerate, say 20:1 thereby giving the Institutions a breathing space in their search for faculties.
3. Post-Graduate students maybe encouraged to undertake teaching assignments for the undergraduate programmes and likewise PhD scholars may take up assignments for the PG classes. The scenario today projects high density of colleges/institutions in certain cities, where a mix of UG Institutions as well as institutions offering both UG and PG courses exists in close vicinity, thus, providing chance for optimal resource sharing in terms of faculties.

Research must be accorded with top priority in Institutions of Excellence such as IIT's, IIM's, IISc, NIT's and Central Universities, with a modest target of producing one PhD per faculty member. This shall go a long way in bridging the gap between the demand and supply for trained and skilled teaching manpower.

One recent welcome change is witnessed with directives to all Universities to start School of Engineering/Technology over and above the existing departments. More such initiatives maybe extended to the colleges/institutions identified as centers with potential for excellence.

Technology enabled learning holds the key to a speedy reform and agencies like NPTEL, DOEACC, REILET, etc. are already focusing towards ICT and e-learning under the aegis' of MHRD and other stakeholders in the field of higher and technical education.

According to Sam Pitroda, going forward technology would be incorporation aggressively into everything from course work, remote access, systems learning, improving contentions, resource management for Universities to be more productive. Government of India has already spend several billion dollars on building the National Knowledge Network, which will connect 5,000 locations with technology facilities to all the Universities, major libraries, and all major R&D centers.

- Though around 50 per cent of the rural population is "literate", more than 90 per cent of the total "poor" are from the villages, and out of the 25,590 villages of Assam, only 2 per cent of the inhabited villages possess any training school — leading to high drop-outs and subsequently, alarmingly high rate of unemployment.
- Of around 2.2 crore population in 23 districts of Assam, covering an area of around 70,523 sq.kms., 37 per cent belongs to the

age group of 01-15s year (*Source:* Planning Commission Report, 2004-05) and would surely get affected by the shortage of technical/vocational training institutes in the region. Thus, the total number of persons expected to be directly touched by this laxity is 0.814 crore during a span of 10 years down the line, when the child of 01 year becomes 10 years old and the adolescent of 15 years becomes a youth of 25 years old. But as a result of mediocre human resource and poor throughput of the Training Institutions, it would be difficult to attract the student towards it as a career.

- In order to establish a linkage between academic, social, and economic activities, it is inevitable that innovative, inter-disciplinary courses are designed and taught — maintaining a balance between (a) theory and hands-on skill, (b) value-based education and business management, and (c) social obligations and profit making. If the high-end research work in the field of Biotechnology could be linked with formation of Agri-clinics, Agri-business-hubs, and other field level activities, the gap between education and unemployment, or school enrollment and drop outs, may be minimized. If the pedagogic research in the laboratories is not matched with action research, it is highly unlikely that companies would come forward to take students as their employees and industries would hesitate to collaborate with the laboratories. Once the gap is reduced, it would ensure a holistic growth of the society through a self-sustaining cycle of : Education — Entrepreneurship Development — Socio-Economic Growth.
- As far as funding is concerned, while State Funding is all the same with other States — apart from few additional schemes through the NEC, and just recently announced special concessions for establishing medical colleges, private finance is low and slow due to:

  (i) High material cost;
  (ii) Law and order problem;
  (iii) Marginal return as a result of poor placement due to lack of industries (recruiters);
  (iv) Lack of efficient manpower; and
  (v) Longer gestation period and high project cost.

- Because of the shortage of human resource (as a result of brain-drain), lack of infrastructure, as well as Fund crunch, it would be always beneficial if the stake-holders agree on sharing resources.

REFERENCES

(*Web as accessed on 10/03/2010*).

1. http://www.articlesbase.com/web-design-articles/north-east-indian-universities-their-race-in-the-web-928228.html
2. http://nagaland.net.in/
3. http://en.wikipedia.org/wiki/Nagaland_Univeristy
4. http://www.kkhsou.org/
5. http://www.rgu.ac.in/
6. http://www.gauhati.ac.in/
7. http://www.dibru.ac.in/
8. http://en.wikipedia.org/wiki/Gauhati_University
9. http://en.wikipedia.org/wiki/Assam_University
10. http://en.wikipedia.org/wiki/Tezpur_University
11. http://www.mzu.edu.in/
12. http://en.wikipedia.org/wiki/Manipur_University"Affiliated_Colleges
13. http://www2.ssc.upenn.edu/about/Higher%20Education.pdf
    (*Indian Higher Education Reform — from Half Baked Socialism to Half Baked Capitalism*, Devesh Kapur and Pratap Bhanu Mehta)
14. http://en.wikipedia.org/wiki/Tripura_University
15. http://news.rediff.com/report/2009/aug/29/india-faces-major-problems-in-higher-education-system.htm
16. http://casi.ssc.upenn.edu/iit/pai
    M. A. Pai, *India in Transition: Higher Technical Education in India at the Crossroads*, 02/08/2009.
17. J.C. Agarwal, *Teacher and Education in a Developing Society*, Vikas Publishing House Private Ltd., New Delhi.

18

VALUE EDUCATION IN THE GOVERNMENT SECONDARY SCHOOLS OF GUWAHATI

Saswoti Baruah Bhuyan

Introduction

Values are a set of principles or standards of behaviour, they are regarded desirable, important and held in high esteem by a particular society in which a person lives and the failure to hold them will result in blame, criticism or condemnation. But with the change of time, decline of values are observed in all the spheres of human life. The very existence of traditional institutions such as family, religion, state and society are being questioned. The urgency and importance of value education has come to lime light because of these increasing conflicts in human life. A compact scheme of value education can be considered as the most potential weapon to fight against this value crisis through its all forms such as formal, non-formal and informal education. It has rightly been pointed out by the National Policy on Education 1986 as "The growing concern over the erosion of essential value and an increasing cynicism in society has brought to focus the need for readjustments in the curriculum for the cultivation of social and moral values".

Methodology: In this study descriptive survey method has been used. An attempt has been made to study, describe and interpret what exists at present.

Objectives

1. To study the opinion of teachers towards the importance of value education.

2. To study whether the teachers are satisfied with the existing curriculum meant for providing value education.

Sample: For the selection of the sample, simple random sampling procedure was used. An attempt had been made to cover all the Government Secondary Schools of greater Guwahati area, talking, atleast six teachers from each school.

Table 18.1: Sampling from Government Secondary Schools of Greater Guwahati

Total No. of Institutions	*Institutions Covered*	*Total No. of Teachers*
5	5	30

Tools: Questionnaires were used to collect information. Both open and closed forms of Questions were included.

Data Collection: To collect data the investigator personally visited each of these institutions.

Analysis and Interpretation of Data: The questionnaires were analyzed in a very simple way. For open ended questions, responses of each question was noted down from all the questionnaires number-wise and then an attempt had been made to generalize it. For closed form of questions percentages were used to analyze data.

Findings

1. The respondents have given different opinions when asked about the meaning and concept of values, with one single perceived conclusion. For them, values are a set of principles to guide the life of the children in the right path and enrich their behaviour with good qualities. Some of the values considered essential amongst the students are honesty, kindness, respect for parents, respect to their teachers, maintaining discipline, sincerity and obedience, etc.
2. It has been opined by the respondents that there is degradation of values in and around the society. Commonly found problems amongst the students are lack of sincerity, lack of concentration, showing disrespect towards their parents and teachers, lack of discipline, etc. However, there are some exceptional cases. But this is again not many.
3. Respondents have pointed out many reasons for the whole process of degradation of values such as materialistic world, stiff competition, parental expectation, corruption, invasion of

electronic media, etc. It has been specially pointed out by the respondents that media to a large extent is responsible for spreading wrong values in the society. They have pointed out as an example that the celebration of *Sarasvati Puja* is purely a religious festival of the educational institution. Instead it has been projected in such a manner that the whole occasion has turned into a kind of fashion extra veganza. Thus, the festival losses its spiritual values.

4. All the respondents are in favour of providing value education to the children. According to them, Value education should find a place in the curriculum meant for school children. Schools are the places where these positive attributes can be cultivated for the betterment of the individual, society and the nation as a whole.
5. All most 80 per cent respondents are in favour of the inclusion of a separate subject to teach values to the children. They have cited the example of moral science which was there in the curriculum, but now it has been removed. Whereas 20 per cent respondents are of the opinion that the inclusion of the subject will not serve much. The students will study the subject only to score marks in the examination. It will fail to achieve its real purpose, as value education is more attitudinal development rather than knowledge or information about what is right or wrong.

Table 18.2: Provision for Separate Subject

Yes	*Percentage*	*No*	*Percentage*
24	80%	6	20%

6. 77 per cent of the respondents are not satisfied with the existing curriculum meant for providing value education. According to them, there is nothing specifically given in the curriculum to teach values to the children. But, the remaining 23 per cent are of the opinion that values are hidden in all the school subjects. For example, in class IX in the subject English (SEBA Course), there is a very beautiful poem called "Character of a happy life" which carries the message of how to become happy in life. It depends on the teacher to apply their mind and find out the values and naturally blend them in teaching, so that children can acquire those values.

Table 18.3: Satisfied with the Curriculum

Yes	*Percentage*	*No*	*Percentage*
7	23%	23	77%

7. According to the respondents lack of co-curricular activities are also creating problem. There is no game period as such. In some of the schools, game period is there but that too only for class-V and VIII Students. Scouts and Guide, N.C.C. is there. But it is optional. In all the schools co-curriculum activities are arranged only once a year. So, it fails to provide opportunity to the children for developing democratic values, self-discipline and their creative talents.
8. Teachers are of the opinion that total no of punishment is also contributing to this degradation of values amongst the students. Teachers are afraid of giving even the minor punishment to the students as they tend to be very sentimental at times. Such, was the state that in a reputed school of the city, letters were sent to the guardians of four students of class VIII informing about their indiscipline behaviour in the school. As a result, the students fled from their homes. Because of which the school authorities had been made to go through a lot of harassment.
9. Teachers try to infuse values amongst the students by citing the examples of great personalities, celebrating important days and events, inviting guests from different fields, etc. In some of the schools after the morning assembly quotations of great personalities are read out and the values it preaches are explained to the students.

Suggestions

1. Parents should be actively involved with this whole process as they are more accessible to the child than any other family members. They should help the teachers as and when required. Parent teacher meeting should be held regularly.
2. Provision of trained teachers should be made to deal with this situation. Counseling activities should form a part and parcel of curriculum. Provision should also be made for meditation and yoga classes.
3. Some teachers suggested the inclusion of Rajyoga the course given by Projapita Brahmakumari Ishwariya Vishwavidyalaya

on value education, as it has already been accepted by the Central Government.

4. A period is to be allotted in the daily time-table of the school for value education.
5. Social Studies can be made a useful tool to inculcate values like cooperation, sacrifice, non-violence, heroism, tolerance, concern for environment, etc. as it is a combination of many subjects like History, Geography, Economics and civics.
6. Co-curriculum activities should be properly organized in the school curriculum. Provision should be made for regular games and sports activities.

Conclusion

The need for values and value education has got prominence at present because of the detoriation of human values. It is more important now than it was in the past. Value education is not just talking about values but our schools should adopt a programme which would help in infusing values that are useful for developing proper value based life.

REFERENCES

Agarwal, J.C., *Theory and Principles of Education*, Vikas Publishing House Pvt. Ltd., New Delhi, 2006.

Dr. D. Vijaya Bharathi, *Value Oriented Education "Initiatives at the Teacher Education Level"*, Neelkamal Publication Pvt. Ltd., New Delhi, 2007.

Dr. Sharma, *Philosophical and Sociological Foundation of Education*, Lakshmi Narain Agarwal, Agra, 2002.

Safaya and Shaida, *Modern Theory and Principles of Education*, Dhanpat Rai Publishing Company Pvt. Ltd., New Delhi, 2003.

19

BHUPEN HAZARIKA
The Singer of the Man and Society

Anup Kr. Deka

Introduction

Bhupen Hazarika is a personality who touches upon almost all the fields of art and culture ranging from singing to film-making; from painting to literature. Though he was a man possessing multi-facet talents, he was basically a singer — his words, tune and voice are enriched with unique characteristics. The field where he likes to identify himself with all the more passion and zeal is the field of songs and music. His songs have been enthralling the millions of audience over the years. Hazarika's voice enriched with melody and power of expression, and all new appeal of the tune of some of his songs have mesmerized the audience in such a way that he had emerged as not only a man of exceptional quality and talent but also a taintless noble soul even before his death (Gohain, Hiren [ed.]). An Article by Kumud Baruah, 2012:21). Initially, Hazarika had inclination towards literature, writing stories and poems. He never thought that music would ever be his life and livelihood. At one point, however, he realized that writing songs had become the orbit of his life, and the primary medium of his thought expression was his song and his voice (Hazarika, Surjya [ed.], 2008:0.4).

Bhupen Hazarika wrote songs not simply for the sake of writing. It was not something premeditated. His songs are the result of impulsive and instinctive reaction of his hypersensitive mind. They are his response to the different social issues. Hazarika said, "Whenever in some moment, a particular thought or matter touches my heart, it springs forth with all force of current to be a song". The subject matter of his thoughts is from the social milieu around him (Hazarika, Surjya [ed.], 2008:0.4).

Songs of Man and Society

In the year 1937, when Bhupen Hazarika was only eleven years old, he wrote his first song. It was a paean remembering Sankardev whose social consciousness built the base for his thought (Madhab, Beni [ed.], 1981:107):

"Kuxumbar Putra Sri Sankar Gurue
Dharisil Nāmare Tān
Nāmare Xurate Ānandat Nāsisil
Pabitra Bardowā Thān
Mor Guru Oi, Pabitra Bardowā Thān
Axekh Jatanā Bhunjilā Sri Sankar, Dharamar Nāmate Tumi
Xakalu Dukhaloi Pithi Dilā Guru, Dhainya Axam Bhumi
Mor Guru Oi Dhanya Axom Bhumi.
Nāmghar Xājilā, Rāijkhan Thāpilā
Ekatār Āxanat Āni
Bhāonā Xonate Borgeet Xuwagā, Prasārilā Devabāni.
Mor Guru Oi Prāsārilā Devabāni
Atupi Dutupi Sakulu Xare Mor Dukhani Saranak Pāi
Axamor Ākāxat Dukhar Rol Uthise
Āji Sri Sankar Nāi
Muru Guru Oi, Āji Sri Sankar Nāi".

(Hazarika, Bhupen, 1993:1)

(*Sankar Guru, the son of Kusumber, set the tune of Naam. And in that tune the holy Bardowa dances. Sri Sankar you had suffered great pain for the sake of religion. You had established 'Naamghar' and united the people. You have spread divine message through 'Bhaona' and 'Borgeet'. I cannot hold back my tears getting your feet. The sound of sorrow reverberates in the sky of Assam that Sankar Guru is now not there to guide the people at the hour of crisis*).

"Since, I was born till today, I have been living leaning on music, and being socially conscious. If I can do something for society through music, I will hold this life of mine to be successful", Hazarika said (Hazarika, Surjya [ed], 2008:490). And this very song of Hazarika reflects his social consciousness and concern. He confessed that he never wanted to be a good singer. He had always wondered whether this society could be uplifted by means of song. He had been obsessed with this idea since childhood. And it was because of this idea and notion in mind he had written this song *Kuxumbar Putra Sri Sankar Gurue* (Hazarika Surjya [ed.], 2011:23).

Here, he acknowledges the contribution of Sankardeva towards the formation and development of Assamese society and culture. Sankardeva's religious and social reformation is also earnestly recognized by him. The last three lines of the song is to be marked as they tacitly express the role Bhupen Hazarika is going to assume in latter course of his life. Hazarika says, "To change society, the fire is still burning in me. I was greatly influenced by Sankardeva. The first lyric I ever wrote was on him. It expressed juvenile anguish at the hatred and violence in society, and also the desire to guide the society towards love and brotherhood" (Dutta, Arup Kumar, 2002:25).

He has accepted Sankardeva as his *Guru* (the mentor and guide) and deeply realizes his importance in the Assamese society. He feels the relevance and need of Sankardeva in the present time of social unrest and disintegration. By recognizing Sankardeva as his *Guru*, Bhupen Hazarika hints at the spirit of a reformist in him. It is the spirit which remains a major force in many of his songs.

The force and spirit of a reformist in his first song has been vehemently asserted in his second song *Agni Jugar Firingati Moicomposed* in 1939 when he was only thirteen years of age. (Hazarika, Surjya [ed], 2008:0.12). The song is replete with a sense of rebellion and social reformation. Bhupen Hazarika in this song identifies himself as a potent force for social change:

Agni Jugar Firingati Moi
Natun Axom Garhim
Xarba Hārār Xarbaswa Punar Phirāi Ānim
Natun Axom Garhim
Nara Kangkālar Astra Xāji
Xoxankarik Badhim. . . .

(Hazarika, Bhupen, 1993:33)

(*I am the spark of a fiery age. I will build new Assam. And I will bring back the lost fortune of all the dispossessed people. I will make weapon of human skeleton and with it I will kill the exploiters and the oppressors*).

(*N.B.* The line *Natun Axom Garhim* had originally been *Natun Bharat Garhim*. The change was made at the suggestion of Bishnu Rabha in 1948, when the song was incorporated into a film called '*Sirāj*') (Dutta, Arup Kumar, 2002:29).

When Hazarika wrote this song, the death and destruction of Second World War and the turmoil and turbulence of India's Freedom struggle were rampant. That was a burning period (*Agni-Jug*) of conflicts and unrest. It is in this period he wanted to be a spark for social change. He wanted to establish a classless society where there would be no difference among people in terms of religion, caste and community. This society, he envisaged, would discard the jingoistic attitude of the people. It would be a society, without any discord. Such society would be a heaven of equality, love and brotherhood. The tone and spirit of radical revolutionary change in the song take Hazarika to the edge of being labelled as socialist realist. He talks of bringing back to the deprived all that were exploited from and striped of them. Again he says that he will forge weapons from human skeletons (*Nara-Kangkāl*) to destroy the exploiters. The image of *Nara-kangkāl* is used to refer to the downtrodden and exploited people of the society. And by weapon of skeleton he means the rise and empowerment of these people. And this takes him to threshold of Marxist Philosophy of social change and equality. However, Bhupen Hazarika says that when he wrote this song Marx never came into his intellectual life (Kumar, Thaneswar, 2011:27). Later on, because of the song's socialist revolutionary tone and message, Bishnu Rabha had included it in his communist book *Mukti Deol*. He, however, replaced the line "*Harijan, Pāhāri, Hindu, Muslimanr, Boro, Koch, Sutia, Ahomor*" of the song with '*Hindu-Muslim*', '*Sikh-Christianar*'.

Bhupen Hazarika declared that he would use his song as an instrument for social change (Hazarika, Surjya [ed.], 2008:0.5). This is of course very natural with him considering his close association with Jyotiprasad Agarwala, Bishnu Prasad Rabha and later on with Paul Robson. During his stay in Tezpur from 1935 to 1940, he came into contact with the cultural icons like Jyotiprasad Agarwala and Bishnu Rabha and the father of modern Assamese theatre, Phani Sarma. Referring to that period Bhupen Hazarika says, "That time in Tezpur, when my artist life began, was the golden age of my life and the most meaningful time for me" (Hazarika, Bhupen, 2011:45). From 1936 to 1948 Hazarika shared very close ties with Jyotiprasad. He said that the prime concern of Jyotiprasad was to discuss how through art and culture the society can be freed of its follies and vices (Hazarika, Surya [ed.], 2008:732). He showed to Bhupen Hazarika where Mahatma Gandhi has similarity and concord with Karl Marx, how people can be an Assamese, while being an Indian. Hazarika calls Jyotiprasad his *Guru* (the teacher) (Hazarika, Surya [ed.], 2008:732).

It was Jyotiprasad who advised him to meet Paul Robson when he left for America for higher study (*Ibid.*, 757). In Paul Robson, Bhupen

Hazarika discovered another Guru in America. He says of Robson, "He was a social singer with the power to change" (Dutta, Arup Kumar, 2002:46). Robson believed that "a guitar is not a musical instrument, it is a social instrument. The strum of a guitar can make a nation think" (Hazarika, Surya [ed.], 2008:759). Bhupen Hazarika confesses, "Like Jyotiprasad and Bishnu Kokaideu (i.e. elder brother), he was responsible for moulding my philosophy of action. I too wanted to be a singer with the power to change society" (Dutta, Arup Kumar, 2002:46). He has seen much similarity between Joytiprasad and Paul Robson. Both of them were against imperialism, both of them accepted their creative power and talent as tool for social change, and employed it against injustice exploitation of people on people (Hazarika, Surya [ed.], 2008:757). Thus the two social artists, one of his own land Assam and another of distant America, with their intense and deep concern for subjugated people of society have undoubtedly expanded the social outlook of Bhupen Hazarika. Here, Hazarika confesses, "Jyotiprasad and Paul Robson will always remain an ideal in my life" (Hazarika, Surya [ed.], 2008:760).

In his songs Hazarika dons himself with the amour of a soldier in the fight against the exploiters. He wants to be an active soldier, a potent force for the uplift of the proletariat. Hazarika talks of a radical and revolutionary change. He is the voice of the people. His songs give vent to the oppressed wish of the people to effect the change from injustice to justice, from hopelessness to hopefulness, from subjugation to emancipation. Here, reference can be made to Hazarika's famous song *Endhār Kātir Nixāte*. Hazarika says that in this song he doesn't merely present the pain and heartening cry of a mother who loses her son. He wants to show how Panei-like thousands of mother can become rebellious and raise storms of revolution (rather than shedding tears while singing lullaby) with the vow to create a new society (Hazarika, Surya [ed.], 2008:1536). A faith in the inherent dignity and nobility of the common man is the very root and basis of Bhupen Hazarika's song. He recognizes the common mass as a power, and asserts their sense of dignity and belongingness, whenever he gets the chance. He wants to remind the poor and exploited labour class that they are the force for social change, the creators of history and path-breakers of the civilization.

One of the major concerns of Bhupen Hazarika's song is the uplift of the proletariat. His songs, as he said, are the means and weapons to bring about a social change which will ascertain the rights, freedoms and justices to this poor exploited working people. This revolutionary spirit for social change and assertion of the dignity of the dispossessed are the elements in his songs which take him close to Marxist idealism.

Like Marx, Bhupen Hazarika also realizes that without economical justice, people cannot live a dignified life. Whenever the economic negligence is felt the feelings of the deprived got violent expression. Without economic freedom people's freedom is not possible. That is why his songs throw light on painful economic condition of the people and show ways and means to overcome it. It is to be marked that Bhupen Hazarika's intense sense of humanism is at the root of the Marxist aspect in his songs. As it has been said earlier, he had written his first song *Agni Jugar Phiringati Moi* before he knew what Marxism was all about. But because of the song's imbibed Marxist spirit and philosophy, it was qualified to find place in Bishnu Rabha's *Mukti Deol*. It proves that whatever he bears of Marxism is corollary to his empathy with the have-nots and exploited. There is universality in his humanism. He sings:

"Mānuhe Mānuhar Bābe
Jadihe Akano Nābhābe
Akani Xahanubhutire
Bhābiba Koneno Kowā? Xamaniā?"

(Hazarika, Bhupen, 1993:369)

(*If men do not think about men with compassion/Tell me who will think?*)

There is no doubt that man, viewed in larger perspective and varied dimension, is the focal concern in Bhupen Hazarika's Song. A primary subject of his song is men and men's society. Hazarika said, "In all countries of the world water is made of parts of Hydrogen and one part of Oxygen. New York, Mascow or Paris, Helchingki, Sivsagar, or Belgium — wherever I go — Man is man, made of one metal" (Hazarika, Surya, 2008:0.15). This song is intended to stir the sense of responsibilities of the haves towards the have-nots. For awakening the sense of human responsibilities this song has been universally embraced. The Bengali version of this song *Mānus Mānuser Janya* has been rated by BBC (Bengali Section) as the best song of the twentieth century (Kumar, Thaneswar, 2011:18). And this further asserts his universal acceptance.

Conclusion

Bhupen Hazarika is a voice and spirit of dynamism, love and universal brotherhood. His love of man is not an end in itself. It is a revolution for eliminating social injustice, for empowering the proletariat and establishing social equality and universal brotherhood. It is a love that qualifies the poor and deprived. While his love has a sense of general acceptance for the broader section of the have-nots around the world, it rejects the general class of the haves. His humanity and fellow feeling recognizes and distinguishes between the poor and the rich, the labour and the owner, the exploited and the exploiter. His sense and consciousness move in two extremes — the anger for the exploiter and oppressor and general human feelings for the exploited and oppressed. And they infuse in him a sense of social responsibility. He views man in terms of society. His humanism is for establishing the general dignity and nobility of the deprived man in general. So, he sings —

"Jiyāi Thākim
Jiyāi Thāki Ekhan Xamāj
Garhibar Mor Man Āse,
Jiyāi Thāki Ekhan Xamāj
Garhibar Pan Āse,
Jot Xonatkoi Mānuhar Dām
Alap Haleo Besi Āse"

(Hazarika, Bhupen, 1993:463)

(*I want to live with the will and promise to make a society where men will be more valuable than gold*).

REFERENCES

Baird, Forest E., and Walter Kaufmann, *From Plato to Derrida*, Pearson Prentice Hall, New Jersey, 2008.

Dutta, Arup Kumar, *Bhupen Hazarika: The Roving Minstrel*, Rupa & Co., New Delhi, 2002.

Gohain, Hiren, *Bhaabi Kaalar Khanikar*, Jyoti Prakashan, Guwahati, 2003.

Hazarika, Bhupen, *Chikmik Bijuli*, Lawyer's Book Stall, Guwahati, 1969.

———, *Moi Eti Jajabar*, S.H. Educational Trust, Guwahati, 2011.

———, *Bohag Mathu Eati Ritu Nahai*, S.H. Educational Trust, Guwahati, 2010.

———, *Prasanga Sundarar*, Chandra Prakash, Guwahati, 2005.

———, *Geetawali*, Bani Mandir, Guwahati, 1993.

Hazarika, Surjya, (ed.), *Dr. Bhupen Hazarika: Rachanawali*, Vol. I-III, S.H. Educational Trust, Guwahati, 2008.

———, *Assam Ratna Bata 2008*, Guwahati: Government of Assam, 2009.

Kalita, Pulin, *Agni Yugar Firingati*, Banalata, Guwahati, 2011, 2007.

Kadir, Abdul, (ed.), *Najrul Rasana Xambhar*, Universal Book Depot, Kolkata, 1965.

Kumar, Thaneswar, *Dr. Bhupen Hazarikaar Geet Aru Kishu Prushangik Katha*, Ashok Book Stall, Guwahati, 2011.

Marx, Karl, *The Communist Manifesto*, <eBook Eden.Com>
———, *Critique of the Gotha Programme*, Foreign Languages Press, Peking, 1972.
Neog, Maheswar, *Asamiya Giti-Sahitya*, Janata Book Stall, Tezpur, 1958.
Pujari Arcchana, *Dr. Bhupen Hazarikar Gitor Mulyayan*, Bani Mandir, Guwahati, 2002.
Rajbongshi, Paramananda, (ed.), *Dr. Bhupen Hazarika: Jiwan Aru Sangram*, Asam Sahitya Sabha, Jorhat, 2012.
Sarma, Satyendranath (ed.), *Jyotiprasad Rachanavali*, Assam Prakashan Parishad, Guwahati, 1986.

20

VAISHNAVISM IN ASSAM IN THE PRE-SANKARITE PERIOD

Marami Choudhury

The eastern most State of Indian Union which is known as Assam at present was called by different names in different periods of history. The most ancient name of Assam was Pragjyotishpura. It was a place of Saivism and Saktism. But *Visnu-sadhna* was also there in the name of *Pancharatra-sadhna*.

"Vaishnavism was established in Assam at a time when Surya worship and Brahmanical culture made considerable progress, and as the evidence shows, the worship of both Visnu and his incarnations was prevalent in the land from early times" (Choudhury, P.C., 1987:409). The association of Visnu-Krsna with Pragjyotisa is a well known fact. In the *Mahabharata*, Visnu is named as Pragjyotisajyestha (Murthy, H.V.S., 1973:12).

The *Kalika Purana* describes clearly about the worship of Visnu-Vasudeva with rituals and also mentions five incarnations of the deity as being worshipped in different places of Assam, *viz.* Hayagriva, worship in Manikuta (Hajo), Fish incarnation, worshipped in the Maysyadhvaja mount to the east of Manikuta, Madhava in the form of Bhairava, named Pandunatha in Raksa-kuta; The boar incarnation in the Citrabaha mount and Vasudeva-Krsna in the Dikkaravasini region. "Banabhatta in his *Harsha-charita* describes the king Bhaskar Varman as belonging to Vaisnava family (Vaisnava vamsa). The Chinese Buddhist pilgrim Yuan Chawang also states that Bhaskar Varman was descended from Narayanadeva" (Murthy, H.V.S., 1973:8).

The origin of Vaishnavism in Assam is said to be uncertain. Hence, from when and how it originates can never be definitely accounted for. The Vaishnava religion must have come to Assam along with the Vedic religion and culture. From legends and history, it is also evident that

Vedic civilization and culture along with Saivism and Saktism was prevalent in Assam since the time of Aryanization.

Vaishnavism was also simultaneously practised in Assam along with Saivism and Saktism. "The *Kalika Purana* in recounting the sacred places of ancient Kamarupa mentions fifteen places sacred to Siva against five sacred to Devi and five sacred to Visnu. Even in Modern Assam, Saivite temples out number those sacred to other Gods and Goddess" (Kakati, B., 1967:10). The antiquity of Visnu in his incarnations is associated with the Hayagriva — Madhava worship in Hajo. According to the *Puranas*, it was Visnu, in his Hayagriva form who killed the demon Jvarasura on the Manikuta, where stood a temple of Hayagriva Visnu. The *Garuda Purana* gives the mode of worship of Hayagriva which was a mixture of the Pauranic and Tantricism faiths. The earliest reference to Visnu worship can be found in the 'Badganga epigraph of Bhutivarman and the King is here mentioned as '*parama daivata — parama bhagavata*'. At that time, the Vaisnava King is referred to as '*paramabhagavata*' and the King who follows the Saivism as '*parama mahesvara*'. It is noteworthy that the King Bhutivarman is mentioned in the inscription as the performer of 'Asvamedha Sacrifice' which indicates that the Vedic culture was in full bloom in his time. But it is also clear from the inscription that he was a devotee of Visnu and in his kingdom Vaisnavism was widespread. The biographer of Sankaradeva mentioned the name of Dharmapala in association with the faith.

The worship of Visnu is as old as the *Rig-Veda*, where he is called "one of the Adityas and Grierson urgently holds that the Bhagavata doctrine was a development of the Sun-worship, common to both the Iranians and Indians" (Choudhury, P.C., 1987:408). But still during that period Visnu was regarded as a minor God and Vaishnavism as a faith, is fully developed at the time of the *Mahabharata*. "There is infact little connection between the cult of Visnu of the *Vedas* and the *Bhakti* cult or what may be called the sectarian Vaishnavism of later times" (Roychoudhury, Hem. Ch., 1936:6f-17f). The name 'Vasudeva' is mentioned in the post-Vedic literature and the name 'Visnu' is cited in 'Panini' and the earliest reference to the Bhagavatas has been made in the *Brahmasutras*. "In any case, the divine character given to Krsna was a later development. Vasudeva had little connection with Visnu of the Vedas, and the origin of sectarian Vaishnavism — cannot be traced to the Visnu cult of the Vedas" (Roychoudhury, Hem. Ch., 1936:6f-17f). But, gradually with the introduction of the idea of incarnation both the cult became synthesized as Vaishnavism. Hence, in course of time,

Visnu of the Vedic period, Narayana of the *Pancaratras*, Vasudeva Krsna of the Satvats and Gopala of the Abhiras became unified and worshipped under the name of 'Visnu' in and through his different manifestations.

The *Yogini-tantra* offers a different account of the origin of the Hayagriva worship in the Manikuta. The *tantra* also gives an account of the systems of worship in different Visnupithas specially Pandu-natha in Raksakuta. The method of worship of Vasudeva-Krsna as shown in the *Kalika Purana* is to some extent similar to the rules laid down in the *Pancaratra Samhitas*. The Vaishnavism enunciated in the *Pancharatra Samhita* is no doubt an early form of Vaishnavism. "The *Samhitas* are historically noteworthy in two ways. They make the first emergence of Sakta principles in the Vaishnavite sects. But they are also notable as being the first manuals formed to express both the beliefs and practices of Vaishnavas" (Farquhar, J.N., 1920:183-186). The *Yogini-Tantra* links Hayagriva image with that of Jagannatha Puri. "However, conflicting the accounts may be, it is certain that Vaishnavism made its way into Assam through the elite part of the society very early sometime before Christian era" (Murthy, H.V.S., 1973:10). "The Aryanised names Pragjyotisa and Kamarupa, which find mention as early as the *Brahmanas* and the *Grihya Sutras*, also point to the same conclusion. Yuan Chawang's testimony that hundreds of Deva temples, evidently of Aryan or Brahmanical Gods, existed in Kamarupa, indicates that during the seventh century A.D., Brahmanical culture or *Aryadharma* was widespread in the land. This is confirmed by the Bidhanpur grant, which states that Bhaskar Varman spread the *Aryadharma* by dispelling the darkness of the Kali age (Choudhury, P.C., 1987:395).

All the different grants which have been discovered in ancient Kamrupa agree on the point that the Kings of Varman, Salastambha and Pala dynasties as descendent of the Boar incarnation of 'Lord Visnu'. "In different Copper plates events which have special reference to the Kings of Kamarupa the King of the Varman and Pala dynasties were mentioned as the defendants of the Boar incarnations of Visnu. Just as the name of Maheswar, Siva whom they worshipped the name of Visnu as the Progenitor of their generation or somehow the name of Visnu was associated with those grants" [Sarma, Banikanta (ed.), 1991:8-9 (article by Sastri, M.R.)].

Like other sources of information the sculptural representation of the period provide us a welcome evidence of the prevalence of Vaishnavism during this period. They give us an indication of the popularity of Vaishnavism from seventh century onwards. "We have extensive archaeological remains of temples dedicated to Visnu and his incarnations and icons of the deity throughout Assam. The remains show that beginning at least with the fifth and sixth century A.D. Visnu was worshipped in his iconographic representations and Vaishnavism was widespread in the land (Choudhury, P.C., 1987:412-413).

A large number of images have been discovered in Assam since early times. "A fine representation of Visnu in his *Sthanaka* variety is found at Deopani" (Choudhury, P.C., 1987:456). Different icons of Visnu discovered from different religiously important places lead us to believe that from very ancient time Vaishnavism or Visnu worship were prevalent in Assam, either of the main deity or the forms of its ten or twenty four incarnations.

It may be noted in passing that the references are made in the *Sankara Carita* of Ramcharana Thakura to the prevalence of Vaishnavism before Sankardeva. It is said that Sankardeva with his relatives shifted from Alipukhuri to Bardowa in the Nagaon district. At the new place when Sankardeva was himself cutting the earth with a *Kodali* (axe) to built the plinth of the proposed *Kirtana-Ghara*, he struck upon a Visnu image of shining black stone. He took out the image from under the ground and explained that everybody will give up the worship of the Devi and take to the worship of Krsna. He installed the image on the platform in the newly built Namaghara (*Gurucharita*-Ramcharan Thakur). To sum up, the facts recounted above definitely prove that Vaishnavism penetrated into Assam even before the Christian era and began to attract the attention of the masses and the state in the succeeding centuries.

Biswa Narayan Sastri in his article "Pre-Sankarite Vaishnavism in ancient and medieval Assam" states "In the Puranic age the story of Krishna, the supreme Lord has been described in the *Visnu Purana, Harivamsa, Matsya Purana, Brahma Vaivartha Purana* and finally in the *Bhagavata Purana*. From the *Visnu Purana* to the *Brahma Vaivartha Purana* is a period of four to fifth centuries and in this period *Krishna Katha* through the *Puranic* stories was made very popular among the people. The process is gradually replacement of Visnu by Krishna" [Mahanta, P. (ed.), 2001:55).

It is evident that 'Bhakti', the main root of Vaishnavism was accepted in the Pre-Sankarian Vaishnavism also. But, there is a distinct difference between pre-Sankarite *bhakti-dharma* and *bhakti-dharma* as preached by Sankardeva. The former was confined among the elite and in the process the image of Visnu or Krishna was worshipped but Neo-Vaishnava movement by Sankaradeva made all the people equal partners of the *bhakti*, which has only one deity in Krishna. Moreover, the *bhakti* cult swept away or submerged the little differences that existed in the performance of ritual *bhakti*.

The social and political condition of the pre-Sankarite period helped Sankaradeva to propound creative humanism in the form of Neo-Vaishnavism in Assam. "On the royal patronage, the expensive ceremonies such as worship, sacrifice, etc. were organized among the aristrocrates with Brahmanian customs. The effort made by Brahmanism to advance the tribals into a wider Hindu society was totally pole" (Bora, Dilip, 2008:108). Again, with the trend of Aryanization, the different religious conceptions entered into the society of Assam, i.e. Saivism, Saktism, Tantrism and Vaishnavism. During this period, kings were the followers either of Vaisnavism or Saivism. "The worship of Siva was prevalent in Assam from ancient times. Siva was the tutelary God of ancient Kings of Kamrupa from the fifth to the twelfth centuries. The *Kalika Purana* and *Yogini Tantra* have mentioned several places sacred to God Siva and there still exist many Siva temples in Darrang and Kamrup districts" (Sarma S.N., 1996:5).

The Siva temples of Hajo (Kedaresvara and Kamatesvara), Biswanath Singari (Guevara), are famous from ancient times. Siva was the exalted God, and even influenced Sankara's home or significantly the name of Sankaradeva was 'Sankara' — the other name of Siva. "Sankaradeva has given Siva too equal status with Visnu. Though, in Harmohana (Kirtanghosa) Siva was degraded to a lower level in comparison to Visnu or miserable condition of Siva was shown in Harihara battle" (Bora, Dilip, 2008:109). Though, Siva has been degraded by the prevalent songs of Siva in Vaishnava society, such as '*ki khai pagala holi. . .*', etc. yet Siva and Visnu are the same in the opinion of Vaisnava people. It seems that behind the conflict between Siva and Visnu, presented through these stories, reflect the contemporary social conflict and in these conflicts superiority of Visnu is established.

Before Sankaradeva, along with Saivism, Saktism and Tantricism were also the pre-dominant trend of the State of Assam. "Saktism was dominant cult of Assam in ancient and medieval times upto the advent of Neo-Vaishnavism, and even today it holds a place next to Vaishnavism" (Sarma S.N., 1996:6). The two Sanskrit works composed in Assam, the *Kalika Purana* and the *Yogini Tantra* have mainly dealt with the Shakti cult. The various forms of Shakti was worshipped in different temples dedicated to her. In this regard, Banikanta Kakati has identified *Dikkara*

Vasini of *Kalika Purana* with goddess Tamresvari or Kecaikhaiti (eater of raw flesh) (Kakati, Banikanta, 1967:21-24). The main radiating centres of Saktism has been the shrines dedicated to Kamakhya and Dikkaravasini.

Eliot defines Saktism in 'Hinduism and Buddhism' as the worship of "a goddess of many names and forms, who is adored with sexual rites and the sacrifice of animals, or when the law permits of men" (Eliot, Sir Charles, Vol. I, 1921:xxxvi). Shakti was worshipped according to Tantric rites and sacrifices in these two shrines situated in the western and eastern parts of the country (i.e. Kamarupa). In Saktism "human sacrifice was also performed in the Jayanyesvari Temple of Jayantapura located in modern Jayantia hills" (Sarma, S.N., 1996:6). The worship of Snake goddess Manasa, who is believed as the manifestation of Shakti in Assamese *Kavyas* was very popular in western parts of Assam. "The *Padma Purana* and the *Beula Upakhyana*, the two Assamese *Kavyas* composed by Mankar and Durgabara during the closing decades of the fifteenth century definitely prove the existence and popularity of this cult on the eve of the Neo-Vaisnavite movement. Besides Kamakhya, Sakti in her different forms like Ugratara, Mangalacandi, Siddhesvari, Bhairavi, Camunda, Burhi Gosani, Durgesvari, etc. were worshipped in different places" (Sharma, S.N., 1996:7). Images of Manasa and other Sakti goddesses have been discovered in Guwahati and Nagaon district.

Though, Vaishnavism prevailed on the eve of Neo-Vaishnavite movement in Assam, it was quite different from the one introduced by Sankaradeva and his followers. Bapchandra Mahanta explain the various form of Visnu worship that prevailed in Pre-Sankaradeva period in Assam.

Supreme Brahman or Lord Visnu

1. Pancharatra Narayana Vishnu in which Visnu is the only tutelary divinity
2. Visnu is to be worshipped with Sakti, according to Ramanuja and other Vaishnava teachers
3. Worshipping of Visnu with pilgrimage fast, *sraddha* ceremony, etc.

(Mahanta, Bapchandra, 1987:33)

Though, *Yogini Tantra* and other textual references have commented on the superiority of Visnu in pre-Sankarite Assam, yet this idea was inclusive in the third form as shown above. Of course, the presence of the second form too cannot be ignored in which Visnu is worshipped with Sakti which is known as Tantric Vaishnavism. The superiority of Visnu as shown in *pancaratra* was followed by tantric path.

In the *Pancharatra* system "Visnu was the only cause of all — The universal ceaseless consciousness of Mahapurusha is the essence of

Bhagavata Purana also" (Mahanta, Bap Chandra, 1987:223). It is worth mentioning that these are some ideas amidst the followers of Vaishnavism, though they centres round *Bhakti* yet they did not deeply consider their hearts as spiritual.

Caste system was prevalent during this period Bap Ch. Mahanta has shown that women in the form of Shakti were worshipped along with Visnu. Moreover, there are many descriptions of ways to accomplishment spirituality like *Tapa, Japa, Yajna*, etc. in different tales of the *Bhagavata Purana* (Mahanta, Bap Ch., 1987:203). "The worship of Visnu in the form of Vasudeva seems to have been prevalent from early times. The Baraganga Rock inscription of Mahabhuti Barma (554 A.D.) which refers to the King as Parama-Bhagavata is the earliest recorded evidence of the existence of Vaishnavism" (Sharma, S.N., 1996:7). But the Umachal Rock Inscription which belongs to an early period refers to the excavation of a cave temple dedicated to Balabhadra Swami one of the *Vyuhes* of Visnu in the *Pancharatra* sect.

According to *Kalika Purana* the adoration of Hayagriva Madhava of Hajo in Assam is performed in accordance with the rites of *Pancharatra* and the name of Vasudeva is mentioned in different places. It is remarkable that Şankardeva has also mentioned about *Pancharatra* in the Kirtanghosa as —

vailaha narada risi name avatara
pancaratra name tantra karila prasar
yaka asarile mohamoksa pada pai
harira kirtana kari phura vina bai

(Kirtanghosa, 16)

[*As Sage Narada didst Thou incarnate, to preach Pancharatra Tantra far and wide. Its practice helped one attain highest seat of liberation; singing Hari's nama on the date thou moveth on*].

"The mode of reign of Tantras of Kamarupa has shown that especially Saivism got expansion here. But during the time of Indrapala, Gauri (Parvati) has got preference to Hara. But the altar of *Dashavatara* at Bamunipahar of Tezpur has proved the supremacy of Visnu. *Kalika Purana* and even *Yogini Tantra* also show that the advent of Visnu has put an end to the misfortunes of the inhabitants of Kamarupa" [Gohain, Hiren, 1987:226(A)]. This statement of *Kalika Purana* and *Yogini Tantra* has indicated of a developed Aryan Culture of later stage. However, Siva, Shakti and Visnu — all three were adorned in ancient Kamarupa and their forms are of two types — i.e., Vedic and Tantric. There may be some ritual differences but its unity of divinity is remarkable. Sivnath Barman has said that Shakti Tantric goddess of *Manusmriti* as shown by Kuluk Bhatta is non-Vedic (Barman, Sivnath, 1989:287).

Thus, we find that Tantrism, was prevalent and the worship of various gods and goddesses with elaborate ceremonies, both esoteric or exotic, was also very popular. "Monotheism and the cult of *Bhakti* did not thrive for want of a proper atmosphere though the belief in one Supreme God was not altogether alien to the learned section of the people" (Sharma, S.N., 1986:11). In order to bring all people of different sects under a systematized religious code and conduct of life to do away with the extreme Tantric rituals connected with Saivism and Shaktism which encouraged sensuality in the name of religion and to supply the mass with a mode of worship which would be simple and accessible to all, Sankaradeva came forward with his Neo-Vaishnavism or *Eka Sarana Nama Dharma.*

"While the cult of Vasudeva mainly flourished in the temples, the Vaishnavism of the Epics appears to have influenced a certain section of the mass. The Assamese translation of the *Ramayana* by Madhava Kandali, the Court poet of the Kachari King Mahamanikya of the fourteenth century and popular translations of several episodes of the *Mahabharata* by Harihara Vipra, Kaviratna Sarasvati and Rudra Kandali, all belonging to the fourteenth century A.D., establish that Vaisnavism as found in the two epics was not unknown to a section of people" [Kakati, B. (ed.), 1959:Ch.-II, 16ff].

Therefore, both literary and archaeological sources signify that the worship of Visnu and his incarnations was established in the land from early times. During the Pre-Sankarite period a large number of poets and writers in ancient Kamarupa professed and actively supported Vaishnavism. A significant number of Vaisnava thinkers wrote on early Vaishnavism and practised it to save the society from further degeneration and disintegration.

Though, Sankaradeva was not the first introducer of 'Vaishnavism' in Assam, yet his thoughts with a new shape attracted the common people and his ideal philosophy of life based on humanism.

REFERENCES

Barman, Sivnath, *Srimanta Sankaradeva Kriti Aru Krititva (Assamese)*, Purbanchal Prakash, Ghy, 1989.

Borah, Dilip, Samaj, *Sahitya Aru Sanhati*, published by Bhabani Offset and Imaging Systems Pvt. Ltd., Rajgarh Road, Guwahati, 2008.

Choudhury, Pratap Chandra, *The History of Civilization of the People of Assam to the Twelfth Century A.D.*, published by Spectrum Publications, Panbazar, Guwahati, Assam, 1987.

Chutia, Dharmeswar (ed.), *Mahapurush Sankaradeva Vakyamrita*, Srimanta Sankaradeva Sangha, Published by Hariprasad Hazarika, Nagaon, 1998.

Eliot, T.S., *Religion and Literature*, London, 1921,

Farquhar, J.N., *An Outline of the Religious Literature of India*, Motilal Banarasi Das, Delhi, 1920.

Gohain, Hiren, *Asamiya Jatiya Jivanata Mahapurushiya Parampara (Assamese)*, Lawyers Book Stall, Guwahati, Vol. I, 1987 (A).

Kakati, Banikanta (ed.), *Aspects of Early Assamese Literature*, Gauhati University, 1959.

Kakati, Banikanta, *The Mother Goddess Kamakhya*, Guwahati 1967.

Mahanta, Bap Chandra, *Aitihasik Patabhumit Mahapurusa Sankaradeva*, Jorhat, 1987.

Mahanta, Pradip Jyoti (ed.), *Glimpses of the Vaishnava Heritage of Assam*, Published by Gagan Chandra Adhikary, Asom Satra Mahasabha, 2001.

Murthy, H.V.S., *Vaishnavism of Sankaradeva and Ramanuja: A Comparative Study*, Motilal Banarasi Das, Delhi, 1973.

Roychoudhury, Hem Ch., *Materials for the Study of Early History of the Vaishnava Sect*, Kolkata, 1936.

Saikia, Purnananda, *Mahapurusa Madhavadeva's Namghosa* (Rendered into English verse), Bora Prakashan, Guwahati, 1997.

———, *Sreemanta Sankaradeva's The Kirttana Ghosa* (An English verse Rendering) Srimanta Sankaradeva Sangha, Nagaon, Assam, 2005.

Sarma, Banikanta (ed.), *Asomar Vaishnava Dharmar Ruprekha*, Published by Bani Prakash Pvt. Ltd., Guwahati, 1991.

Sharma, S.N., *The Neo-Vaisnavite Movement and the Satra Institution of Assam*, Lawyer's Book Stall, 1996.

21

THE SATTRAS OF MAJULI
Its Arts and Culture

Biju Rajkhowa

The contribution of the *sattras* towards the religion, culture and the lifestyle of the natives of Assam is always worth a mention and undeniable. The way the *sattras* established in different parts of the State have influenced the inhabitants of those particular places, similarly, the *sattras* of Majuli have been able to strike the attention of the people of Assam and the world. Geographically, socially and culturally, Majuli is one of the biggest inhabited river islands in the world. Majuli is a sub-division of the Jorhat district of Assam. Majuli, situated on the heart of the mighty Brahmaputra, is made of a landmass of 350 years old and was once the largest river island in the world with tranquil waterline. This river island has been inhabited by many different of tribes that go above a population of almost one and a half lakhs. Each of the tribes and community living in the island have shared a bond of unity by keeping their traditions and cultures intact amidst the colourful *Sattrīyā* culture of the land. It seems that the whispering winds of the river island and the rhythm of *Bargīt, Bihu gīts* and *oinitom* has built a strong bond between its inhabitants and the Mother Nature. That is why, perhaps, social activist Sanjay Ghosh had expressed once:

"The land of the river and whispering wind
Sweet rice and plenty of fish
Where the sun rises to the sound of a hundred birds and
Evening resonate of the music of cymbals and kirttans".[1]

Cultural Significance of Majuli

Majuli is the heart of the *Sattrīyā* culture. On speaking about the *sattras* and their cultural significance, the Neo-Vaishnavite and the two Vaishnava Saints Sankaradeva and Madhavadeva have to be named. The golden period of 1522 AD when the Sankaradeva and Madhavadeva came into the terms of each other is noteworthy. It was at Dhuwahat Belguri where the great personalities met each other and was later marked as the 'Manikanchan Kshetra' in the history of Vaishnava religion. It was in Dhuwahat Belguri, situated towards the west of the Ahatguri division where the first *sattra* was established and later with time the land erosion of the Bramaputra river bank, shifted it to the north.

In Majuli there are all together sixty-five *sattras* which turn Majuli into a *Sattrapith* (the land of *sattras*). Some of those *sattras* got shifted to different locations due to several reasons and consequently, at present there are a total of 22 big and small *sattras* keeping the heritage of the land intact. It is in these *sattras*, one can witness the cultural contributions of the two Vaishnava Saints along with their disciples, their matchless creations, invaluable compositions and the hundreds of years old manuscripts written on the skins of *sānchi*.

The very view of the *sattras* is kaleidoscopic and spiritual with the little huts of the disciples spread in all four sides East, West, North and South and the *nāmghar* based right in the centre under the conduction of the *sattradhikar*. The timely and regular practice of *nritya-gīt* right from the sunrise to even after the sunset creates a melodious and spiritual atmosphere in these *sattras*.

The term *Māti-ākharā* is used to denote the primary stage of practicing *nrityas* like *Natuwā, Cāli, Jhumurā, Ojāpāli, Nādu-bhoṅgī* and *Apsarā nāc*, etc. The significant cultural practices like *Bargīt, Bhatimā, Tutoi, Sopoi*, etc. have been composed in a pure spiritual and devotional atmosphere and in the rhythms of the prayers. Along with the regular practice of *Gāyana-Bāyana* and *Sūtradhāra*, it has been a habit to exercise and study the *Aṅkia-bhāonā* introduced by Sankaradeva in the *sattras*. It has been an inseparable tradition of the *sattras* to be indulged in *Soidhya Prasanga* (reciting the fourteen clauses of the *Bhāgavat*), *Saran, Bhajan*, etc. Amongst the cultural functions of the sattras, staging of *Rāsalīlā* on the full moon night in the autumn season, *nāt, pālnam*, etc. are notable.

The river island of Majuli is said to be the land of unity and brotherhood. It has the same rhythm and tune for different community songs and numbers even if it is *Bargīt, Bihugīt* or the *Oinitom*. Built on a diversity of the social limitations of the people living in this river island, their myths, traditions and their thought processes; the culture of Majuli has reached its present stature. It changes its colour with the change in the seasons and the agricultural tribes welcome a new festival every time in a new season. The best instance of unity in diversity of the place is its celebration of every community festival together under one roof, be it is *Bihu, Norācigā, Oinītom, Pohrāg, Kebang, Ali-Ai-Ligāng* or the *Bāith Pujā*.

Art and Culture of Majuli

For Majuli and its people, celebration of *Rās* is one of the major social and devotional functions. The entire river island is found drowned in a different mood and world of the melodious rhythms of the *Rās gīt* and *nritya* with the local business also gaining a momentum. On the auspicious day of the full moon, *Sri Krsna Rāslīlā* commence with the different sattras of Majuli like Dakshinpat, Samoguri, Auniati, Gormurh, Bengenaati, Notun Kamalabari, Uttar Kamalabari, Bhogpur, Bihimpur, Narasiṅgha, etc. observing it in their own particular ways. Except for the Gormurh Sattra, most of the other *sattras* practice male oriented acting in *Rāslīlā*. In fact, apart from the sattras, almost fifty other stages are built on which *Rāslīlā* is staged from three to four days. The annual *pālnām* observance in the Auniati Sattra draws more of a gravity and holiness to the entire Majuli. The tradition of *pālnām* practice in this *sattra* started way back in the days of the fifth *Sattradhikār* Sri Sri Haridev.[2] The whole scene and surrounding of the *Sattra* with the disciples taking part in the *kirttan*, playing *Khol, Tāl, Doba, Soṅkho*, etc. and their auspicious rhythms along with the trade fairs arranged all around turns to be pretty joyous and cheerful. The tradition of *pālnām* practice commenced in the days of Sankaradeva is still prevailing in the *Sattras* of Gormurh, Dakshinpat, Notun Kamalabari, Uttar Kamalabari, Bengenaati, etc.[3]

Bhāonā, a creation of Sankaradeva, has been able to make an incredible impression on the cultural life of Majuli. Sankardeva holds up unmatchable instances of architecture and sculpture to the people of Assam through the use of locally found goods at its best. The masks made of bamboo, bamboo cane, clay, cloth, paper and natural colours like *heṅgul* and *haitāl* are some instances of incredible artistic calibre of the Vaishnava Saint. The creation and use of the *Cho-Mukha, Lotokai Mukha* and *Mukh Mukha* (some kinds of masks) have not only adorned the *bhāonā* and *Rāslīlā* but these have also added a charm and richness to the exhibitions, museums, etc. These masks use to be very light and are easily movable to places. The tradition of mask culture found and started since the seventeenth century is still gloriously maintained in *Sattras* like Notun Samoguri, Puroni Samoguri, Bihimpur and Alengi Narasingha, etc. The mask culture of Majuli has been able to make a place of its own in different places of India. As an acknowledgement to the mask culture, artist pension was provided to Rudrakanta Dev in 1988 and *Sangeet Natak Academy Awards* was delivered to the *Sattradhikar* of the Notun Samoguri Sattra Sri Sri Krishnakanta Dev Goswami in 2002. In 1980, another renowned artist Hemchandra Goswami founded a mask making training institute named '*Sukumar Kalapith*'.[4] Of the masks made, the ones like *Narasimha, Ravana, Putna, Basuki, Gorur,* lion, tortoise and crocodiles, etc., and also the bamboo made gateways are outstanding.

A kind of peaceful spiritual *aura* prevails in Majuli during the Assamese month of *Bhādo.* The *sattras* and villages of Majuli celebrate special occasions like the birth ceremony of Lord *Sri Krsna* and the *tithīs* of the saints with great devotion and sanctity. Each of the *nāmghar* indulges in *nām kirttan.* Some of the *sattras* perform *Gāyana-Bāyana* as well. The *sattras* have very well maintained the tradition of performing *soidhya-prasanga* in the *nāmghars* all round the year in addition to performing it in the Assamese month of *Bhādo.* Most of the villages and *Sattras* based in Majuli hold religious ceremonies like *Borhobāh* during the Assamese month of *Jeth-Ahār. Borhobāh* is performed in five stages called *Ushakirttan, Gopini Prasanga, Duporiya Prasanga, Kirttan Pāth* and *Rahashya Bhakti* and towards the nights, *Bhāonā* is enacted. Quite many of the *sattras* regularly observe some other functions and occasions like annual *Pholgus-utsava (holi), Bihu, Harikirttan* (prayer to *Lord Krsna*), etc.

The art and culture of Majuli is further enriched and enhanced by the cultural practices like *nritya gīt* of the *sattras.* A variety of dance forms like *Cāli Nāc, Notuwā Nāc, Jhumurā, Nādu-bhoṅgī, Ojāpāli, Sūtradhārī, Rojaghoriyā Nāc, Bhāonā*, etc. and the *Apsarā nāc* of the Auniati Sattra have been regularly practiced in Majuli. In addition to *Bargīt, Ankar gīt*, etc., particular *sattras* have been practicing *Ojāpāli gīt* and *Hājovāliā gīt*[5] as well.

Majuli is rich in terms of handicrafts as well. Along with the bamboo cane made hand fans of the Auniati sattra and Notun Kamalabari sattra, *kuhila* made mats of the Bhogpur sattra and the wooden sculpture of the Narasingha sattra; the *sattras* and the local inhabitants of Majuli does commendable job in making other things like *Siṅhsan, Xorai*, bamboo cane made products, *Gosa, Thoga, Jopa*, etc. The rare possessions of the *sattras* too are symbols of the folk culture of the place. Some such rare things that are being tried to be preserved are a Golden *kalsi* studded *Borjāpi* of the Dakshinpat sattra, a bronze *Xorai* with silver flower works on it, an ivory made *Xofura* of Gormurh sattra, a four storied *Raha Xorai*, the royal attire of Gadadhar Singha found in the Bengenaati sattra, *Rajchakra*, an ivory made mat of Auniati sattra, wooden *Borxorāi*, bamboo cane made *jopā* and also the things that were once used by the Vaishnava Saint are found in the Notun Kamalabari and North Kamalabari sattra. The notable ones among such things include the *Chitra Bhāgawat, Hastibidyarnava, Srīhastamuktāvalī, Nitilankur*, etc. The *Sattradhikar* of the Notun Kamalabari sattra Sri Sri Narayan Chandra Goswami's production the '*Arjun-Bhanjan Nāt*' and '*Sanchipatiya Ankawali*' in cooperation with an artist from Nagaon Mridu Mausam Bora have revitalized the trend of pictured books very well.

The indigenous tribes inhibiting in Majuli like the Deori, Mishing, Sonowal Kachari, etc. through their one-of-a-kind cultural practices, have been able to make Majuli a culturally colourful and rich land.

The Sattras of Majuli

Majuli is the heart of the *sattras*. Several castes and tribes like Brahmin, Koch, Kachari, Baniya, Kumar, Nath, Moran, Motok, Mishing, Deori, etc. have been inhabiting in this land since time immemorial. Vaishnava Saint and reformer Sankaradeva began uniting the diversified Assam right from Majuli through his revolution of devotion. Sankaradeva planned and decided over the major functions of the *sattras* by establishing a model of *sattra* at Belguri Dhuwahat located towards west of Majuli. It is at this place where Sankara-Madhava met each other for the first time. It can be claimed very well that it is in Majuli of upper Assam where the replica of the *sattra* was founded for the first time ever (1520-1540 A.D.).[6] Henceforth, Majuli is the place where the Vaishnava Saint, through this revolution of devotion brought the common men together and united them by providing them with a simple lifestyle, equality, independence, non-violence, abolition of untouchability, implementing simple norms in terms of religious practices and equal rights for all. People used to sit together in same level on the ground in the *Nāmghar* or *sattras* irrespective of their caste and creed to get delved into the *kirttan* of the God and were thus tied by one religion. Although Sankaradeva had to leave upper Assam due for not being in good note of the Ahom King and took shelter in the kingdom of Koch King in lower Assam yet, upper Assam was never out of his mind. In the meanwhile gosains like Gopaladeva, Jadumonideva, Bodula Padmaata set-up *sattras* in upper Assam and started spreading *Ek Xaran Nāmdharma* (believe on one Lord only). At a point of time, on being approved and accepted by the Ahom rulers, several *sattras* were being established in different parts of Majuli for the spread and practice of Vaishnava religion.

Edward Gait stated: "The Vaishnava religion obtained a strong footing in the country in the later part of the fifteenth century when Sankaradeva (1449-1569) the foundation lead of the *Bhāgawati* movement in Assam appeared on the scene during the reign of the Ahom king Suhungmung. From Jayadhaj Singh (1649-1663) to Ratnadhvaj Singh (1679-1681), the Ahom kings with a few exemptions showed due respect and courtesy to the Vaishnava gosains and accepted initiation. They made grants and endowments for the maintenance of Vaishnava monasteries and the most important sattra of Eastern Assam were set-up under their patronage".[7]

The geographical environment of Majuli was adequate for setting up the *sattras* and the gosains were influenced by the lifestyle of its inhabitants and the beauty of the Mother Nature. This is why, perhaps, Sankaradeva preached and started the *Bhāgawati* movement from this place. Right since the day of establishing the *sattras*, these have not only been preaching religion but it has left its mark on the field of education, politics and culture too in Assam's social system. There were a total of 64 *sattras* established in Majuli comprising of the ones that gained political grants and the ones deprived of it. The problem of land erosion in the Brahmaputra River has led to only half of the *sattras* remaining in the land. At present, the *sattras* that are alive and are under the Majuli district Sattra Mahasabha include Sri Sri Auniati Sattra, Sri Gormurh Sattra, Sri Sri Natun Kamalabari Sattra, Sri Sri Uttar Kamalabari Sattra, Sri Sri Bhogpur Sattra, Sri Sri Bengenaati Sattra, Sri Sri Dakshinpat Sattra, Sri Sri Alengi Tokoubari Sattra, Sri Sri Narasingha Sattra, Sri Sri Bahjengani Sattra, Sri Sri Dikhoumukhia Bor Alengi Sattra, Sri Sri Ananta Kalsila Sattra, Sri Sri Samoguri Sattra (ancient), Sri Sri Dalani Samoguri Sattra, Sri Sri Notun Samoguri Sattra, Sri Sri Bihimpur Sattra, Sri Sri Adi Bihimpur Sattra, Sri Sri Belesindhiya Sattra, Sri Sri Adhar Mahora Sattra, Sri Sri Owa Sattra, Sri Sri Majuli Bor Alengji Sattra, Sri Sri Bor Alengi Sattra, Sri Sri Majuli Adi Alengi Sattra, Sri Sri Madhya Majuli Kamalabari Sattra, etc.

Although the list of these *sattras* is being prepared with the help of the Sattra Mahasabha, yet not all of these *sattras* possesses the features of being a complete and independent *sattra*.

Some of the Important Sattras in Majuli

1. **Gormurh Sattra:** It is at the district headquarter of the present Majuli, Gormurh where this *sattra* is located. Banshigopaladeva's adopted son Mitradeva and Jayharideva used to live in the Kuruwabahi Sattra. On the demise of Gopaladeva, Mitradeva became the *sattradhikar* of the Kuruwabahi sattra and then Harideva founded the Gormurh sattra separately. Almost half of the unmarried gosains of the Kuruwabahi sattra came along Harideva to the Gormurh sattra.

   History says that the Lahdoigor that was built by the Ahom King Swargadeu Pratap Singha to protect his state ends near this *sattra*. This part of the Gor in Majuli is called as the Sewatol Gor. And as this *sattra* was set on an ending point of the Gor, it was named as the Gormurh sattra. The main image of God in this *sattra* is Baṅshigopala Mahaprabhu.

   No particular time can be traced regarding the formation of this *sattra*. According to the *Charitraputhi*, it was set up during the days of the Ahom king Jayadhvaj Singha. Maniram Dewan, in '*Burañjī Vivek Ratna*' has mentioned that after the establishment of the Kuruwabahi Sattra, a brother of Gopaladeva with the support and grant of Jayadhvaj Singha founded the Gormurh Sattra. Whatever it is, the present *sattradhikar* of the sattra Harideva Goswami have also said that Gopaladeva's brother have established the Gormurh sattra with due patronage of Jayadhvaj Singha.

   The festivals celebrated in the Gormurh Sattra are the death and birth ceremonies of the *Sattradhikars* and Sankara-Madhavadeva, *Phalgu-utsava, Rās, Pālnām* and the three *Bihus*.

   The branches of the sattra are the 1. Nagaon Phulaguri Branch, 2. Puranigudām Branch, 3. North Guwahati Middle Section Branch, and 4. Tokolai Branch Sattra.

2. **Sri Sri Auniati Sattra:** On 1575 (1653 AD) Ahom King Jayadhvaj Singha established the Auniati sattra in a place called Auniati. For setting up the *sattra*, he brought a statue of Govinda (Lord Krsna) from Kuruwabahi and donated it to Niranjan Dev along with many other things real-estate, money, bedding, property and bronze plates, etc. This *sattra* follows the principle of celibacy. With almost 10 lakh of disciples from all around Assam Dr. Sri Sri Pitambar Deva Goswami is the *sattradhikar* of this *sattra* and Sri Sri Devananda Deva Goswami is taking charge as a young

sattradhikar. At present, approx. 280 Vaishnava Gosains are associated with this *sattra*.

The major function observed in the Auniati sattra is *pālnām*. It is celebrated for a total of five days from 25th to 29th of the Assamese month of *Kati*. Along with it, the *sattra* also celebrates other festivals like *Janmastami* (Lord *Krsna's* birth ceremony), *Rāsjātra* (a procession on the occasion of *Rās*), the three *Bihus*, the birth and death ceremonies of the Vaishnava saints and of the *sattradhikars*, joint celebration of *Boiragi Nām Utsava, bhāonā*, etc. every year. Currently, a well-designed library is being built in the *sattra* to preserve the antique manuscripts of *sānchipāt* and all very priceless books of the *sattra* and by the *sattradhikars*. Amongst such preserved books *Hastividyarnava, Srīhastamuktāvalī, Mahābharata, Rāmayana, Bhāgawat*, etc. are noteworthy. The museum of the *sattra* possesses ivory made mat (which is one and only in the world), silver made *Māihang, Mān Xofura, Borjapi*, silver made *Xorai* of the royal ages, bronze plates, *Bheru, Kali*, etc. almost hundred such things.

The total number of *nāts* (drama) composed by the *sattradhikar* and the gosains of the Auniati sattra are 104. The present *sattradhikar* has published his composition of seven *nāts* and an *nritya-nātika* (dance-drama) named *Natyagīti Tarangīni*. Some of the research books by the *sattra* are — *Sattrīyā Utsavar Tatporjya aru Iyar Porichay, Axom'r Nām Anusthān, Geeta Abhigyan, Bhāgawat Darpan, Chinar Lijiyangot*, etc. Through the formation of the religion publishing machine in the *sattra* by Dattadeva in the year 1871 and by publishing journals like *Assam Bilasini, Assam Tara, Assam Dipika*, etc., he has made unforgettable contributions to the media world. At present, the *sattra* publishes a tri-monthly magazine called '*Sanskriti Pallava*'.

3. **Dakshinpat Sattra:** It is one of the major *sattras* of Majuli. The surrounding the *sattra* reflect mesmerizing natural beauty with the age old Gor made in the days of the Ahom King along with the splendour of the Chandramala Aideu's pond. In 1576 (1658 A.D.), in the Assamese month of *Puh*, Ahom King Jayadhvaj Singha invited Bonomalideva to offer the Bhotiyapr pond and set-up a *sattra* for him at Rngolibhar Ptnagar. In the meantime, Mirjumla attacked Assam due to which the process of foundation of the *sattra* had to stop and it only completed during the reign of Chakradhvaj Singha.

The Sanskrit note of Sridhar Swami and the 103 paged almost deteriorated *Bhāgawat* written in the year 1493 that was being gifted in a golden scroll by saint Sankaradeva to Damodaradeva is the invaluable possession of the *sattra*. The *sattra* also has other antique goods like the image of God of the pre-Ahom age, bronze plates, royal *Bortup* (bigger bombs), *Hengdāng* (a sort of long and heavy sword used by the Ahom kings), *Lakhuti* (walking stick), metal made things, *Krsna-Balaram* crown made of gold and silver, *Bhogjarā, Jalghari* (water watch), *Kingkhap*, etc. Dakshinpat Sattra's contribution in the field of dance, song, drama, *ojā, gāyana-bāyana* is commendable. Currently, the *sattra* is known for practicing *Rajāgharīyā nṛtya, Indravishek nṛitya, Notuwā, Ojapāli, Beheruā, Phalgu-utsava, Krsna Mangal, Ramcaraniya* and so on. The image of God in this *sattra* is Jadava Rai.

Along with the Koch, Kachari and the Ahom Kings Jayadhvaj Singha, Chakradhvaj Singha and other royal officers, three of Assam's ex Chief Ministers too were disciples of this *sattra*. At present as well, several tribes of Assam and the North-East like Duonia Naga, Khamti, Mishing, Bodo, Bhutiya, Nepali, Mismi, Singpho, Oka and Dophola are disciples of this *sattra*. A branch of Dakshinpat Sattra is located at Nuxali of Majuli. It is a rule to import the *sattradhikar* from this branch to the *sattra* following celibacy.

4. **Kamalabari Sattra:** Bodula Padma ata, on the instruction of his mentor saint Madhavadeva came to upper Assam with an intension to preach Vaishnava religion and ended up setting the Kamalabari Sattra in 1673 at Majuli. It is one of the *sattras* that believe in definite oneness. A number of twenty *sattradhikar* came in charge and conducted the *sattra* respectively after Bodula ata. At a point of time, it got divided into Uttar Kamalabari Sattra and Notun Kamalabari Sattra.

Uttar Kamalabari Sattra: When Krishnadeva took charge as the *sattradhikar* of the Kamalabari sattra, a sort of conflict took place amongst the gosains to remove the Brahmins. They made the two claimants of the *sattradhikar* position, Sambhunath and Jagannathdeva parted off and set-up a new *sattra*. Sambhunathdeva went towards the north of the *sattra* along with some disciples to set-up his *sattra* at a fully licensed plot on the north bank of the Tuni River. But by resting the charge of the *sattra* on the shoulders of his brother Bishnudeva he passed away before the *sattra* could come into existence. After that, Bishnudeva set-up the new *sattra* in cooperation with his disciples in 1837. As it was based on the north of the main *sattra*, hence, it got its name *Uttar* (north) Kamalabari sattra. "As the area of the *sattra* was not sufficient enough, it shifted for the second time under the patronage of Raibahadur Dinanath Bezbaruah under the conduction of Muhikanta Deva in 1881. In 1923 for the third time and then in 1956, under the conduction of Kamalakantadeva, it shifted for the fourth time to the present place due to land erosion.[8]

The Uttar Kamalabari sattra has made unmatchable contributions towards introducing the *Sattrīyā* culture in the international platform. Parmananda Barbāyana of this *sattra* who is also known as the magical player of the Khol, won the *Sangeet Natak Academy Award* in the year 2000. Some of the endangered things found and preserved in this *sattra* are the manuscripts of *sānchipāt*, the *Xofura* that Sankaradeva used for keeping his betel-nuts, the *Jopmālā* of Madhavadeva, the *Sagarjuli.*bowl of Badula ata used while having his meal, *Padasila*, etc.

Notun Kamalabari Sattra: When in 1856, the gosains faced difference of opinion with the *sattradhikar* Chandrahsdeva, a total of 120 gosains split from the main *sattra* to set-up the Notun Kamalabari Sattra in 1858. They availed a government permission of 440 *bighas* of land for the formation of the Notun Kamalabari sattra. This particular *sattra* have been able to succeed in spreading the *Sattrīyā* culture to places and have attained national credits as well. The main dances practiced in the *sattras* are *Cāli, Jhumurā, Nādu-bhongī, Sūtradhār, Ojāpāli, Rojaghoriyā Cāli*, etc. Maniram Datta Bayan in 1963, Bapuram Bayan ata in 1979, Rosheswar Saikia Borbayana in 1981 won *Sangeet Natak Academy Awards* for this *sattra*. In 2004, *sattradhikar* Sri Sri Narayana Chandra Deva Goswami won the honourable Sankaradeva Award of the Assam Government.

5. **Bhogpur Sattra:** Is a notable *sattra* in Majuli. The second *sattra* that Vaishnava saint Sankaradeva set-up by lighting an earthen lamp is the Bhogpur Sattra. On the bank of the old Dikhou River of the Bengenaati post office, the Bhogpur sattra was established in the year 1441 A.D. (1519). Earlier on, this place was known as Dinapur. Saint Sankaradeva while leaving for King Naranarayana's court lighted an earthen lamp in this place and rested the charge of the *sattra* on his disciples. As Dinapur used to produce plenty of

edibles without any scarcity for anything, it later got named as Bhogpur. Bipra Damodaradeva was the first *dharmachārya* of the Bhogpur sattra. It presently holds a huge number, i.e., forty-five thousands of disciples in it and follows celibacy.

The *Sattrīyā nrityas* practiced in the Bhogpur sattra particularly are *Cāli Nāc, Jhumur Nāc, Nādu-bhongī, Satradhār* and *Ojāpāli.* A total of 44 *sānchipāt* manuscripts are preserved in this *sattra.*

Conclusion

Majuli has made uncountable contributions towards the cultural and social life in Assam. It is the *sattra*-culture of this river island that has been able to strike the attention of the world. Known as the land of fusion of the saints Sankara-Madhava, it seems Majuli is a place of never ending art and culture. The locals of Majuli have always been celebrating and rejoicing the *Rās* festival which even makes the people living out of the river island for professional and other purposes rush home back for the celebrations. In fact, not only from Assam, but from places outside India too, tourists come to enjoy the festival. The whole atmosphere of the place along with its local business gains a momentum during these days. Each of the *sattra* based in Majuli, namely Gormurh, Dakshinpat, Bhogpur, Auniati, Bengenaati, Notun Kamalabari, Uttar Kamalabari, Narasingha, Samoguri, etc. celebrates *Sri Krsna Rāslīlā* on the full moon of autumn. Except for the Gormurh Sattra, majority of the other *sattras* perform male oriented *Rāslīlā.*

With specialization in handicrafts, the villages and *sattras* of Majuli have been playing a lead role in the making of things like *Singhasan, Xorai, Gosa, Jopa*, bamboo cane made things, etc. Each of its *sattras* have a special quality in handicrafts, like Auniati Sattra and the Notun Kamalabari sattra are known for its bamboo cane made hand fans, Bhogpur Sattra for *Kuhila* made mat, Narasingha Sattra for wooden sculpture and so on.

NOTES

1. Hazarika, Ananda, *'Majuli'*, Annual Issue-1, *Majuli: Ek Antorjatik Nadidwip.*
2. Sarma, Tirthanath, *Auniati Sattrar Buranji*, 1975, p. 123.
3. Nath, Gunamoni, "Majulir Raas aru Palnaam Utsava", *Majuli*, Editor: Prasanta Kumar Mahanta, 2001, p. 138.
4. Hazarika, Dulal, *Majulir Kala-Sanskriti: Majuli*, Annual Issue-1, p. 62.
5. Goswami, Pabitrapran, *Majulit Raag Sangitor Sorsa: Majuli*, Editor: Prasanta Kumar Mahanta, 2001, p. 135.

6. Rajkhowa, Tulasi, *Majuli*, Annual Issue-1, p. 87.
7. *A History of Assam*, p. 289.
8. Rajkhowa, Tulasi, *Majuli*, Annual Issue-1, 2001.

REFERENCES

Baruah, Birinchi Kumar, *Asomiya Bhakha Aru Sanskriti*, 7th Edition, March 1992, p. 89.

Bejbaruah, Laksminath, *Sri Sri Sankardeva Aru Sri Sri Madhavadeva*, Banalata Publishers, November 2012.

Bora, Debabhusan (Editing), *Majuli*, Annual Issue-1, Katha Publication, Katha-Readers' Forum-2011.

Das, Amulya Chandra, *Alok*, Assamese Deptt., B. Barooah College, Ghy, May 2013.

Deka, Dinesh Chandra, *"Assam" — The Land of Red River and Blue Hills*, Directorate of Information and Public Relations, Government of Assam.

Gait, E., *A History of Assam*, Lawyer's Book Stall, Guwahati, 1984.

Hazarika, Biman, *Ekabinxa Xotikar Axom't Nava-Vaishnav Sattra (Somoshya Aru Sombhavana)*, 16th August, 2013.

Hazarika, Dipak, *Juganayak Srimanta Sankardeva*, Banalata, Panbazar, Ghy, 14th October, 2013.

Mahanta, Prasanta Kumar, *Majuli*, 3rd Edition, May 2013, (Editing), Grantha Sanskriti, Torajan, Jorhat, Assam.

Neog, Maheswar, *Pabitra Asam*, 4th Edition, 8 March, 2008.

———, *Guru Carit Katha*, 2nd Edition, University Publication Deptt., Guwahati University, 2013.

Sarma, Tirthnath, *Auniati Sattrar Buranji*, p. 123, 1975.

22

SOCIO-ECONOMIC STATUS OF TRIBAL POPULATION IN THE LIGHT OF EDUCATION

Gitika Das

In our country the Scheduled Tribes are recognized as the weakest section of the society and constituting about 8.6 per cent of total population in India as per 2011 Census. During the period 2001-2011 the population grew by 23.7 per cent. Tribal communities live in about 15 per cent of the country's total area in various ecological and geo-climatic conditions ranging from plains and forest to hills and inaccessible areas. These tribes belong to different ethnological groups, possess diverse socio-religious characteristics and are at various levels of socio-economic development.

Since, Independence, several plans and programmes have been introducing to uplift socio-economic status of the tribal communities in India. However, some special provisions have also been made in the Constitution of India to provide socio-economic and political guarantees to the tribal communities. The Ministry of Tribal Affairs has also been introducing various Schemes and Programmes, which are largely focused on improvement of living standards, education, health care and skill up-gradation of the tribal people without any gender bias. But most of them are still remained backward and development programmes seem to have achieved only limited success in bringing about improvement in the quality of life of tribal people.

The North-Eastern region of the country comprises the States of Arunachal Pradesh, Assam, Manipur, Meghalaya, Mizoram, Nagaland, Tripura and Sikkim. All these units, excepting the two former princely states of Manipur and Tripura, constituted the erstwhile composite State of Assam. North-Eastern India has been historically subject to the penetration by the people of Mongolian origin and culture in the same way as the north-western passes of the Himalayas had provided for the entry of the Aryans.

These Mongolian people, after their successive waves of migration to this part of the region settled in the valleys, hills, mountains and also in difficult terrains. They were later known in different names. In erstwhile Assam they were known as Kacharis or Boro Kacharis, Rabha, Hajong, Mishing (Miri), Garo, Dalu, Karbi (Mikir) Tiwa (Lalung), Sonawal, Thengal, Saraniya, Tai-Phake, Tai-Khamti, Tai-Khamiyang, Turung, Singpho, Dimasa, Naga, Khasi, Jayantia, Pnar, Lakher, Hmar, Kuki, etc. and many more. The tribal people of this though originated from a single stock, yet they are not homogenous in their language, culture, food habits or other such socio-economic life. The people living in different geographical set-up practice their way of life according to their own cultural prescription. For instance people living in difficult hilly region practice jhum, terrace cultivation. They are purely dependent on forest. On the other hand, the plain dweller practices both wet and dry cultivation. They are animistic by their religious faiths and customary practices regulate their social behaviour. Hereditary chiefs or village chiefs are rule maker and decision-maker. Women and men have little difference in execution of daily family life. Tradition acts as guiding factor in their normal way of life. They are often at loggerheads with one another and with outsiders as well, for which all of them suffer in many ways.

Seemingly, this people are marked by under development, inaccessibility, isolation, low density of population compared to caste people, low socio-economic and educational development, high cost of living and lack of developed infrastructure and very painfully often suffer from intra and inter tribal conflict for uneven resource distribution and evil impact of terrorism.

Assam is one of the States of India and located in North-Eastern corner of India. With a geographical area 78,438 sq.km., Assam accounts for about 2.4 per cent of the country's total geographical area. The present Assam State is bounded by latitudes 24°08′10″N and 27°58′15″N and longitude 89°42′05″E and 96°01′14″E (*Assam State Gazetteer*, 1999:3).

According to 2011 Census, the total Scheduled Tribe population of India is 10,42,81,034, in rural area it is 9,38,19,162 and in urban area is 1,04,61,872. Assam is 38,84,371 (Males 19,57,005, Females, 19,27,366), constituting 12.4 per cent of total 3,12,05,576 population in the State.

The Scheduled Tribe communities of Assam may be divided into two broad categories, namely — plains Tribes and Hill Tribes. There are fourteen (14) Tribal groups in the State of Assam, including Bodoland Territorial Areas district and excluding Autonomous Districts of Karbi-Anglong and North Cachar (Dima-Hasao) hills and total fifteen (15) Tribal groups in the list of Autonomous Districts of Karbi-Anglong and North Cachar hills as per Annual Report of Ministry of Tribal Affairs 2007-08. Table 22.1 shows the Tribe-wise distribution of Population of Assam as per 2001 census.

Table 22.1: Tribe-Wise Distribution of Population of Assam

Sl. No.	*Name of Scheduled Tribe*	*Total Person*	*Male*	*Female*
1.	Boro Kachari	1352771	682710	670061
2.	Barmans in Cachar	15877	8024	7853
3.	Mising (Miri)	587310	299790	287520
4.	Deori	41161	20809	20352
5.	Rabha	277517	140614	136903
6.	Tiwa (Lalung)	170622	85964	84658
7.	Karbi (Mikir)	353513	180136	173377
8.	Dimasa	110976	56876	54100
9.	Kachari, Sonowal	235881	119470	116411
10.	Mech	8997	4597	4400
11.	Hojai	1882	932	950
12.	Garo	21112	10739	10373
13.	Khasi	12722	3654	6368
14.	Any Kuki Tribes	28273	14666	13607
15.	Man, Tai Speaking	739	375	364
16.	Any Naga Tribes	21706	11077	10629
17.	Any Mizo Tribes	2957	1504	1453
18.	Hmar	14460	7429	7031
19.	Hajong	256	139	117
20.	Chakma	2478	1329	1149
21.	Lakher	11	5	6
22.	Syntheng	336	164	172
Total ST population		3308570	1678117	1630453

Source: Census of India, 2001.

Among the total Scheduled Tribe population Boro Kachari Tribe registered highest (40.9%) position in the State. On the other hand, the Mishing tribe occupies second position constituting 17.8 per cent of the total scheduled tribe population in the State. Other major Tribal groups are the Karbis (10.7%), Rabhas (8.4%), Kachari, Sonowal (7.1%), Tiwas (5.2%) Dimasa Kacharis (3.4%) and Deoris (1.2%) etc.

Schumacher has gone a little ahead by saying "Development does not starts with goods, it starts with people and their education, organization and discipline". He also says that "without these three, all resources remain latent, untapped and potential". Therefore, education is the backbone of socio-economic development of a nation and a community in micro sense. Education of the community members focuses the inner development scenario of a state and a nation as well. There is some important measuring scale which gives a glimpse of socio-economic status of the people at large. The scheduled tribes of Assam living in both hills and plains are socio-economically in a better position compared to its hills counterpart residing in other parts of North-Eastern states and the country as well.

Educational Attainment Indicator

Within the social sector, the influence of education is the most important and education impacts of all types of human development outcomes. Education is an important input as well as an outcome indicator influencing other development indicators like health, nutritional status, income and family planning. Women education is the path way to women empowerment and it paves the way to improve quality of life. It helps in women to enter into the political, economical, and social spheres with confidence (Pathak, 2009). Among different parameters of educational attainments, literacy is the most fundamental, as it paves the way for further learning and training (India, HDR, 2011). Literacy is the first step in knowledge building and hence, literacy indicators are important in the assessment of human development. It reflects the socio-economic development picture. It is to be noted that literacy rate in general and female literacy in particular is considered as the best indicator of the socio-economic development. Female literacy in particular is of vital importance for the future of the nation, as child's health is crucial linked to the mothers' literacy (India HDR, 2011:181).

Literacy Rate

Census 2001 recognized a person aged 7 years and above who can both read and write with understanding in any language is to be taken as literate. A person who can only read, but cannot write is not literate. Literacy rate of population is defined as the percentage of literates to the total population age 7 years and above. Literacy is an indicator of socio-economic status and highly essential for the economic development as well as social development. Although, there has been a visible increase in the literacy rates of Scheduled Tribes the gap between the literacy rates with the general population still persists. The total literacy rate of Assam as per 2011 Census is 72.2 per cent, where total male literacy rate is 77.8 per cent and female literacy rate is 66.3 per cent respectively and very remarkably the Scheduled Tribes literacy is also almost same, i.e. 72.1 per cent. In respect of male and female literacy rate among the Scheduled Tribes population of Assam, the percentage being 78.9 and 65.1. There is a huge gap (19.9% points) between male and female literacy rate. Scheduled Tribes female literacy rate is 2 per cent point lower than the overall female literacy (54.4%) of Assam. The Scheduled Tribes female literacy is well ahead (17.6% points) of national female literacy rate (34.8%). The detail comparison of literacy rate is shown in Table 22.2.

Table 22.2: Comparison of Literacy Rate (Excluding age group 0-6 years)

Sl.No.	*Category*	*Literacy Rate (%)*		
		Person	*Male*	*Female*
1.	All STs of Assam	62.5	72.3	52.4
2.	Assam All	63.3	71.3	54.4
3.	All STs of India	46.01	59.1	34.8

Source: Census of India, 2001.

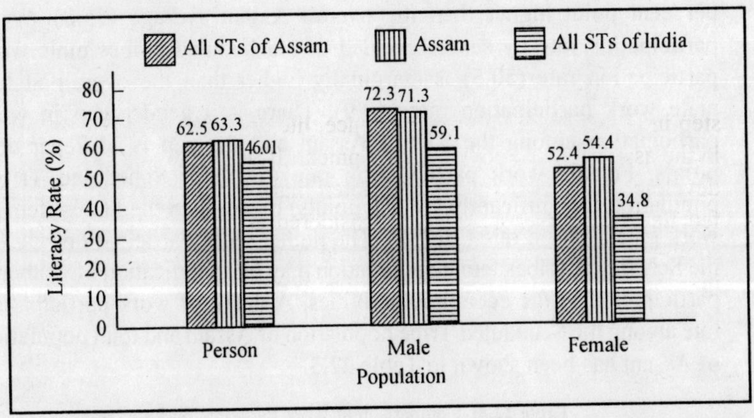

Figure 22.1: Comparison of Literacy Rate (Excluding age group 0-6 years)

Thus, education has a dominant impact over the socio-economic development of the tribal people since they are still lacking proper awareness of developmental programmes.

Economic Participation of Mising Women

Economic empowerment of women can be understood through assessing economic participation of women in different economic activities. Economic empowerment for women means empowering women for availing new employment opportunities, for generating income, self-employment and entrepreneurship development. Joshi (1998) pointed out that Women's folk work participation rate and her being economically independent is very vital for determining the economic status of women. The work participation rate indicates the access of the people to the means of livelihood.

Work Participation Rate

Work participation rate, is defined as the percentage of total workers (main and marginal) to the total population. Higher work participation rate is the indication of participation of economic development. Singh (1986:141) pointed out that "the proportion workforce in the tribal population in India is comparatively much more than that of non-Tribal's". However, it does not really mean that Tribal's are better placed in terms of employment, according to him.

The percentage distribution of workforce revealed that the work participation rate (43.2) among the Scheduled Tribe population is 7.4 per cent point higher than the overall Assam average (35.8). Work participation rate by sexes revealed that Scheduled Tribes male work participation rate (50.5) is marginally higher than the overall States' male work participation rate (49.9). There is a gender gap in work participation among the STs of Assam and the gap is 11.7 per cent points. Female work participation rate (38.8) of Scheduled Tribes population is significantly (18.1% points) higher than the States' female work participation rate (20.7%). The higher work participation rate for the Scheduled Tribes female population may be an indication of women's participation in the economic activities. A detail of work participation rate among the Scheduled Tribe population of Assam and total population of Assam has been shown in Table 22.3.

Table 22.3: Comparison of Work Participation Rate

Sl.No.	*Category*	*Work Participation Rate (%), as per 2001 Census*		
		Person	*Male*	*Female*
1.	All STs of Assam	43.2	50.5	38.8
2.	Assam (All)	35.8	49.9	20.7

Source: Census of India, 2001.

From Table 22.3, data it is clearly seen that females are contributing largely in their family income in tribal areas.

Problems of Tribal Areas

The main problem of Tribal areas is that their educational institutions are not within their easy reach. Moreover, most of the tribal families cannot afford primary, secondary education and also higher education because of their economic conditions. As a first generation learner, their parents are uneducated so their children are deprived of guidance, their children also feel handicapped because their parents do not take any interest in what they are doing at schools and colleges.

Another problem of tribal's area is that primary schools follows mainly Assamese medium syllabi, hence, students find it difficult to follow because they speak their own dialect. Assamese language is rarely used in their day-to-day conversation. So, they cannot communicate with others and after someday they stopped of going to school, such situation is a major problem of tribal societies causing the problem of large school dropouts.

Most of the primary schools in villages are without teachers or one or two teachers, school are running with very poor infrastructure. Education is closely related to economic condition of the family, so without improving the economic condition, quality of education will never be improved. Ignorance and lack of skill in trade greatly hamper the economic growth of the tribal people. Traditionally, they are engaging in agriculture, horticulture, sericulture with primitive technology. Their traditional technique in cultivation does not help them in their economic prosperity. So, they need assistance and training in modern technique of agriculture for improving their quality of life and economy. Moreover, training on various vocational trades should be given to the tribal people.

The main cause of the low level literacy of tribal in Assam may be summarized as follows:

1. Lack of awareness of the tribal people as to the benefits of education.
2. Our education system is designed to meet the requirement of average ability and it is alien to tribal life and culture for this tribal children dropping out from school.
3. Regarding the question of distance between home and school as a barrier for schooling, tribal parents found inconvenient to send their children to school as they have to pass through thick forest and hills, etc.

4. There is a prevailing notion that education of a girl is luxury and should be avoided.
5. The conditions of schools are far from satisfactory and the number of schools is inadequate.
6. Poverty is also a problem in this issue. As the parents cannot provide text books, school dress and other educational requirements and needs.
7. As a first generation learner they are deprive of guidance.
8. The parents are not motivated for their children education. Their major interest of earning money not in education.
9. Communication system is not suitable in that area.

Besides all these problems, there are many other problems which the tribal's are facing in day-to-day life. For improvement of the people the following points may be taken into consideration.

1. Education should be made compulsory and educational institutions should be established in every village of the tribal communities.
2. Library and girls' hostel should be attached to each educational institution.
3. Parents should be conscious about the benefit of the education.
4. Communication should be improved on that area.
5. Improve the condition of electricity, water supply, sanitation, standard of living in the remotest tribal area developmental schemes should be introduced in the tribal area as per their need.
6. Adult education centres for tribal should be opened separately.
7. Special attention should be paid to the tribal women.

Government sometimes launches ambitious plans and programmes for the development of tribal people as well as general people but the favour does not reach to the needy people because of their ignorance.

Presently, Government of India with the help of State government giving importance for educational development to the weaker section of the society. The major programmes are Sarba Shikha Abhiyan (SSA), National Programmes of Nutrition Support to Primary Education (NPNSPE), National Literacy Mission (NLM), District Primary Education Programmes (DPEP), National Adult Education Programmes (NAEP), etc.

Now, the Constitution of India provide free and compulsory education to all children in the age of 6-14 years as fundamental right. The Right of

Children Free and Compulsory Education (RTE) Act, 2009 is based in the 86th Amendment of the Constitution under Article 21-A and RTE Act came into effect.

On the other hand, Government of India with the help of State government is taking several steps to improve the living standard of the tribal population. The Assam Tribal Development Authority was set-up in 1983 under the Act of State government. It was set-up for the socio-economic development of the tribal people in Assam to formulate schemes for their development. Assam Tribal Development Corporation has been established to look after the economic development of the BPL people.

Efforts made from the beginning of the first Five Year Plan through various developmental plans, policies, strategies and programmes, have registered definite quantitative improvement in the socio-economic status of the tribal people. However, progress made by them could not bring them anywhere nearer the mainstream society. As the gaps in the socio-economic status continued to prevail, the Government of Assam and the Government of India are taking different measures by providing more funds to minimize the gaps in near future.

REFERENCES

Bordoloi, B.N., *Constraints of Tribal Development in North-East India*, Assam Institute of Research for Tribals and Scheduled Castes, Guwahati, 1990.

———, *Tribals of Assam*, AIRTSC. Guwahati, 1991.

Das, Bhaswati Baruah and Saswati Baruah Bhuyan, *Emerging Issues of Indian Education*, Ashok Book Stall, Guwahati, 2012.

Das, Girindra Nath, *India, Tribal Development in North-East*, Assam Institute of Research for Tribals and Scheduled Castes, Guwahati, 2008.

Hazarika, N.A., *Tribal Women and Development*, published by N.A. Hazarika, Guwahati, 2007.

Venkateswaran S., *Principals of Education*, Vikas Publishing House, New Delhi, 1993.

Census Report 2001, 2011.